PUBLIC SAFETY

90 0628214 1

Also by Richard Clutterbuck

ACROSS THE RIVER (*as Richard Jocelyn*)
THE LONG LONG WAR
PROTEST AND THE URBAN GUERRILLA
RIOT AND REVOLUTION IN SINGAPORE AND MALAYA
LIVING WITH TERRORISM
GUERRILLAS AND TERRORISTS
KIDNAP AND RANSOM
BRITAIN IN AGONY
*THE MEDIA AND POLITICAL VIOLENCE
*INDUSTRIAL CONFLICT AND DEMOCRACY
CONFLICT AND VIOLENCE IN SINGAPORE AND MALAYSIA
*THE FUTURE OF POLITICAL VIOLENCE
*KIDNAP, HIJACK AND EXTORTION
TERRORISM AND GUERRILLA WARFARE
TERRORISM, DRUGS AND CRIME IN EUROPE AFTER 1992
*INTERNATIONAL CRISIS AND CONFLICT
TERRORISM IN AN UNSTABLE WORLD
*DRUGS, CRIME AND CORRUPTION

**Also published by Macmillan*

Public Safety and Civil Liberties

Richard Clutterbuck

Security and Political Risk Consultant, and
Honorary Research Fellow
University of Exeter

Foreword by Sir Robert Mark, GBE, QPM

formerly Commissioner of the Metropolitan Police

First published 1997 by
MACMILLAN PRESS LTD
Houndmills, Basingstoke, Hampshire RG21 6XS
and London
Companies and representatives
throughout the world

ISBN 0–333–61185–3 hardcover
ISBN 0–333–61186–1 paperback

A catalogue record for this book is available
from the British Library.

This book is printed on paper suitable for recycling and made from fully managed and sustained forest sources.

10 9 8 7 6 5 4 3 2 1
06 05 04 03 02 01 00 99 98 97

Printed in Great Britain by
The Ipswich Book Company Ltd
Ipswich, Suffolk

Contents

List of Tables

Foreword

This book is timely; indeed, perhaps overdue. It brings together many of the different threads in the pattern of what is loosely called 'law and order' and poses questions which will sooner or later have to be answered.

After twenty years as a chief police officer and a further nineteen in contemplative retirement I believe that law and order is for the first time a problem more worrying to ordinary people than any other. That is not to say that Maastricht, a single European currency, racism, Northern Ireland and so on will not continue to monopolize the headlines. But crime and public order affect many of us more immediately and arouse emotion, argument and unease. It is also unique among our more serious problems in that its public image has always been misleading. Reality has been obscured by complacency and the laws relating to libel and contempt of court. In no other area of public affairs is enforced obscurity so harmful to the public interest.

The latent factor common to each of the problems discussed in this book is the expectation or assumption of effective law. By effective, I do not mean severe or punitive. I mean a system of law which offers a reasonable probability of conviction, which would do more than anything else to still hysterical demands for retribution. I am sorry to say that our present system of criminal justice does not justify that assumption. On the contrary it has reached a level of ineffectiveness positively harmful to public confidence. That situation is aggravated by the mistaken assumption that acquittal necessarily implies innocence, provoking an unjustified suspicion that the prosecution process is badly administered or unfair. Most worrying of all, the system offers no deterrent to the criminally inclined or to those who offend against public order for political or industrial reasons. Indeed, research into the latter would probably show that, with the exception of the Cambridge Garden House case (1969) and that of the Shrewsbury pickets (1972), both of which provoked hostile comment, the prosecution of public order cases could be seen as a waste of limited police resources serving no useful purpose.

The public must be persuaded, and legislators compelled, to accept the reality that even the most enlightened and well-intentioned proposals to improve the administration of justice must all fail unless founded on effective law.

It is sad to reflect that attempts to improve that effectiveness in the post-war years, notably the abolition of peremptory challenge of jurors and majority verdicts, have all been opposed by lawyers, with one or two exceptions. It seems to me essential that decisions relating to the criminal process should reflect the views of society as a whole, not just of those closely involved in its administration. 'No man shall judge his own cause' runs the famous dictum and it is just as true in relation to the criminal process itself. This book will stimulate wide interest in the problem and, I hope, encourage others to address it.

The author is an academic with many years' experience in this subject, with the unusual advantage of having been engaged in law enforcement as an army officer serving overseas. He is not committed to the prejudices or viewpoint of any of the professions or services concerned with criminal justice in Britain and might well be regarded as uniquely qualified to speak for the thinking, caring private citizen. I hope his book will arouse wide interest among just such a readership. It well deserves it.

ROBERT MARK

Preface

In 49 out of every 50 crimes committed in Britain, the criminals walk free. I am supposed to explain in the Preface why I wrote the book. Is this reason enough?

Crime more than doubled in 1981–93, though it has been clawed back a bit in 1994–96. The most worrying thing is that one-third of all crimes were committed by people under 21, including 60 per cent of the robberies and 55 per cent of the car thefts. I have tried, like many others, to work out why this was so – what makes young people turn to crime.

I have looked both at our intelligence methods and at our criminal justice and public order laws, and especially at how we deal – or fail to deal – with persistent criminals and with intimidation of witnesses and juries. I have compared the British system of law enforcement and justice with some others and considered whether we should develop more of the alternatives to prison. I have suggested some changes and challenged some sacred cows, especially our hallowed adversarial system of law, and have assessed some of the technology now becoming available for law enforcement. I have tried to strike a balance between effective law enforcement and civil liberties, including the civil liberties of the victims of crime.

In examining the interplay of all these factors, I know that different readers will have different interests, so I have tried to ensure that each section – young people, drugs, intelligence, the law, technology, and so on – can stand on its own, relying on a full table of contents and a balance between repetition and excessive cross-referencing.

I had a problem over genders – he or she. Every Act of Parliament uses 'he' to incorporate both genders in every phrase referring to criminals, rioters, and so on, which seems fair enough as the great majority of criminals are male. Some of the Acts have been in force for over a century and others only since 1996, but they all do the same. Where my sentences contain the wording of the law ('if he uses or threatens violence . . . his . . . him . . .') I gave up the attempt to find tortuous ways round, and followed suit.

As with a number of my previous books, I started by seeking advice from Lord Scarman, whom I look up to as the wisest and most far-sighted judge I have known in my lifetime. I have also talked to many serving police officers, often in the context of lectures and seminars. Among these I am especially grateful to John Grieve, who is now head of the anti-terrorist branch and, before that, was Director of Intelligence at New Scotland Yard. I have not named any of the other police and intelligence officers I spoke to as I know that they would prefer this.

I have quoted freely from the work of Sir Robert Mark and the outstanding research done by Alison Jamieson, by Jon Silverman (BBC Home Affairs Correspondent) and by the National Association for the Care and Resettlement of Offenders (NACRO). But neither they, nor Lord Scarman nor John Grieve, will necessarily agree with my analysis or conclusions, for which I must take full responsibility.

I owe a special debt of gratitude to my copy-editor, Christine Firth. She has now edited six of my books and improved every one of them beyond measure.

RICHARD CLUTTERBUCK

List of Abbreviations

For foreign acronyms and in other cases where it is judged to be more helpful to the reader, an English description (in parentheses) is given instead of spelling out the words.

ACJDTU	Andean Commission of Jurists, *Drug Trafficking Update*
ACPO	Association of Chief Police Officers
ACSO	Assistant Commissioner for Special Operations
AD	*Action Directe* (France)
AFR	Automatic Fingerprint Recognition
ALF	Animal Liberation Front
ANL	Anti-Nazi League
APC	Advance Passenger Clearance
ASF	Automated Search Facility
ATM	automated teller machine (in a bank)
BA	British Airways
BAA	British Airports Authority
BCCI	Bank of Credit and Commerce International
BGS	(German Border Guard)
BKA	(German criminal intelligence office)
CANPASS	(Canadian biometric travel pass)
CCTV	closed circuit television
CDCU	Central Drugs Coordination Unit
CE(NI)A	Criminal Evidence (Northern Ireland) Act (1988)
CIA	Central Intelligence Agency (USA)
CID	Criminal Investigation Department
CJA	Criminal Justice Act (1988)
CJPOA	Criminal Justice and Public Order Act (1994)
CJPU	Criminal Justice Protection Unit
CPS	Crown Prosecution Service
CRI	(Dutch police intelligence office)
CS	Conflict Studies
CSO	Central Statistical Office
CTR	Currency Transaction Report

2D	two-dimensional (barcode)
DDU	Drug Dependency Unit
Digi-2	(two-finger digital biometric identification system)
DINCOTE	(Peruvian police anti-terrorist intelligence unit)
DIS	Defence Intelligence Service
DNA	(genetic molecule in body fluids)
DPP	Director of Public Prosecutions
DSS	Department of Social Security
DST	(French Surveillance Service)
DTOA	Drug Trafficking Offences Act (1986)
EAASP	European Association of Airport and Seaport Police
EDU	European Drugs Unit
EGIS	(a brand of vapour detector)
ELO	European Liaison Officer (Europol)
EU	European Union
Europol	European Police Office
FAST	Future Automated Screening of Travellers
FATF	Financial Action Task Force
FBI	Federal Bureau of Investigation (USA)
FCO	Foreign and Commonwealth Office
FP	fingerprint (digital biometric identification system)
G7	Group of Seven (Canada, France, Germany, Italy, Japan, UK and USA)
GBH	grievous bodily harm
GCHQ	(British international radio intercept service)
GDP	gross domestic product
GNP	gross national product
HAC	Home Affairs Committee (House of Commons)
HG	hand geometry (digital biometric identification system)
HGV	heavy goods vehicle
HMSO	Her Majesty's Stationery Office
ICAO	International Civil Aviation Organization
ID card	identity card
IMG	International Marxist Group
INS	Immigration and Naturalization Service (USA)

INSPASS	INS Travel Pass
Interpol	International Police Organization
IRA	Irish Republican Army
ISDD	Institute for the Study of Drug Dependence
JFK	J.F. Kennedy International Airport, New York
JIC	Joint Intelligence Committee
KGB	(Soviet intelligence service)
LSD	(synthetic hallucinogenic drug)
MCP	Malayan Communist Party
MDMA	(Ecstasy – synthetic hallucinogenic drug)
MI5	Security Service (colloquial title)
MI6	Secret Intelligence Service (colloquial title)
MRI	machine readable identity (card)
MRP	machine readable passport
MRV	machine readable visa
MRZ	machine readable zone (on card)
NACRO	National Association for the Care and Resettlement of Offenders
NAPO	National Association of Probation Officers
NCIS	National Criminal Intelligence Service
NDIU	National Drugs Intelligence Unit
NF	National Front
NHS	National Health Service
NICRA	Northern Ireland Civil Rights Association
NI(EP)A	Northern Ireland (Emergency Provisions) Act (1973)
NKVD	(Soviet intelligence service – predecessor of KGB)
OAS	(French Secret Army Organization) (1950s–1960s)
OCR	Optical Character Readable (lettering)
PACE	Police and Criminal Evidence Act (1984)
PIN	personal identification number
PNC	Police National Computer
POA	Public Order Act (1936 and 1986)
PSIS	Permanent Secretaries' Committee on the Intelligence Services
PTA	Prevention of Terrorism (Temporary Provisions) Act (1989)
PT(AP)B	Prevention of Terrorism (Additional Powers) Bill (1996)

RCCJ	Royal Commission on Criminal Justice (1993)
RCS	Regional Crime Squad
Risc	reduced instruction set computers
RISCT	Research Institute for the Study of Conflict and Terrorism
RUC	Royal Ulster Constabulary
SB	Special Branch
SEA	Single European Act
SFO	Serious Fraud Office
SIS	Secret Intelligence Service
SL	*Sendero Luminoso* (Shining Path) (Peru)
STP	Schiphol Travel Pass
SWP	Socialist Workers' Party
TDA	taking and driving away (of vehicles)
TEC	Training and Enterprise Council
TREVI	(EU Ministerial Security Committee)
ULTRA	(British code-breaking system – Second World War)
UNDCP	United Nations Drug Control Programme
VIVID	(a brand of enhanced X-ray detector)
Vopos	*Volkspolizei* (East German Police)
WTTC	World Travel and Tourism Council
Y Service	(British radio intercept service – Second World War)
YT	Youth Training

Part I
Introduction

1 Questions and Dilemmas

Crime does devastating damage to civil liberties; it kills, wounds, deprives people of hard-earned possessions and may do severe psychological damage to its victims (especially where sex or violence are involved) as well as physical damage. The central dilemma is how to take effective measures to prevent or detect crime without also unacceptably eroding people's civil liberties.

The prime challenges are to increase the rate of detection and conviction, and to prevent the miscarriage of justice by intimidation or corruption of witnesses and juries, including intimidation of the victims themselves. Only 1 crime in 4 is reported, 1 in 50 results in a conviction and 1 in 750 in someone going to prison.[1] This greatly encourages criminals, who regard the small chance of being convicted as well worth the risk, particularly as crime pays so much better than most jobs or unemployment benefit. So they commit more crimes and more victims suffer.

The most disturbing element in the pattern of crime is the preponderance of young criminals. Over 60 per cent of those arrested for robbery (or muggings) and 55 per cent of those arrested for car thefts are under 21, and a high percentage of drug abusers and street drug sellers are also young.

Why do so many young people turn to crime – some of them permanently? Of young offenders (under 21) 75 per cent of the boys and 53 per cent of the girls are convicted a second time within two years. And one-third of all young people convicted for burglary have already had at least three previous convictions.

How do children turn into criminals? Are some born evil? Are the seeds of delinquency sown before they go to school? They seem to germinate through truancy and petty crime at primary school and blossom through teenage alienation from society. So to what extent are their parents and brothers and sisters to blame? One can imagine the effect it must have on a child to be brought up in a deprived home with an unemployed father and older siblings who have never had a job and never expect to get one.

The Thatcher revolution in the 1980s transformed the economy, converting Britain from being the 'sick man of Europe', despised for the 'British disease', into one of the fastest growing economies in the European Union. The median wage grew by 35 per cent in real terms and that of high earners by 50 per cent. The philosophy was to give incentives and rewards for success and 90 per cent of the population shared in that growth, so they elected the Conservatives four times in succession – in 1979, 1982, 1987 and 1992. But the price of the 90 per cent becoming more prosperous (and more greedy?) was to let the devil take the hindmost. The poorest 10 per cent, most of them on unemployment benefit, and an inordinate number of them black, saw their standard of living actually decline between 1979 and 1991 by 17 per cent in real terms. Has this landed Britain with a pool of alienated people who see little worth doing other than to turn to crime? If so, what should be done about it now?

Drug abuse and crime are closely linked. Of the money spent on drugs on the streets, 90 per cent is acquired by crime, and this alone accounts for 50 per cent of the theft and burglary in Britain. Of the population, 6 per cent take drugs at least once each year and 22 per cent have taken drugs before they are 16. Selling drugs is extremely rewarding; a street dealer can easily earn £1000 a week and some of the importers and distributors are in the £250,000 to £1 million a year bracket. Why on earth would they consider going back to unemployment benefit?

What is the answer? Tougher suppression? Compulsory treatment? To allow drugs to be sold like alcohol, heavily taxed, controlled and licensed? If so, how can they be kept out of the hands of teenagers, many of whom have their lives ruined by them? And what can be done to curb the crime which is generated by the drug trade? If licensing drugs would put the drug trafficking gangs out of business, would it also result in more young people becoming addicted to drugs?

Ten million pounds of illegal money go into circulation in Britain every day. Of the money passing through the City of London, 10 per cent is believed to be the laundered proceeds of international crime. This is made easy by the client confidentiality guaranteed by some international banks. How can governments and the banking community put this right?

Success in fighting crime depends on spotting and targeting criminals. Chapters 6, 7 and 8 of this book are devoted to intelligence. Intelligence gathering depends on observation and surveillance and on recruiting informants by giving incentives and rewards to people within the ranks of the criminal and terrorist gangs. How is this intelligence built up? How are the potential informants spotted? How effective are these activities? Are they fair? And how well does the counter-terrorist legislation work and does it infringe civil liberties? Is it still necessary?

The Public Order Acts of 1986 and 1994 revised the laws concerning processions and assemblies and created new offences classed as 'trespassory assemblies'. The Employment Acts of 1980, 1982 and 1984 have had the effect of outlawing secondary and mass picketing, which has dramatically reduced the number of strikes and the violence on picket lines. This has certainly played a part in the growth of the economy, but has it curtailed civil rights and freedoms? And what effect has it had on police relations with the public?

The Police and Criminal Evidence Act of 1984 and the Criminal Justice and Public Order Act of 1994 changed the powers of arrest and detention and modified the right to silence, or at least the interpretation of it. All these laws are analysed in Part IV of this book to assess their effects on civil liberties.

The figures for trials (only 1 crime in 50 resulting in a conviction) were mentioned earlier. Is our law too heavily weighted in favour of the accused at the expense of past and future victims of crime? How much do we suffer from unscrupulous lawyers and bent coppers? How can we protect witnesses and jurors from intimidation and corruption? Is our adversarial system still the best or would we do better to shift towards the continental inquisitorial system?

Does prison work? Why do so many criminals go on offending again and again, particularly young criminals? Should Britain try more of the alternatives to prison, as many Scandinavian and other European countries do?

First offenders are treated leniently, but should they be forgiven a second time? And a third? And a fourth? Perhaps the baseball rule 'three strikes and you're out' is going too far, but should sentences for repeat offences be escalated more steeply?

Modern technology offers many new powers to those who enforce the law. The use of digital biometric data, unique to each individual (based on fingerprints or – better – hand geometry) is being tested in extensive trials for processing air travellers through immigration; this opens up the possibility of speeding the passage of airport passengers, while reducing the chances of illegal immigrants, international criminals and drug smugglers getting through undetected. But could this technology be used in other ways which might erode civil liberties?

Most of the other countries in Europe have identity (ID) cards. In some they are compulsory, but where they are voluntary, as in France and Italy, the advantages are so great that virtually the whole population chooses to get them. Should Britain follow suit? If so, should they be combined with driving licences or passports? Should an ID card contain coded medical, benefit entitlement or police data – or all on one card for convenience? Or would there be a risk of unauthorized people getting access to confidential data about individuals? Some commercial firms would be happy to pay a lot for this. And should ID cards contain digital biometric data to prevent thieves or forgers getting through the net by impersonation?

Is there an inherent right to conceal identity? Some would say that there is. But is there any civil right to impersonate someone else? And could ID cards be used for harassment by unscrupulous officials or be too easily forged by criminals?

There is a lot of emerging technology in the field of access control and surveillance, especially the proliferation of closed circuit television (CCTV) to deter and detect shoplifting, trespass, football hooliganism, drug trafficking and street crime. This helps to protect the public, but does it unduly invade privacy?

Semtex explosive emits so little vapour that detecting it is equivalent to detecting a glass of whisky in Loch Ness (one part in a million million). Equipment to detect vapour to this level is now in use at most major airports and the noses of trained dogs can be even more sensitive. The equipment and the dogs can also be used for detecting drugs and illegal immigrants concealed in heavy goods vehicles (HGVs) or cargo containers. The potential benefits to the community seem to be considerable but could they, like other technologies, be used to invade privacy?

The fundamental question is how to deter and prevent crime and to detect and convict criminals and terrorists without unduly eroding civil liberties. Different people's civil liberties may conflict: that of prisoners accused but not yet convicted; that of suspects not yet cleared; that of innocent bystanders inconvenienced or stopped, searched and detained; and that of future victims of crime. If the law enforcement system lets guilty criminals go free, it is sentencing more innocent people to suffer from their crimes. How and where should the lines be drawn?

Part II
Crime and its Causes

2 Patterns of Crime

THE BOTTOM RUNGS OF THE CRIME LADDER

What kinds of people become habitual criminals? To what extent is this due to inborn characteristics, such as aggression and dishonesty? Or failure to civilize and educate children early in life so that they become generous, thoughtful, mutually supporting and caring for the community, rather than grabbing what they can from it for themselves?

Criminals can be considered in three levels, mainly characterized by the scale at which they operate: individual or petty criminals; organized criminal gangs; and Mafia-style organizations. There is some overlapping and people graduate from one to the other.

Petty crime is sometimes committed by a loner but more often by a group of two or three, and usually against victims within or close by their own communities. One man in three (but many fewer women) is found guilty of at least one petty crime by the age of 35,[1] but most of them keep away from it once they get a steady job. A very small minority, however, make it a persistent means of livelihood, being sentenced and released again and again. One-third of those convicted of burglary have at least three previous convictions.[2] A large proportion of burglaries, thefts and robberies are committed by a very small percentage of the population – young and old.

Most of them start poor, in deprived neighbourhoods, in which it is difficult for households on income support to meet their bills for basic needs – rent, food, fuel and clothing. For young criminals, however, the pattern soon becomes very different from that of the nineteenth century, when they stole to avoid starvation. More commonly, they are initially aiming to pay for small pleasures, such as better food, tapes, videos, and so on, or to bring a little excitement into otherwise bleak and frustrating lives. For some, this excitement will involve drugs and, if they become regular users, they may have to raise £400–500 a week to pay for them –

from crime. Shoplifting is usually a loner's crime, while burglary generally involves at least two people and probably a third. Car theft and 'joy riding' are the most exciting.

ORGANIZED CRIME

From this, some get involved in the second category, organized crime, initially on the fringes of an established gang. Organized criminal gangs are typically from six to ten strong but sometimes up to fifty or a hundred.[3] Their activities may include distributing and selling drugs and, if burglary is involved, they will have established contacts ('fences') for getting rid of stolen goods. A member of an organized criminal gang typically makes about £1000 a week and, if caught and sentenced, is more likely to return to this source of income rather than seek boring and low-paid work or apply for social security.

As they rise in the hierarchy of organized crime, young criminals (predominantly male) graduate to an affluent and sometimes flamboyant lifestyle, with a smart car (BMWs are popular), gold and jewellery, liquor; some, to assert their success and *machismo*, cultivate the reputation of having a different woman every night.[4] Some still live at home, especially if their fathers or brothers are also criminals, but most live with others in the gang or on the fringe of it.

By no means all the members of organized gangs come from deprived communities. Some of the leaders have organizing and leadership experience and come from an environment which would enable them to earn a successful living, but they are attracted by the prospect of getting rich quickly and of having a more exciting life. This type are particularly to be found in drug trafficking gangs or as leaders of professional car-theft organizations. They sometimes work on an international scale, especially in the export of stolen vehicles – or fraud.

Financial fraud and counterfeiting are particularly lucrative forms of crime, and these criminals know their way around the business world – again often internationally. Few of them were ever deprived and are never likely to be so. They probably do more harm to the community than burglars, thieves and robbers, and may employ hit squads to deal with rivals or informants, but the professionl fraudsters seldom themselves use violence or threaten personal safety; yet they do contribute indirectly to other forms of crime against persons and property including violence and drug trafficking in their capacity as money launderers (see Chapter 5).

A growing and lucrative form of organized crime at its lower end is post office fraud. The gang leaders recruit thieves among post office sorters, initially by offering a share (usually 10 per cent) of the proceeds and later, if the sorters become uneasy and want to pull out, by threat of betrayal to the police or of physical violence. The thieves are taught how to spot letters likely to contain large cheques, for example, in printed envelopes addressed to credit card companies for payment of monthly accounts. These are then passed to the forgers who have sophisticated equipment for obliterating the payee and substituting another to which they cannot easily be traced. This type of fraud was believed to have netted £100 million in the UK in 1995.[5] Theft of credit cards, bank cards or charge cards can be even more lucrative.

MAFIA-STYLE CRIME

In the third category are Mafia-style criminal organizations. So far there have been no British Mafias but there have been occasional attempts, usually shortlived, by Italian and American Mafias to open up subsidiaries in Britain.[6] The characteristics of Mafias, in Italy or Russia, is that they have a hierarchical structure through which, by means of intimidation and corruption, they gain control of substantial sectors of industry and commerce and, in due course, of local, municipal and (as in Italy) national political power. Thus the key difference between Mafias and other organized criminal gangs is that Mafias are seeking power as well as money. Their power and their money feed off each other.

The classic example is *Cosa Nostra* which, from 1944 to 1994, had virtual control of Sicily, both political and economic. It comprised some 5000 men (women were kept to the fringes) organized in 180 'families', each of which was comparable in size to an organized criminal gang. Recruits to the families were subjected to an initiation ceremony in which they took the vow of silence (*omerta*), acknowledging that the penalty for breaking it was death. These families were grouped in provinces, each of which had a *capo commissione* (chief). These chiefs in turn formed a *super-commissione* headed by a *capo di capi* (chief of chiefs) – a position periodically contested in 'mafia wars'. From the early 1980s, until his arrest in January 1993, the *capo di capi* was alleged to be Salvatore 'Toto' Raiina. *Cosa Nostra* influence spread into Rome and the industrial north, with many senior public figures accused of complicity – having accepted bribes in the face of threats to their own or their families' lives.

Of the other main Italian Mafias, *Camorra* (Naples) in 1993 had about 7000 members in 130 'clans' and '*Ndrangheta* (Calabria) about 6700 in 126 *n'drini*, which were based more on blood ties than those in *Cosa Nostra* and were more independent.[7]

Since the collapse of Communism in 1989, the emergence of a black market in the gaps left by the disintegrating command economy led to a rapid growth of organized crime in Russia where, by 1994, there were over 5000 organized criminal gangs, each between 10 and 100 strong.[8] Some of these have now coalesced into regional groupings on mafia lines, exercising political, industrial and financial power in their regions though not (up to the time of writing) on a national scale. They are often led by former members of the *nomenklatura*, who moved into the black market when they were unhorsed by *perestroika* and knew the ropes sufficiently well to be able to gain control of many of the newly privatized companies.

In the USA in the 1920s, during Prohibition (of alcohol) criminal gangs based on the Italian-American Mafia, with strong links to *Cosa Nostra* in Sicily, gained control of bootlegging, especially in Chicago and New York. Through intimidation and corruption they extended their control to a number of industrial, commercial and local political leaders.

The Medellin and Cali drug cartels in Colombia also have many Mafia characteristics, including control of a number of politicians, whose compliance they ensure by offering, as the Colombians put it, a 'choice of silver or lead'.

At present there seems to be no likelihood of British organized criminal gangs coalescing with Mafia-style hierarchies, but the police and intelligence authorities are constantly aware of this possibility, initially focused in certain regions, as happened in Russia and is threatening other central European countries such as Poland. The first indications would be suspicious behaviour by some of the local councillors or officials or of leading figures in regional business and industry, who were succumbing to intimidation and corruption.

THE PATTERN OF SERIOUS OFFENCES IN BRITAIN

'Notifiable offences' are serious offences, including most 'indictable offences' (which have to be tried by a crown court), most 'triable either way offences' (triable by crown court or by magistrates) and some 'summary offences' such as unauthorized taking of a motor vehicle, notifiable on account of the possible risk to life. Statistics of notifiable offences are published annually and give a fair indication of the pattern of crime in Britain.[9] Table 2.1 shows the number of notifiable offences recorded and the clear-up rates for England and Wales and for the Metropolitan Police area.[10]

The weakness of these figures is that only about a quarter of crimes are reported at all. Thus the average clear-up rate, 26 per cent of recorded crimes, probably means about 6 per cent of the total number of crimes, of which only about 2 per cent result in convictions. It was mentioned earlier that only 1 crime in 50 results in a conviction and 1 in 750 in imprisonment.[11] Clear-up rates are lowest for offences affecting property, though higher for violent and sexual offences.

In March 1996, figures were published by the Home Office (*The Times*, 26 March 1996) showing that there was an encouraging trend, in that the total number of recorded crimes had fallen slightly in each of the years 1993, 1994 and 1995. This amounted to a total fall of 8 per cent over those three years, reversing a steady rise in the years 1981–92 totalling 111 per cent (i.e. more than doubled). Most of the types of recorded crimes had fallen in 1995, though reported robberies increased by 14.7 per cent in the year; but this may well have been due to a higher proportion of victims deciding to report that they had been robbed.

Table 2.1 Recorded crime (notifiable offences) and clear-up rates

Notifiable offences	*England and Wales 1994* Number recorded	% of total	Clear-up rate (%)	*London Metropolis 1994–95* Number recorded	% of total	Clear-up rate (%)
Violence against the person	220,000	4.18	77	42,679	5.09	69
Sexual offences	32,000	0.6	76	6,820	0.81	64
Robbery	60,000	1.14	22	26,139	3.12	22
Burglary	1,261,000	24.00	21	166,120	19.84	20
Theft and handling stolen goods	2,561,000	48.75	24	394,344	47.10	17
of which theft of vehicles	534,000	10.16	19			
of which theft from vehicles	844,000	16.06	13			
Fraud and forgery	146,000	2.77	52	32,472	3.87	43
Criminal damage	930,000	17.70	17	159,854	19.09	14
Others, including drug trafficking	43,000	0.81	99	8,777	1.04	86
Total	5,253,000		average 26%			average 22%

Sources: Compiled from CSO, *Social Trends 1996*, London, HMSO, 1996, pp. 160 and 168; Metropolitan Police, *Report 1994–95*, London, Metropolitan Police, 1995, pp. 70–1.

The ages of those found guilty or cautioned for indictable offences in 1994 in England and Wales are shown in Table 2.2. This shows that 522,500 were found guilty or cautioned, of whom 426,800 (82 per cent) were male and 95,700 (18 per cent) were female, and that 42 per cent of the males and 47 per cent of the females were under 21.[12]

The likelihood of first offenders reoffending was very high, particularly among young offenders (those who were under 21 at the time of the second conviction). Of young offenders, 75 per cent of the boys and 53 per cent of the girls were convicted of a second offence within two years. Among those over 21, 47 per cent of the men and 38 per cent of the women were reconvicted within two years.[13]

Table 2.3 shows the number of arrests in 1994–95 for notifiable offences in the London area (national figures were not available). These show what a high percentage of those arrested were under 21, including

Table 2.2 Ages of offenders found guilty or cautioned (England and Wales)

Percentages	*Males aged*					*Females aged*				
Indictable offences	*10–13*	*14–17*	*18–20*	*21 & over*	*% of all 10+*	*10–13*	*14–17*	*18–20*	*21 & over*	*% of all 10+*
Violence against the person	10	13	10	13	12	8	14	9	9	10
Sexual offences	1	1	1	2	2	0	0	0	0	0
Robbery	2	2	1	1	1	1	1	0	0	—
Burglary	18	17	13	8	11	3	3	2	1	2
Theft and handling stolen goods	60	47	36	37	40	85	72	62	61	66
Criminal damage	6	4	3	3	3	1	2	1	1	1
Drug offences	1	10	22	16	15	1	4	11	9	7
Other offences	2	6	15	21	16	1	4	14	18	12
Total %	100	100	100	100	100	100	100	100	100	100
Total offences (thousands)	22.8	80.6	75.3	248.1	426.8	9.4	23.0	12.3	51.0	95.7
% of offenders belonging to each age group	5	19	18	58	100	10	24	13	53	100

Source: CSO, *Social Trends 1996*, pp. 162–3.

Table 2.3 Arrests (Metropolitan police) 1994–95

Notifiable offences	*Age group of persons arrested*					
	Not known	*10–20*	*21–30*	*31–40*	*41& over*	*Total*
Violence against the person	3,473	2,811	2,908	2,426	1,242	12,860
Sexual offences	275	302	407	339	434	1,757
Robbery	331	1,856	619	222	53	3,081
Burglary	895	4,304	2,858	886	271	9,214
Theft and handling stolen goods	5,899	16,484	14,209	7,064	4,382	48,038
of which motor vehicle thefts	240	1,387	668	173	78	2,546
Fraud and forgery	710	1,243	3,466	1,875	1,046	8,340
Criminal damage	1,925	3,983	3,211	1,577	760	11,456
Other notifiable offences	275	1,977	2,755	1,272	610	6,889
Total Notifiable offences	13,783	32,960	30,433	15,561	8,798	101,635
Other recorded offences (non-notifiable)	6,470	12,963	16,755	7,372	3,259	46,819

Source: Metropolitan Police, *Report 1994–95*, p. 81.

22%	of those arrested for violence against the person
60%	for robbery
47%	for burglary
34%	for theft and handling stolen goods
55%	for car thefts
35%	for criminal damage

Some of the reasons why so many young people turn to crime and how the problem might be tackled are discussed in Chapters 3 and 14.

Of those convicted for indictable offences in 1994, fewer the one in five received immediate custodial sentences:

20%	were discharged
31%	were fined
28%	were sentenced to community service
1%	received fully suspended sentences
17%	received custodial sentences (16% under five years)
2%	received other sentences

Of these, some offences averaged a higher percentage of custodial sentences – for example, robbery 65 per cent, burglary 34 per cent and violence against the person 22 per cent. The average was brought down by lower percentages of custodial sentences for theft and handling stolen goods (11 per cent) and criminal damage (10 per cent).[14]

Of adults (people over 21) who are sent to prison, the average lengths of sentences are shown in Table 2.4.

The great majority of victims of violence are young. In particular, young males (16–29) are nearly 20 times as likely to be attacked than people over 60. Victims of violence in 1994–95 included:[15]

less than 1% of all people over 60
4% of all people aged 30–59
8.3% of females aged 16–29
14.5% (one in seven) of males aged 16–29

OFFENCES ENDANGERING LIFE

Of the notifiable offences listed in Table 2.1, the most likely to cause death are violence against the person and robbery

Table 2.4 Average custodial sentences – adults (over 21)

Offence	*Males*	*Females*
Violence against the person	23 months	21 months
Sexual offences	39 months	33 months
Robbery	50 months	31 months
Burglary	17 months	15 months
Theft and handling stolen goods	11 months	9 months
Fraud and forgery	15 months	11 months
Criminal damage	28 months	30 months
Drug offences	30 months	35 months
Motoring offences	9 months	7 months
Other offences	12 months	10 months
Average – all offences	22 months	18 months

Source: CSO, *Social Trends 1996*, p. 167.

(mugging). In addition to these, a number of homicides are as a result of taking and driving away (TDA) a motor vehicle. A substantial number of deaths and other crimes also arise from the trafficking and abuse of drugs, which are discussed in Chapter 4.

Britain has – and has traditionally had – an enviably low rate of murder compared with other countries. This is largely due to the police (and consequently most criminals) being unarmed. In 1992, recorded murders per million of the population were 910 in Colombia, 155 in Russia, 90 in the USA, 40 in Germany, 25 in Britain and 12 in Japan.[16] Of the 42,679 crimes of violence against the person in the London Metropolis listed in Table 2.1, only 191 (0.4 per cent) resulted in death, 3363 (8 per cent) in serious injury and over 90 per cent in slight injuries or no injuries at all. In more than 80 per cent of cases, no weapons were used; and when they were used they were mainly blunt instruments (8 per cent) or sharp instruments (6 per cent). In only 693 cases in all (1.6 per cent) were firearms used.[17] This is in striking contrast to the USA, where 50 per cent of the murders are drug related and most are carried out with guns.[18]

In addition to the 191 murders and manslaughters, 30 people were killed by reckless driving, including TDA. These accounted for over 10 per cent of the 291 people killed in motor accidents in the Metropolis.[19]

Recorded theft and unauthorized taking of motor vehicles in the Metropolis in 1994–95 amounted to 63,286 (16 per cent of all theft and handling stolen goods – 394,344). Thefts from a motor vehicle added a further 119,623 (30 per cent), which indicates how big a part motor vehicles play in all forms of crime, lethal or otherwise. Burglaries (166,120) and robberies (26,139) are listed separately from the 394,344 thefts, and so on. The clear-up rates are, for burglaries 20 per cent, for theft, etc. 17 per cent and for robbery 14 per cent, but for car thefts under 8 per cent and for TDA 16 per cent.[20] With only a quarter of offences being reported by the victims and recorded by the police, this suggests that between 95 per cent and 98 per cent of robbers, thieves and burglars get away with it.

TDA ('joy riding') is a cause of particular concern because of the risk it poses to life. Joy riders are mostly under 17 and hold no driving licences or car insurance. One of their main motivations is to show off to their friends (male and female). But, because of their youth, magistrates tend to deal with them leniently, even when they repeat the offence many times. There have also been notorious cases of criminals under 15 who have committed up to 70 offences, and the judiciary has been dismally unsuccessful in protecting the public from them. The same applies to the punishment of young burglars, who sometimes get sentences of less than a year even after ten previous convictions. These problems will be discussed further in Chapters 3 and 14.

Drug trafficking also causes loss of life, through overdoses, violence on a high or on the way down from a high, and gang fights. The drugs business, with possible ways of tackling it, is examined in Chapter 4.

The murder rates on p. 19 are clearly linked to gun ownership. There were 212 million guns held privately in the USA, including 67 million handguns. Gunshot wounds kill 38,000 people each year, about 60 per cent by suicide or accident. Of 16,000 murders with guns in USA in 1993, 13,000 were with handguns. By contrast, 54 people were being murdered annually with guns in the UK. The chance of dying from gunshot wounds in USA was 70 times greater than in the UK and 100 times greater than in Japan; and British gun laws were tightened in October 1996 (see Postscript, p. 230).

3 Why Young People Turn to Crime

GOOD CHILDREN, BAD CHILDREN

This chapter looks at how British children grow up and how their home life, education, training and environment can launch them on the way to becoming either considerate and responsible or anti-social; and at how and why some become habitual criminals in their teens or even earlier as truants from primary school.

A number of children are born devious and dishonest (a mercifully small percentage) and it will be very difficult for their parents and their schools to develop them into good citizens. Many of these may end up as confidence tricksters, fraudsters or successful professional criminals, as they are often intelligent, plausible and sometimes charming. With so small a percentage of crimes resulting in conviction (see pp. 15–20), some of them become rich and powerful, and their skill, cunning and articulacy are such that they do not get caught. Their crimes are mainly large-scale frauds whose proceeds may be in millions rather than thousands.

The great majority of children, however, are born neither evil nor devious. Some may get into trouble under the influence of other children but the ones who have good parents and an environment which gives them opportunities are likely to become reasonably responsible citizens. If, however, circumstances beyond their control throw them into a deprived sector of the community (the poorest 10 per cent) a combination of adverse conditions will frustrate them and convince them that society is unfair and hostile to them. Many of them will then turn to crime as the only way they can see to get their fair share from what is, by world standards, an affluent society.

AGGRESSION AND CIVILIZATION

Every animal has some aggressive instincts. This has been an essential part of Darwinian natural selection and survival of the fittest over the past 40 million years. The human species was first recognizable about 2 million years ago, when the 'naked apes' emerged from the forests on two feet,[1] able to survive on the open plains among predators who were fleeter of foot and more powerful with tooth and claw. The humans prevailed by superior intelligence and an exceptional ability to cooperate in hunting groups. Along with other mammals whose propagation depended on sexual mating, human males have competed, so that the strongest and cleverest took the choice of breeding with the most desirable females, who themselves competed to attract the most desirable males. So have deer and wolves – but humans have developed one very unpleasant difference from the others.

It is relatively rare for mammals other than humans to kill their own species. When stags lock horns, once they have established which one *could* kill the other if the fight proceeded, they disengage, and the losers accept the winner as the leader of the herd. A fight between male wolves ends when the winner has his jaws poised over the loser's throat; he does not close them; the loser is spared and accepts his subordination, though he is free to breed with females the leader does not want. So the pack goes on growing.

Humans do kill others of their own species, sometimes as invividuals but more commonly as members of a group, a tribe or (more recently) a nation. This arises less from personal conflicts than from socialization – from the intense urge to be accepted and admired within the group. This accounts for the high murder rate in some countries, for the astonishing phenomenon of war, for ethnic cleansing and, at street level, for gang warfare. This human characteristic developed from our hunting groups over a million years ago.

There is a tendency to exaggerate the effects on the development of human behaviour of our recent socialization – neighbours, school, life in the fields and streets and now the images projected by the media. These are important but our deeply rooted instincts outweigh them.

This is perhaps easiest to visualize by equating years to distance, watching naked apes evolving into intelligent human beings. Equating 1 metre to 1000 years, the naked apes emerging from the forest 2 million years ago trudged into view 2000 metres away. For over 99 per cent of that time, they evolved as hunter-gatherers, cooperating in small groups, helped by dogs needing their mutual support, and eventually getting the idea of throwing missiles and making tools and weapons – the first major distinction from most other animals. Only 12,000 years ago, in the last 12 metres of that 2 km trudge, they discovered agriculture, began to settle in villages and develop the rudiments of collective security, defending their villages from nomads outside who coveted their comfort and prosperity. Collective security created the need for chiefs and henchmen. This started a major social change, but the fundamental characteristics of the human species had already long been established. Then, 6 metres (6000 years) away, the city states appeared around Babylon, beginning what became culture and civilization.

Greek and Roman civilization, with the development of literature, drama and democratic government, and a huge advance in the ability to organize for war, perfected the notion of modern nation-states and empires, at about 2 metres (2000 years) – spitting distance away. The Renaissance came at 50 cm (500 years), the industrial revolution at 20 cm (200 years), mass education and a popular press at 10 cm, public TV channels 5 cm and the Internet, E-mail, etc., almost scratching our nose at half a centimetre.

So the influence of civilization, of the industrial society, education and the media can be exaggerated. On the other hand, there is only a limited amount we can do about the 2 million year evolution of our innate instincts except to understand them. One of the aims of the 2000 years of post-Greek civilization has been to seek ways of channelling and modifying these instincts (for example, the instincts of self-preservation, competition for a livelihood, and greed), by social engineering and mind bending to shape a chosen form of society. Unfortunately the social engineers and mind benders have often themselves been motivated more by self and sectional interests than by a wish to benefit the community. Though they may delude themselves otherwise, few have done much to improve the lot of others if it was to be at the expense of their own. But, all the way through, the learning of the parents made a big difference to the next generation.

HOME AND SCHOOL

The process of education begins long before school. The Basic Skills Agency did a valuable research project, studying a group of 20 year olds for whom information was collected at various stages of their lives from the year of their birth, 1970, through to 1991. Their results are summarized in Table 3.1. Among other things, they found that the chances of a 21 year old acquiring adequate reading skills depended to a startling extent on the level of education reached by their parents. Of 21 year olds in 1991 having a 'very low' reading skill, 69 per cent (over two-thirds) had parents neither of whom had any educational qualification. The proportion of parents having no qualification in 1970 (40 per cent) was obviously much higher than now, but the handicap carried by their children was horrific. If one parent had even a basic vocational qualification, the son or daughter had more than twice the chance of avoiding illiteracy; if one parent had a GCE O level, three times the chance; if one parent had an A level, over four times the chance; and if one parent had a degree, over seven times the chance.[2]

The reasons for this lie much deeper than just the ambitions and attitudes the children acquire from their parents towards school attendance and what school is worth. The effects start from earliest childhood. The poorest parents living in the most deprived conditions tended (again more in 1970–80 than in the mid-1990s) to have quite a lot of children with not much room to move, since their lives offered few satisfactions other than child-bearing. The chance of the parents finding time or space for meaningful conversation with their children before they reached school age was very small; their most frequent communication would probably be 'get out of my way'. As soon as the children were old enough they would escape onto the streets with

Table 3.1 Effect of parents' education on reading and numeracy of 21 year olds

	Literacy and numeracy of 21 year old whose better educated parent had level shown here				
	Highest qualification of either parent				
	NIL qual.	*Vocational*	*0 level or equiv.*	*A level or equiv.*	*Degree or Cert. Ed.*
Percentage who reached literacy and numeracy levels below at age 21					
Reading skills of 21 year olds					
Very low	69	13	12	4	3
Low	59	11	17	7	6
No apparent problem	34	17	23	11	16
Numeracy skills of 21 year olds					
Very low	52	17	19	6	4
Low	64	11	14	6	5
No apparent problem	36	16	22	11	15
Percentage of parents one of whom had qualification as shown	40	16	21	10	13
Relative odds against the child being literate (parent with degree = 1)	7.47	3.52	2.47	1.73	1.0

Source: Compiled from data provided by Basic Skills Agency cited in CSO, *Social Trends* 1996, p. 67.

their friends, learning to be streetwise but not much else.

By contrast, the children of educated parents would have been having a steady trickle of culture impinging on them from earliest infancy. Their parents would choose toys, pictures and books which encouraged dexterity and intelligence. As they moved around the kitchen they would talk to their babies, who would become aware of what and why and how things happened. When they went for a walk, without particularly thinking about it, the parents would explain what they saw, what it meant and, later on, how it came into being. They would go to places like the Tower of London or the Roman walls in York as well as to the swings and roundabouts. By the age of 7, most of their children would know the pleasure and value of reading and become inquisitive, pursuing what they found interesting. In other words, the process of education and civilization, superimposed on the basic instincts with which they were born, had begun in the first year of their lives.

The behaviour of very young children, before upbringing and socialization have begun to take effect, can give a useful clue about the canvas on which we have to paint a better society. Apart from the very small percentage of natural deviants mentioned at the start of this chapter, children of up to 3 years old playing at home or in play groups will compete (perhaps for toys or affection) and may squabble and hit each other; but they very rarely use 'weapons', like hard edges or sharp pencils, to do serious damage to each other; and if they do draw blood, they are generally frightened and upset. Like the deer and the wolves they have no instinct to kill or seriously harm their own kind, which is reassuring.

For all except orphans or children in care, a child's first group is the nuclear family. The years from 1 to 5 are crucially important, not only for education but also for interaction with others. In families of two parents and two or three children, they grow up accustomed to living together, with respect for the interests of others, not always getting their own way and learning the mutual benefits of cooperation. With good parents, they also learn to accept advice. Occasionally, however, families can have a negative influence, if parents and older brothers and sisters are unemployed, frustrated, cynical, resentful of deprivation and advocating a right to help themselves to what they consider to be their due – or what they want.

Even when they are at school, from 5 to 16 or 18, home remains, for most, the strongest influence. Of 6000 conscious hours in the year (16 hours a day) they spend only about 1000 hours at school compared with 5000 hours with their families or neighbourhood friends, including evenings, weekends and holidays – that is, five waking hours under the home influence for every hour at school. This continues right through until they move out of daily range of home, to go to work or university.

There are now, however, many more one-parent families (as many as 49 per cent of Afro-Caribbean families). Other families have unemployed fathers and rely on part-time work by the mother, with social security benefits, to survive; so these children grow up with no understanding of a 'work ethic'. Very often, families on benefit can find no way to cope without fiddling or petty crime or both, and this too has an inevitable effect on children growing up. The number of children raised in families on income support rose from 955,000 in 1979 to 3 million in 1993.[3]

PRE-SCHOOL CARE

Pre-school child care can help enormously in preventing children from getting onto the doomladen conveyor belt leading to truancy, illiteracy and thence to a life of crime. This is vitally important for the children of working mothers and those from broken homes or in other circumstances which give them little chance of keeping off that conveyor belt. Help can take the form of day nurseries, crèches, child minders (or nannies), play groups and private nurseries.

The government provides day nurseries for about 33,000 children in the UK. Most of these come from homes where child abuse, poor parenting or poor home conditions make such care necessary, and this is reflected in the fact that over half the 33,000 have speech, health or behaviour problems – four times as many as in nursery schools and ten times as many as in play groups,[4] not an ideal atmosphere in which to grow up.

Nearly 900,000 3 and 4 year olds attend play groups in the UK. Most play groups, however, provide no more than a respite for mothers lasting a few hours, often only two or three times a week, not giving them the opportunity to take up full-time or even part-time employment. The play groups do, however, provide valuable education for the children in learning to live together and developing basic social skills and confidence. Many of them are cooperative ventures by the mothers of the children concerned, and they either take turns to run the play group or share the expenses of paying someone else to do so. But these are usually the better mothers in any case, and their children are therefore the least likely to have behavioural problems; so they all benefit from each other and enjoy a good preparation for school.

About 250,000 children have places with registered child minders; these are generally the children of working mothers, of whom many more have informal arrangements with unregistered child minders. Because the parents work and have a sense of responsibility, these children are, again, generally not the ones who get into trouble later.

Local nursery schools, or nursery classes in state schools, are provided for about 400,000 children but, of these, fewer than 50,000 are full time. Most mothers have to pay but other children from unsatisfactory homes are sent there at public expense, so the percentage of problem children is more than double that in play schools, though very much less than in day nurseries.[5]

Crèches are often provided by companies free for the children of their employees. Most of these are excellent because the companies know that this attracts good people to work for them.

The government recognized the importance of day care and pre-school education when it introduced vouchers for them in 1995, and future governments may or may not continue with these, but they will all fund nursery education in some way.

There have been some constructive experiments in the USA, of which the Perry Pre-School Project is the best known. It has now published findings of the effects on people who went through the programme in the mid-1960s. All were children from 'multiply deprived' backgrounds and they were given a high quality 'active learning' programme. Their subsequent lives were then compared with those of a control group of children of similar age and background. The Project children had significantly less trouble with the police, 7 per cent having five or more arrests compared with 27 per cent in the control group; 71 per cent completed twelfth grade (age 17) or higher education compared with 57 per cent; and 29 per cent earned $2000 or more per month compared with 7 per cent. Allowing for the saving in costs of law enforcement, prison, and so on, it was estimated that, over the lifetimes of the participants, the taxpayer was saved $7.16 for every dollar invested.[6]

TRUANTS AND LOW ACHIEVERS

Of children aged between 5 and 9 at primary school, it is estimated that 21 per cent of the mothers work full time.[7]

Up to 1 million children in this age group are believed to come home to an empty house after school and many are often unsupervised during holidays. This lack of parental supervision, formally in controlling the children's independence, and informally in partaking in their leisure activities, has been shown to be closely related to offending behaviour,[8] especially truancy, shoplifting and vandalism. There is an urgent need for public expenditure to counter this, for example by providing attractive after-school programmes in school premises after they would normally close at 3.30 or 4 p.m., adventure playgrounds, and holiday play schemes.[9] This also underlines the need for adequate play facilities in the vicinity of bleak blocks of low-cost inner city housing, where the children have nowhere to go, so they range around in gangs, getting into trouble.

Parental supervision remains important when children go on to secondary school from age 11 onwards, particularly in ensuring attendance at school. Helping families who are having trouble with teenage children is not a statutory duty for the social services, and the constraint on their resources, ironically, often means that children have to commit a crime before the family gets any help.[10] Solving these problems is not helped by the youth culture created by television companies seeking high ratings, and other advertisers trying to stimulate teenage demand.

Today's teenagers are, or should be, tomorrow's parents. Many young people, especially boys, grow up in an environment in which they see little prospect of ever earning enough income to marry, make a home and have children. Some break away and live rough (62 per cent of young people sleeping rough on the streets of London in 1994 were black)[11] and both they and many others are damaged in such a way that, if they do have children, in or out of wedlock, they are sadly unlikely to make good parents.

The danger signs in a child's development become clearly recognizable in primary school when, usually under the leadership of older children from homes in which the anchor of family influence is weak, regular truancy begins. This does double damage, both depriving children of education (as was shown in Table 3.1) and leading them into street crime, both for the money and the buzz. This early deviance should be tackled much more firmly than it is. Absence from school should be reported and followed up, and community police officers should give a high priority to questioning children of school age seen at large during school hours. Truants should be initially punished by loss of privileges and, if they persist, they should be moved to special schools with stricter discipline and training designed to get them back into the main stream. As the Perry Pre-School Project has shown (see p. 28), this will be cheaper in the end than if they are allowed to become criminals, and some, at least, may be saved from this. We should not abandon them to their fate at the age of 10.

East Asian culture, in Japan and China, with Singapore and the other 'little tigers', produces more disciplined children than contemporary Western culture. In China this is still excessively influenced by the rigidity and ruthlessness of the Communist Party and the state. In Japan and the others the influences are more healthily balanced, with economic incentives buttressed by a powerful ethos of respect for parents. These influences lead to a much lower crime rate and to an unmistakably happier disposition among young people at work, contrasting with the cynical or apathetic outlook of many of their equivalents in Western societies. Singapore is probably the best model of all.

There is no substitute for good parenting, and one of the most valuable additions to our curriculum would be to teach children the arts of parenting right through school. This could be extended, where necessary, to further education of parents themselves – perhaps compulsorily where children are truants and committing offences early in their lives.

Truancy is usually a street gang activity and when gang members do attend school they despise the staff and the other children, often getting sadistic pleasure out of bullying the smaller ones, acquiring a sense of power and a taste for violence. The Home Office Prison Survey of 1991 found that 30 per cent of prisoners had regularly played truant after the age of 11, compared with 3 per cent of the population as a whole.[12]

Low achievement is a cumulative disease. Truancy – illiteracy – inability to absorb education – non-cooperation – and a perverse macho pride in being a 'bad boy'. By the age of 15, such children already know the rewards of crime and the small chance of conviction. To stop their rot before it is too late requires intense efforts by dedicated people who have the art of building a rapport with difficult children; the best are often former delinquents themselves. They can hope to rescue only a minority, but every success will save the community more than their pay. Where they fail the children will grow up with a contempt for society and its values; they will believe, often with good reason, that many of the fat cats who run that society do so only in their own interests and that their so-called values are hypocritical; they see little prospect of being offered either work or opportunities and they believe that they have a right to help themselves, like they see some of the fat cats doing. Their aim is therefore to acquire the skills to beat that rotten society and its law enforcers and, in doing so, to enjoy the buzz and the affluence – a luxurious lifestyle, cars, sex and drugs – through crime. It sounds good, but the price will be paid by their victims (who will seldom be the fat cats).

FINANCING BETTER EDUCATION

If Britain is to check this slide, it will be vitally important to spend more on education at every level. As well as alleviating illiteracy and alienation at the bottom end of the educational range, better teaching is needed to keep up with the competition and the pace of technological change. In education Britain is badly behind France, Germany, Japan and Singapore.

All three main political parties in UK agree on the need for better and more widely available nursery schooling and differ only in the ways they plan to achieve it. They also agree that it is essential to attract better quality teachers to primary and secondary schools. This means higher pay coupled with enforcement of standards and a fair system for removing any who are not good enough. Delinquency and poor teachers produce a vicious circle: violent and abusive children deter many of the best people from teaching in urban schools where they are most needed; weak and ineffective teachers allow truancy and delinquency to flourish.

To break this vicious circle will mean a lot more money over the whole range from nursery through primary to secondary education. (University education should be made to finance its own improvement by replacing student grants by student loans, to be repaid over the years out of the higher salaries which graduates should earn. This process has already begun.) There is much to be said for the Liberal Democrat proposal to raise the money by an extra 1 per cent on income tax. For tactical reasons, this should be raised not by increasing the basic rate of income tax, but by imposing a separate 'education levy' of 1 per cent on all incomes taxable at or above the basic rate (currently 24 per cent). This should go into a dedicated fund, additional to the current education budget increased annually by the inflation rate, to be spent and accounted for only for specified educational purposes, notably on raising the pay and quality of teachers and financing universal pre-school care and education. The great majority of the public would welcome it if it were done in this way. It might even be possible to bypass our antiquated adversarial political system; if one party leader could persuade the other two to guarantee this levy as in the national interest whichever party were in power, that leader would gain enormously in public esteem (see also Chapter 13).

INEQUALITY

It is too early yet to pass a final judgement on Mrs Thatcher's administration (1979–90). Its achievements were a remarkable overhaul of Britain's economy which it had long needed, and the end of the 'British disease'. In the 1970s Britain had lost ten times as many working days from strikes as Germany, whose investment per worker in industry and commerce was double that in Britain, with an obvious effect on productivity and growth. British people were either pitied or despised in Europe. By 1991 all that was past: Britain had survived the depression of the 1980s better than most EU countries and emerged with one of the healthiest economies and the lowest strike rate. Unemployment, though still too high, was lower than most. And events like the resolution of the Iranian Embassy siege in London (1980) and the Falklands War (1982) had revived British pride and confidence on the international scene.

The social price of these successes was, however, very high. The overall balance sheet of the credit for economic progress against the debit for damage to society, in terms of deprivation of the poorest 10 per cent and the crime rate, cannot yet be finally assessed. This price can best be summed up as a widening of inequality. The Department of Social Security (DSS) reported that, between 1979 and 1991, the available income after housing costs of the richest 10 per cent grew by 62 per cent, while that of the poorest 10 per cent declined by 17 per cent in real terms.[13]

It would be an exaggeration to say that this was deliberate, but it could be ascribed to a philosophy that Britain's economic success depended on giving incentives and rewards to those who contributed to that success and a kick up the backside for those who failed, to give them a spur to break out of it or suffer the consequences – the devil take the hindmost.

These poorest 10 per cent more or less coincided with those on supplementary or unemployment benefit (unemployment varied between 8 and 15 per cent during 1979–91). Perhaps some of the Conservative Members of Parliament may have looked at it dispassionately in terms of votes: 'the 10 per cent unemployed will not vote for us anyway; but 10 per cent unemployed means 90 per cent with jobs; if we ensure that those in work become more prosperous every year, the majority will vote for us in a secret ballot, however much they complain about the Headmistress'. And vote they did – in 1983, 1987 and, fading a bit, in 1992.

As a further illustration of the growing inequalities: at the start of the 1980s the richest 20 per cent of the population were four times richer than the poorest 20 per cent; by 1991 they were six times richer.[14] The Joseph Rowntree Foundation noted that, after 1978, the lowest hourly paid wages hardly changed in real terms and by 1992 were actually lower than in 1975; median wages in the same period grew by 35 per cent and higher wages grew by 50 per cent;[15] in other words, the prosperity of the hourly paid workers rose on average by more than one-third and that of the highest by half, while that of the poorest declined. The Foundation also noted that the proportion of the workforce defining themselves as self-employed rose from 8.8 per cent in 1971 to 12.5 per cent in 1993.[16]

UNEMPLOYMENT

Even more significant in accounting for juvenile crime were the figures for youth unemployment: for 16–17 year olds unemployment was 7 per cent in 1975, 13 per cent in 1991, and for 18–24 year olds it was 6 per cent in 1975, 16 per cent in 1991.[17] Immigrants were hardest hit. By 1988–90 (as a three-year average for the period of lowest unemployment) 8 per cent of all men were unemployed but the rate was 14 per cent for ethnic minorities, including 31 per cent of Pakistanis aged 16–24.[18] These were particularly concentrated in deprived urban areas: while 5 per cent of the UK population was black or Asian, the proportion was 35.4 per cent in Tower Hamlets (London), 21.5 per cent in Birmingham and 15.6 per cent in Bradford.[19] The effects were exacerbated by the fact that 49 per cent of Afro-Caribbean families were headed by single parents.[20] So it was hardly surprising that 26 per cent of the prison population was black (over five times their proportion of the population). This was a reflection not of criminality but of deprivation, since there is no evidence that black people are any more likely to commit offences than white people living in similar areas on similar incomes.[21]

Young people, and especially young black people, are always the worst hit by unemployment. During the second recession, 1990–93, there was a decline in jobs for young people: employment of 16–19 year olds fell by 29 per cent, of 20–24 year olds by 17 per cent but of 25–49 year olds by only 1 per cent. Put another way, 72 per cent of the net fall in employment in that recession was among under 25s, who became twice as likely to be unemployed as older adults (20 per cent compared with 10 per cent); young people from ethnic minorities were twice as likely to be unemployed as whites; being black added, on average, 31.4 per cent to the expected duration of unemployment in August 1991.[22]

Attempts to improve this by youth training had varying success. The government's Community Programme for 1982–88 was one of the more successful; it enabled long-term unemployed people to do work for the practical benefit of the community for 12 months at the 'rate for the job'. In 1988, the Social Security Act replaced income support for school leavers (16 and 17 year olds) with a guaranteed offer of a Youth Training (YT) vacancy, and a training allowance for the unemployed. Parents were expected to continue to provide some financial support for their children. In theory, all 16 and 17 year olds were supposed to be in full-time education, employment or YT. However, unemployed people who were not participating in education or training were not automatically eligible for benefit, so they often disappeared from the statistics, preferring to remain anonymous, in some cases no doubt living by crime. Even for those who had registered for YT, places were not always available; the number fell from 389,000 in March 1988 to 274,000 in 1993.[23]

In 1991, regional Training and Enterprise Councils (TECs) were made responsible for funding training schemes in their regions, with stringent targets for delivering the YT guarantee. Nevertheless, the quality of much of the YT training was poor and did not lead to a job. Many who started YT dropped out before the course was finished. The proportion entering a job on leaving YT reached a peak of 67 per cent in December 1988 but fell to a low of 48 per cent in October 1991 and only just topped 50 per cent in February 1995.[24] Will Hutton, in *The State We're In* (1995), stated:

> More British students finish their education at 18 than in any other industrialized country; fewer have formal educational qualifications; and their mathematical ability is poor. By international standards, there are fewer places for them on vocational training schemes and the levels of technical competence demanded to achieve given qualifications are at the lower end of the spectrum.[25]

Failure to deal with truancy and delinquency at school means that one in every seven adults has difficulty with reading and writing and this is often accompanied by uncooperative attitudes to discipline and work. People from ethnic minorities for whom English is a second language also have special requirements. The reduction of the funds permitted to be spent per trainee has led those providing the training to take on the people who are easiest and least expensive to train ('creaming'); so those with special needs, above all the semi-literate, tend to miss out or to become so frustrated that they drop out. Here is another nudge along the road to disillusion and resort to crime.

On the other hand, the establishment by the TECs of Modern Apprentice Training for two to three years for about 150,000 people was an encouraging development. Once again, however, there is every risk that those with special needs may get left out.[26]

Though unemployment in the UK by 1995 was low by European standards (8.9 per cent compared with 11.3 per cent in France and 12.1 per cent in Italy),[27] there has since the mid-1980s been a hard core of long-term unemployed who have never worked, who live in households in which no one works,[28] or in which the only one in work is the mother and she only part time. Many young people in such families have settled with the idea that they never will work so they seek other means of survival; the temptation to escape from the misery of life in a poor home, having no hopes for the future, becomes irresistible. Young people in those circumstances will either rot or turn to crime.

This chapter has been about how to prevent young people from becoming criminals. Helping them to avoid committing a first offence needs patience, compassion and perseverance. This is worth continuing through a second offence. At that stage, however, they should be warned that, if they commit a third offence, their treatment will become very different; that they will be watched, caught and locked up, and priority will be given to protecting the public from ever having to become their victims again. Faced with a situation where the majority of crimes are committed by people who have been convicted before, policing policy has shifted increasingly to proactive and intelligence-led policing. This is discussed in Chapters 6 to 8. Punishments – secure training orders for children aged 12 to 14, detention, prison and its alternatives – are discussed in Chapter 14.

4 Drug Trafficking in the UK

DRUG ABUSE AND CRIME

Drug trafficking probably constitutes the most serious threat to the quality of life in Britain, partly due to the damage done by drugs to the health and personality of the drug takers (predominantly young) but at least as much due to the crime it generates. An estimated 200,000 to 300,000 regular drug abusers spend between £2 billion and £3 billion each year on British streets buying drugs.[1] Of this, 90 per cent – £1.8 billion to £2.7 billion – is acquired by crime. About half the thefts and burglaries in Britain are carried out to get money to buy drugs.[2]

Anti-drug education should start with children at the age of 10, or preferably earlier. The Institute for the Study of Drug Dependence (ISDD) estimated in 1993 that, among young people, 6 per cent had tried drugs or solvent sniffing by the age of 11, 11 per cent by 14, 19 per cent by 15 and 22 per cent by 16; that by the age of 20, one-third of young men and one-fifth of young women had abused drugs; and that between 2.5 million and 5 million people had taken illicit drugs at some time in their lives. In October 1994 the British government's Green Paper, *Tackling Drugs Together*, estimated that 6 per cent of the population (3 million people) take at least one illegal drug in any one year.[3]

A heavily addicted drug abuser may spend £100,000 a year on drugs, the average addict spending £33,000.[4] Heroin and cocaine, including crack, costs about £60 per gram on the street, cut (i.e. diluted) to an average purity of 50 per cent (ranging from 40 to 70 per cent). A normal dose is one-quarter of a gram (£15). Cocaine, especially in crack form, is a stimulant. Heroin, sometimes sniffed but more often injected, initially produces intense euphoria, followed by a deep feeling of relaxation and drowsiness. A quarter-gram rock of crack, inhaled as smoke, induces an intense high in a few seconds, but it lasts only about 15 minutes. A fashionable package on the streets is 'one-plus-one' – a quarter-gram rock of crack followed by a quarter-gram of heroin injected on the rebound – at £15 each.

The most dangerous of the synthetics is Ecstasy (MDMA), classed with heroin and cocaine as a Class A drug. The cost per dose is about the same, £10–15 for a tablet of Ecstasy. *The Economist* estimated that in 1993 £700 million was being spent on Ecstasy each year, at raves which were attended by half a million young people every week.[5] And every year a number of them are killed by it.

Class B drugs include cannabis, a single dose of 4 g again costing £10–15. Cannabis is not physically addictive but is the most widely consumed.[6] Other Class B drugs are amphetamines (Speed and Ice) at about £10 per dose and LSD at about £2. New synthetics are being developed all the time and come in and out of fashion.

The heaviest spenders are probably the crack addicts, because of the intense shortlived high giving rise to an urgent desire for another dose, within the hour. A weekend binge of 50 or 60 rocks might cost £1000 and a heavy daily user might consume double that amount (£2000) every week, costing £100,000 a year. One addict, convicted at the age of 19 in London, was spending £300 a day on crack, cannabis and LSD; he admitted to 600 burglaries (average 3 per day), 130 street robberies and 220 car break-ins – 959 offences, the largest total ever tried at the Old Bailey. He was aspiring to join a Yardie gang as a crack dealer. He got 10 years.[7]

One of the insidious features of drug abuse is that it spreads. Clever dealers will sell consumers 5 g for the price of 4, encouraging them to recruit four more clients and thereby get their own 1 g free. This will seem less arduous and risky than financing their habit by petty crime – and it may lead them on to becoming dealers earning a big profit. So drug addiction can be a contagious disease.

IMPORTERS AND COURIERS

Taking the lowest estimate of annual drug expenditure on the streets of Britain – £2 billion – approximately £1.5 billion remains in the hands of criminals within the UK – the importers, couriers and distributors. Nearly all the remainder – £500 million – goes into the hands of the drug barons and cartels in Asia and Latin America, the manufacturers of synthetic drugs in Europe, and the drug trafficking gangs and courier systems worldwide. On average, there are eight middlemen between the farmers who produce the cocaine paste in Peru or the opium gum in Myanmar and the consumers on the streets. Out of their takings, these middlemen have to run laboratories or to pay couriers, pilots, boat captains, and others; they may pay bribes to officials to turn a blind eye and fund terrorist movements to threaten to kill those who do not.

All these middlemen sell for about double what they paid for the consignment, out of which they pay their employees or subcontractors and launder the remaining profit for themselves. Thus the price doubles at each handover (eight middlemen plus the consumer) so the price hike is 1, 2, 4, 8, 16, 32, 64, 128, 256. Put another way, out of every gram of cut cocaine or crack sold on British streets for £60, the farmer in Peru gets 23 pence. The other £59.77 (99.5 per cent) goes into the hands of criminals in the UK and worldwide, their employees, corrupt officials or terrorists.

The only people in this chain who deserve even a modicum of pity are some of the couriers. Most of the drugs are smuggled in fairly large consignments (10–20 kg upwards) in containers and other sea, land and overland cargoes. For these, the smugglers, whether corrupt cargo handlers or professional criminals, are well enough paid to minimize the risk of them giving way to police persuasion or incentives to talk about it.

Much of the rest, however, is smuggled by individual couriers, most (though not all) of whom are naive, and have little idea of what profits their employers (exporters and importers) are making. They accept fees which seem huge to them but are small compared with the risks they are taking. Some are backpackers who agree to smuggle a few hundred grams – sometimes 1 or 2 kg – out of Thailand or Malaysia and face the risk of the death penalty. Many others are West Indians or Nigerians.

For a Nigerian woman in a poor village, a fee of £1000

would seem to be inconceivable wealth, likely to set up her family for years to come. Nigeria is a much used transit route for cocaine across the South Atlantic and heroin across Southern Asia. Many Nigerians have relatives in Britain and can get tourist visas to visit them. Most of the couriers are women, preferably with babies, as their employers believe that mothers are less likely to be meticulously searched. Some carry drugs concealed in condoms, which they swallow, sometimes as many as 100, taking pills to block their bowel movements. They excrete them later after passing through customs. If caught with even a fraction of 1 kg they are likely to get four years in prison, or ten years if they smuggle several kilograms in their baggage. Though drug smuggling cannot be excused, these people are ruthlessly exploited, become involved in a judicial system which bewilders them, and are condemned to several years in prison thousands of miles from their families.[8] The people who need catching are their employers.

West Indians are similarly exploited. A Jamaican woman living in England may want to show her baby to her family at home. For an air ticket and a few hundred pounds for a holiday in Jamaica, she will undertake to smuggle, say, 250 g of pure cocaine back to the UK in a condom in her vagina. This will eventually be sold as 500 g of 50 per cent cut cocaine or crack for £30,000. The importer who employs her will probably make £8000 profit on it. Often, however, having agreed to carry 250 g, she is ordered to carry perhaps 2 kg in her baggage worth about £240,000 on the street, with no increase in fee. She dare not refuse for fear of violence or being betrayed to the police.

Sometimes these small-scale couriers carrying a few hundred grams are set up as 'sacrificial lambs'. The importer knows that British customs often put in sniffer dogs to check incoming flights from Jamaica, and that if they pick up the scent of drugs, they will do a vapour check on the passengers; so he makes sure that the woman will be the one spotted, diverting attention from a much bigger and better concealed consignment.[9]

DISTRIBUTORS AND DEALERS

The farmers' cocaine paste and the cut cocaine sold on the street each contain 40–70 per cent cocaine. The paste is refined in the Colombian cartel's laboratory, and is then smuggled pure to save bulk. It is diluted again by the distributors or dealers to make their profit. A similar equation applies to heroin.

The worldwide annual narcotic turnover is $500 billion, some estimates putting it as high as $800 billion. Every cent of this comes in as screwed-up notes on the streets, just as the billion dollar earnings of a big supermarket chain all come through the high street checkout tills.

The importers, distributors and dealers certainly deserve none of the pity which may be felt for the exploited couriers. Importers are likely to become millionaires; they commonly import in 5 kg bags, buying for about £40,000 per bag and selling for £80,000, having paid the pittance to the couriers. They will probably sell it in smaller lots, usually of 1 or 2 kg, to distributors they know and trust. The distributors may dilute 1 kg of pure drug with another 1 kg of inert white powder (talcum, bleach, etc.) so that they have 2 kg of the diluted product to sell. This dilution has two purposes: it has in any case to be diluted as the pure drug can be lethal, especially heroin; and by diluting they make their profit. Distributors may sell each diluted gram at the same price as they paid for 1 g of pure drug so, with twice the weight, they will make 100 per cent profit. If they handle that much each week they may make half a million pounds a year. But if rival distributors are poaching their customers by selling a stronger mixture at the same price, they may have to dilute less and make less profit.

Distributors provide their regular dealers with little packages of a few grams which they can sell in the streets, bars and brothels or, with the aid of a mobile phone number, in taxis or through the windows of cars in a public car park. Dealers with half a dozen regular clients can expect to make £500 to £1000 a week – up to £50,000 a year. Short sentences by the courts, repeated again and again, will not deter them, nor induce them to revert to unemployment benefit or a low-paid job.

In some places, particularly in large housing estates in cities such as London, Manchester and Liverpool, with a high Jamaican population, drug trafficking may be conducted by large rival distributor/dealer gangs linked to even larger gangs ('posses') in Jamaica. Such gangs in British cities, 30 or 50 strong, fight for their territory, often with fatal results – though the comparative rarity of firearms makes these far less lethal than they are in the USA, where it is estimated that 50 per cent of the murders are drug related.[10] There are some excellent case studies of drug-related gangs in Manchester in Jon Silverman's *Crack of Doom*.[11]

Police intelligence and anti-drug operations are discussed in Chapter 8 (pp. 85–90).

THINKING THE UNTHINKABLE

We are manifestly losing the war on drugs. We are failing to educate our children about drugs and failing to prevent their sale in the schools. We are failing to control drugs in prisons, so that many prisoners come out as addicts, and are also convinced that drug trafficking is an easy option for becoming rich. We are failing to deter persistent drug traffickers. And the public as a whole suffers from the doubling of theft and burglary in Britain to finance the purchase of drugs on the streets.

To go on just doing more of the same is to act like the generals in 1917 throwing another 10,000 men at the barbed wire on the Somme. If what we are doing is not working, what else can we try? There are broadly three policies worth looking at: first is the Dutch approach, best described as 'discretionary law enforcement'; second is extending compulsory treatment; third is licensing drugs like alcohol. But, for reasons which will become apparent, we shall still need to keep our full powers of suppression as well.

First, the Dutch. They permit the open sale of cannabis in approved cafés, over 300 in Amsterdam alone. Trading in heroin and cocaine remains illegal but, since 1985, the police have been instructed not to enforce the law against street traders. As a result, they know where most of the popular venues are – street corners, bars, cafés, brothels –

well known also to the consumers. The police keep these under surveillance, much more easily than if they drove them underground. So they can identify the users, guide them towards treatment and prevent them from putting the public at risk by violence or by driving cars under the influence of drugs. More important, they can spot the street dealers and put them under surveillance to lead them to the big distributors and importers – the people they really want to arrest. (The British police also discreetly use this as an intelligence technique: see Chapter 8.) Despite much criticism from their neighbours, the Dutch have a lower addiction rate than Italy or Britain.

Second, we could extend the licensing of doctors to carry out compulsory treatment of identified drug abusers. We already have about 100 doctors licensed to prescribe narcotics to treat volunteers in the NHS Drug Dependency Units (DDUs). The NHS and pharmaceutical companies also buy quantities of coca and opium products and synthetics for medical use as anaesthetics, tranquillizers, painkillers, and so on. Pure heroin and cocaine, bought direct from the commercial pharmaceutical refiners and manufacturers, cost them about £6 per gram. The DDUs can prescribe substitutes like methadone to wean their clients off heroin, or they may prescribe decreasing amounts of the hard drugs themselves. When they do prescribe heroin or cocaine, it is 50 per cent diluted, so the pure drug content costs only £3 – one-twentieth of the street price. Volunteers pay only normal prescription charges, or nothing if they are on income support, so many addicts do volunteer for treatment; and more of them than is generally supposed would be glad to break the habit anyway.

There is a strong case for making this treatment compulsory for people identified by police or doctors as regular drug users, not least to prevent them from recruiting new users to finance their addiction. Under this system, any identified addicts who refused to cooperate or to undergo periodic tests to monitor progress could be made liable for treatment in custody, though this should be done as rarely as possible, as it would be both abrasive and expensive.

So to the third possibility: licensing drugs like alcohol. They would be sold, heavily taxed, by licensed dealers – ideally by the qualified dispensers in high street pharmacies, who are trained and equipped to store and dispense dangerous drugs.

The tax on heroin and cocaine might be set at 150 per cent on the pure drug content, in the same way as alcoholic drinks are taxed (at 200 per cent) on the pure spirit content, which is 40 per cent in whisky and around 12 per cent in wine. On the 150 per cent basis, with an import price of £6 per gram of the pure drug and a reasonable allowance for handling and profit margin for the dispensary, the average dose of a quarter gram of 50 per cent diluted cocaine would cost £2.50 across the counter – about the same as a double tot of whisky in a pub. That price (£10 per gram of the diluted drug) would still be only about one-sixth of the street price; the proceeds from the tax would be available for spending on anti-drug education.

The dispenser would be barred, like the publican, from selling to anyone under 18. Adults identified by their doctors as addicts should be sold drugs only on prescription, so this scheme would work only with some means of identification. Unless Britain later issues ID cards, sales could be made conditional on producing one of the new driving licences (containing a photograph) or a benefit card.

A good start would be a pilot scheme permitting sales of controlled drugs *only* on production of a doctor's prescription. A maximum would be imposed, tightly restricted by the doctor in the case of addicts, with controlled amounts for other adults but, of course, no prescriptions for anyone under 18.

As the pilot scheme progressed, sales of drugs on licence could be extended gradually, with provision to rein in immediately if, in any district, it were having undesirable effects. Eventually, other pressures will almost certainly necessitate Britain having ID cards, probably voluntary to start with, and preferably with digital biometric data to prevent impersonation. This would facilitate control and remove most of the risks. (The issue of ID cards is further discussed in Chapter 15.)

As the scheme progressed, with drugs available at one-sixth of the illegal street price, regular users would soon opt for this, driving most of the current importers, distributors and street dealers out of business. This would cut out not only much of the street violence but also a great deal of the theft and burglary in Britain.

The risks would be far less than many might expect. The Repeal of Prohibition in the USA in 1933, except for a brief blip, did *not* increase alcohol consumption. It did, however, undercut the New York and Chicago Mafias, who had been spawned and sustained by bootlegging. The USA has had reason to regret ever having introduced Prohibition, but has never regretted its Repeal! Britain may well feel the same if it has the courage to repeal the 'zero option' on drugs.

TACKLING THE TEENAGE MARKET

Whatever schemes we try, however, we shall still need to keep the full suppressive apparatus in force because teenagers, barred by the authorized dispensers, would still demand drugs. A rump black market would therefore persist to serve them and they would go on stealing as much as was needed to raise the money to buy them.

With or without any of these schemes, Britain should be much tougher on drug traffickers, particularly on the importers. An addict consumes on average 7 g a week – 350 g a year, 50 per cent cut. People consuming that amount will certainly become addicted if they are not addicted already. An importer proved to have handled even one 5 kg bag in a year (10 kg when cut) will therefore have made or kept about 30 people addicted – and most importers handle a lot more than one 5 kg bag a year. People who ruin 30 (or with 10 bags 300) teenagers' lives, some of them permanently, deserve at least 10 years in prison for a first offence and, if they do it again, 40 years or perhaps 'life meaning life'. The public has a right to be protected from them for ever. (The whole question of escalation of sentences for repeat offences is discussed in Chapter 14.)

There are, of course, strong moral arguments against easing the present total ban on narcotics. It might send a dangerous message to teenagers. If it were to increase drug abuse, it might ruin even more lives. That, however, is unlikely. Repealing Prohibition did not increase alcoholism in the

USA. An intense programme of anti-drug education financed by the heavy tax on licensed drugs could be very effective, particularly if targeted on children early enough in their lives. Campaigns against smoking and drink driving financed by tobacco and alcohol taxes have had some success. Moreover, the huge profits available today to drug traffickers enable them to go to any lengths to promote sales; these profits would be cut out so the sales pressure would be reduced – except that targeted on teenagers. So the entire anti-drug resources of the police, intelligence and other authorities could be concentrated on smashing the teenage black market.

At all events Britain, as an island, is better placed to try bold experiments than the Netherlands or other Mainland European countries. We should have the courage to test out all these alternatives under tight control, always keeping open the option of reversal. In the event, they would almost certainly reduce drug dependency and would unquestionably reduce crime.[12]

Taking some of these risks would be far better than just carrying on as we are, seeing more and more of our teenagers wrecking their lives and being drawn into crime.

5 Money Laundering

FAST MOVING CASH

The suspicion that people are persistent burglars, thieves or street drug dealers is often first aroused when they are spending more than they seem likely to be legitimately earning. One of the most important skills of professional criminals is therefore to find ways of lodging the proceeds of their crimes in such a way that these could plausibly have been legitimately acquired but are still accessible for them to draw upon when they want the money.

The total amount of money from criminal sources entering circulation in Britain is at least £4 billion a year, which is more than £10 million every day. About half of this is money paid on the streets for drugs, most of which was originally acquired by the drug user from theft and burglary (see pp. 37–8). The rest is acquired by other forms of crime, most of which is turned into cash by selling stolen property. In either case, for a street drug dealer or a persistent thief or burglar, a typical amount of cash to be disposed of is £500 or even up to £2000 a week. Some, of course, they will spend on consumer goods and a more exciting lifestyle, but they cannot risk making this too flashy, and several hundred pounds a week under the mattress would make them vulnerable to crime themselves.

How do individuals who probably lack education (though they may have made up for this by becoming streetwise in their teens) convert the property they steal into cash? And how then do they (or the street drug dealer) stash this cash safely away to avoid detection?

First, the disposal of stolen property. Most burglaries are carried out by two or three people, usually young; two will enter the house, the third acting as a lookout and driving a getaway car if there is one. They will pick up small high-value items which they can easily conceal, either in their pockets or in a small shoulder bag or shopping bag. Electronic goods are particularly valuable and easily disposed of. If they are sure in advance that the house will be empty, they may work on a larger scale, loading up a car or masquerading as furniture removers or maintenance engineers. They choose items which should be hard to trace and can be quickly converted into cash; for example, at a car boot sale or by a second-hand dealer in video cassette recorders, car radios or hi fi equipment; or sometimes a junk shop selling cheap antiques, ornaments or jewellery. Or they may just go down to a pub where they can pick up £50 or £100 for a car radio. No names, no paperwork, no trace.

Getting rid of the cash, be it from sales of stolen goods or drugs, is likely to be more complicated. People who are known to spend a lot of time around car boot sales and dealers in second-hand goods may be able to give plausible explanations for having a few hundred pounds to spend each week, but people who are handling much more than £1000 a week may have to find other means.

The best way is to have credible cover as a partner in a small business with a high cash turnover, such as a second-hand shop openly selling similar goods on the high street, a used car dealer, a betting shop, a fast food bar or a tourist agency for cheap accommodation, guides or coach tours. The essential ingredient is a high legitimate turnover in cash, no cheques and a minimum of paperwork, typically buying food or goods one day and selling for cash the next day. The cash proceeds of crime or drug sales can then be concealed among a lively and apparently legitimate trade.

Supposing that there are, say, four or five partners in the legitimate business, they will regularly bank their cash takings, perhaps around £10,000 a week, which is easy enough to explain as trading profits even if half of it is from stolen goods or drug sales. It will then be perfectly credible for partners to be seen to acquire a car, smart clothes, and so on; they will in any case probably pay for them directly in cash to reduce the amount that has to appear in the documentary or computer records of a bank.

There are many other ways of laundering money. 'Cycling' is one common device, through vending machines or mail order business. As a front, a stock of real goods is held, and bought and sold again and again to provide credible activity in the event of a police or customs investigation. In addition, especially in mail order businesses, goods circulate on paper, round and round, in the names of different members of the gang, or by the use of aliases, whereby individuals can buy and sell from themselves to themselves, showing a paper profit each time. Most of the sales are fictitious, though there should be enough actual movement of the stock to allay suspicion. The cash 'profits' are mostly money from the sale of drugs or stolen goods, and are banked along with the legitimate takings. The partners live the lives of successful business people.

One drug seller ran a one-man international art business. In a typical operation, he commissioned a French artist to do some modern paintings at £200 each. He then destroyed the paintings, having forged receipts from 'buyers' in the UK for £2000 each and paid the £1800 'profit' (in fact the takings from his drug sales) into his art dealing bank account, impeccably backed by the real receipts for £200 and the forged receipts for £2000 each. Had there been a query, the French artist would in good faith have confirmed that he had painted and sold the pictures.[1] If the drug dealer had handled 30 pictures in this way, he would successfully have laundered £54,000 of his drug takings. His forgery was detected, but there must be many similar ones which are not.

Other common tricks are to receive 'fees' for fictitious 'services' (say, as a tourist guide) or for an employer to record payments to staff who do not exist, or to 'buy' nonexistent goods to match the 'sales' purporting to account for the money that is banked. These transactions are concealed among the day-to-day operations of the cover business. Betting shops and casinos are excellent for laundering because it is very hard to prove how much money was staked and who won or lost.

Some of those who want to sell drugs try to become minicab or taxi drivers (though in London the rigorous tests for black cab drivers would make this very unlikely in their case). Drivers of a radio minicab can not only sell drugs with minimum danger of detection (other than by a sting), but also launder the money by recording enough bogus fares to cover it; they can enlarge their business by getting trusted clients to give the minicab mobile phone number to other drug users so that they can call the driver to pick them up.

A prostitute has precisely similar opportunities. Who can ever prove how many clients she had that day and how much they paid?

As the criminal activity grows and, with it, the legitimate business, the gang will gradually move up into the realm of organized crime, and will have to reorganize its money laundering methods to fit.

SHELL COMPANIES AND BANK TRANSFERS

The organized criminal gangs, the big disposers of stolen goods and the drug importers, may be handling annual turnovers measured in millions rather than thousands. One way of concealing the origins of such money is by absorbing it into the assets of multinational corporations whose money flows through the international banking system, passing through several different national jurisdictions in a single day. It has been estimated that as much as 10 per cent of the money passing through the London money market is laundered money originally acquired by crime. Among the vast number of electronic transactions each day, the dirty money is unlikely to attract particular attention.

A common technique is to form 'shell companies' – a larger scale version of the junk shops and fast food bars. Since their real purpose is to cover the lucrative criminal cash flow, they can afford to operate their legitimate trading at little or no profit, so that they undercut competitors trading in that field and gain a larger market share with a bigger legitimate cash flow in which to hide the laundering of the criminal money. If they are handling export or import of drugs or other international crime, they usually run subsidiaries in the foreign countries in which they operate, with whom they can exchange goods and services which are either fictitious or inflated. An added advantage is that all these transactions can be concealed in a central corporate bank account which the foreign subsidiary can use freely for drawing or depositing money – a perfect way of covering international transfers.

Fictitious or inflated invoicing are common methods of concealing the criminal origins of money. In a typical case in the early 1980s, the fictitious export of non-existent fruit from Sicily to an equally fictitious fruit juice manufacturer in London enabled £30 million from heroin trafficking to reach a bank account in Switzerland.[2] In another case, the 'kidnap' of a Sicilian drug launderer and the payment of a £2 million ransom may well have been entirely fictitious as a means of laundering money.

In 1985 the Sicilian Mafia, *Cosa Nostra,* controlled a large part of the heroin traffic and sales in New York. They arranged for a number of fast food bars to be bought by New York Italians on whom they knew they could rely to cooperate through a mixture of incentives and fear of retribution. Dollars from street sales of heroin were banked along with the cash taken across the counters of the fast food bars, in which bills and receipts were neither requested nor given. One of the launderers, Luigi Montalcini (not his real name) had cash delivered to his room in an expensive New York hotel. In the space of nine weeks, he made seven cash deposits totalling $5.2 million (£3.5 million) into the account of a property and raw materials company in the New York branch of a Swiss bank. The bank became suspicious owing to the large number of small denomination notes and Montalcini's reluctance to enter the bank vaults himself, presumably because he knew that he would be routinely recorded by the security cameras. In the same period, another $8.5 million (£5.6 million) was paid in cash into other New York banks.

Another activity used to cover money laundering is usury or 'loan sharking'. Companies and individuals trying to avert bankruptcy may take out loans with little or no collateral security, paying interest of up to 40 per cent. Deals of this kind are kept as secret as possible in order not to prejudice confidence in the liquidity of the borrower, so they can be easily and credibly simulated to provide explanations, if demanded, for the transfer of money.[3]

To hamper the banking and transfer of illegal money, the USA led the way in 1986 by introducing compulsory Currency Transaction Reports (CTRs) to document every individual transaction exceeding $10,000 for domestic and $5000 for international deposits or transfers. Other countries, including Britain, followed suit.

To get round this, organized criminal gangs and drug traffickers customarily spread their profits between accounts in a large number of banks, into each of which they deposit sums within the CTR limits, and ensure that international transfers are also made in small sums which the banks are not obliged to report. This practice is known as 'smurfing'. Some banks, however, are reluctant to complete CTRs. One reason is that they are expensive (typically $17 each in a New York bank); another is that, if criminal gangs are involved they might take violent revenge.

FISCAL HAVENS

A major problem, as yet unsolved, is the plethora of 'fiscal havens' around the world, mainly in small newly independent states or offshore islands. Because this brings so much lucrative (albeit shady) business to the islands, their governments make laws guaranteeing banking secrecy and prohibiting by law any investigation or disclosure of any bank account in their territory. They also have company laws which enable foreign companies to open branches in the territory with minimal annual corporation or registration fees and no obligation for accounts to be audited. Most of the islands also run their own national banks.

Foreign companies can therefore set up subsidiaries or holding companies which in fact need comprise nothing more than a small room containing a telephone, a fax and a computer terminal. They can then transfer large sums of money, electronically, into the accounts of these subsidiaries with separate instructions to redirect them – if necessary within a few minutes – into accounts in other fiscal havens with similar banking secrecy guarantees, and thence to a second or third, so that the money is untraceable.

It is also possible to use a computer programming code which instructs the software to erase itself immediately after the transfer is complete; originally developed by hackers to evade detection, this technique is now also used for illicit electronic bank transfers. There is evidence that the Colombian drug cartels have arranged for some of the many small banks in Africa to be equipped for electronic transfers to widen the options available.[4] The laundering process can be further disguised by splitting the money from the start (smurfing) between several banks, each thereafter shifting it along a different chain. So long as all the banks in all the chains guarantee banking secrecy, there is no way in which the source of the money can be proved. It can then be distributed into impeccable assets such as blue chip shares, property, luxury cars, antiques or jewellery, either in the original country of origin or any other in which the criminals have access to it.

MEASURES TO COMBAT MONEY LAUNDERING

Official prying into private bank accounts arouses acute misgiving among innocent and guilty alike. Yet, from 1986 onwards, all the leading banking countries found it necessary, in view of the burgeoning of crime and drug trafficking, to provide access, on condition that the police could satisfy the courts that there was reasonable ground for suspicion that the account might contain money acquired by criminal means.

Every criminal who is caught and convicted by this is likely to have caused 50 or 100 innocent people to suffer. If violent criminal gangs are concerned, as is usually the case with international drug trafficking, many other innocent people unwittingly involved may be put in fear of reprisals if they report their suspicions. So the greatest good for the greatest number clearly justifies effective monitoring. Dirty money significantly undermines national and international economies. But it is also important for the courts to ensure that the power to monitor is not abused to the detriment of the civil liberties of of the innocent people.

Following the introduction of CTRs in 1986 by the USA (see pp. 51–2), Britain passed the Drug Trafficking Offences Act (DTOA) late in 1986,[5] making similar provisions, including the obligation to report transactions above a certain value. In December 1988, the Basel Declaration was signed by the Central Banks of the 12 leading banking countries – the Group of Seven (G7) countries (Canada, France, Germany, Italy, Japan, UK and USA) plus Belgium, Luxembourg, the Netherlands, Sweden and Switzerland. They committed themselves to take steps to identify their clients and the sources of their assets; to report any suspicions to the authorities; and to collaborate with the police and the courts in patrimonial investigations.[6] Unfortunately, however, a number of banks in some of the countries (including Switzerland) found ways to evade these measures. Their reputation for doing so spread through the drug trafficking and other criminal fraternities, so these banks do good business.

The UN Vienna Convention against illicit traffic in drugs was also signed in December 1988. By March 1989, 89 countries had signed it, but some were slow in ratifying it and it did not come into force until November 1990. It committed ratifying nations to introduce the crime of money laundering; to forbid bank secrecy when this offence was suspected (though there will still be some banks which will evade these laws); to make provision to freeze suspected assets during investigation and to seize them if the offence were proved; to extradite offenders on drug trafficking charges; to cooperate internationally in investigation and prosecution; and to suppress drug trafficking by sea and air.[7] This later led to the formation of the United Nations Drug Control Programme (UNDCP), based in Vienna.

In 1989, the 12 signatories of the Basel Declaration plus the EC Commission, Australia, Austria and Spain set up the Financial Action Task Force (FATF). This analysed money laundering, assessed national and international measures and made recommendations, which were later accepted by the governments of 16 countries.[8]

In March 1992, Interpol established an Automated Search Facility (ASF), giving access to data held by national police and intelligence systems, but with the proviso that members can lay down which countries may or may not have access to specific bits of their information.[9]

PROBLEMS OF CONFISCATING ASSETS

Thus far, the freezing and confiscation of assets has had only limited success. Though a bank account or other assets may be frozen as soon as an investigation is ordered, they are not liable to confiscation until and unless their owner has been convicted of a crime of which those assets were alleged to be the proceeds. This applies not only to money laundering but also to other forms of fraud, extortion and racketeering. Unlike other accusations made in courts of law, the onus of proof lies on the accused to prove a legitimate source for the assets. If they have been expertly laundered, they are likely to be or have been in the form of profits of publicly quoted corporations; they may appear to be the proceeds of legitimate trading, buying cheap and selling dear, and these may be recorded in the audited accounts of corporations which had no reason to suspect unlawful origins of the money changing hands.

In an attempt to prevent dirty money from evading the net, British law regards all assets acquired during the six years prior to conviction for drug trafficking as proceeds of that crime unless the accused can prove otherwise.[10] If further assets come to light in the six years after conviction, the prosecution can apply to the court for their confiscation too, subject again to the accused failing to prove that they have a legitimate source.

If the accused manages to abscond before the trial, confiscation cannot be ordered without the presence of a guilty party. This can sometimes be overcome if a number of defendants have been convicted of conspiracy, but it would be better if Britain were to follow the continental procedure for trial *in absentia,* whereby frozen assets could be confiscated if the accused were to fail to appear in court to prove their legitimacy.

Professional criminals and their equally professional accountants and lawyers can find many ways of obstructing the realization of their assets. The current estimate is that, of the money collected by drug traffickers in Britain, only 5 per cent is subjected to confiscation orders and only 1 per cent successfully realized and collected. There is a long way to go.

ATTACKING SECRET BANKING OF CRIMINAL MONEY

The most intractable problem in depriving large-scale criminals of the proceeds of their crimes is the ease with which they can use the secret banking provisions of fiscal havens (and of some other banks which ought to know better) to prevent their origins being traced. There is really only one answer to that, which should be set in motion by the 12 major banking countries which signed the Basel Declaration in 1988 (see pp. 53–4). Having first put their own houses in order, their governments should make it illegal for banks in their countries to have any financial dealings with banks or branches of banks in countries whose governments do not legislate to order investigation of accounts if a qualified court judges that there are reasonable grounds for suspicion that they may contain criminally acquired assets.

This would have to be supervized by a body with UN authority to investigate and if necessary override the local authorities. The precedent for this is the International Civil Aviation Organization (ICAO) which lays down standards in dealing with aviation security and air crimes such as hijacking. In the case of aviation, the enforcement of these has been effectively achieved by the G7 countries in their Bonn Declaration of 1978, which warned that any country which failed to carry out certain specified action regarding hijacked aircraft, crews and passengers would be boycotted jointly by all the G7 countries. The boycott would mean that none of the G7 aircraft would land at the offending country's airports; nor would G7 airports receive any aircraft of the offending country's airlines, nor any aircraft of any country which had touched down in the offending country's airports. Since the G7 countries operated about 80 per cent of the world's commercial air traffic, this boycott would have had a devastating effect on the country's economy and would have bankrupted its airports and airlines. In the subsequent 17 years, the boycott has never had to be applied, since the mere threat of it has been enough to persuade any country contemplating defiance to take the required measures, for example, to arrest the hijackers and release the aircraft to return to its country of origin.

The proposed boycott on financial dealings by the 12 Basel Declaration signatories, who similarly dominate the international banking world, would be equally effective. The mere threat of it would probably be enough to force the governments and bank branches in the fiscal havens to comply or go out of business. The 12 could if necessary extend the boycott to any branch of any bank anywhere which had dealings with a boycotted bank. The enforcement of such a boycott on an international scale would require a powerful and comprehensive agency, provided either by the UN or by the G7 or Basel countries setting it up jointly on the UN's behalf. Nothing less than this is likely to be effective in countering the money laundering role of fiscal havens and of other more devious secret banking.

As with other crime, the detection and conviction of money launderers depends on intelligence, and this will be the subject of the next three chapters.

Part III
Intelligence

6 Intelligence Organization and Background Intelligence

SOURCES OF INTELLIGENCE AND CIVIL LIBERTIES

Intelligence is the decisive element in fighting professional crime. Sophisticated criminals are adept at concealing their identity and their activities within urban societies and the chance of finding them without good intelligence is no better than the chance of finding an experienced terrorist gang living in dense jungle or in the honeycomb of shanty towns around a Latin American city.

Acquiring intelligence, however, is one of the fields which poses the greatest hazards to civil liberties. To be successful it has to be clandestine and often requires calculated deception. It involves spying on people who do not know that they are being spied upon, many of whom will prove to be innocent of any connection with wrongdoing. The police may, in the course of clandestine surveillance, discover information about innocent people's private lives which are not criminal but whose misuse or release to unauthorized people could do them a lot of harm, for example, by damaging their reputation for integrity or credit worthiness, or prejudicing their prospects of getting or holding a job. Unscrupulous police officers could use such information to harass or intimidate people they dislike or regard as potentially disruptive; they are often accused of doing this to ethnic minorities, young people, gypsies and vagrants.

Ultimately, much of the most valuable intelligence comes from informers or informants. In common terminology an 'informer' is someone who gives casual information about something he or she has seen or heard, whereas an 'informant' is someone with inside contacts who is persuaded to give information in the future on an ongoing basis. In practice an informant is almost always someone who was or still is a member or associate of a criminal gang, and more often than not has already been detected committing a crime.

So the motive for becoming an informant is often a desire to 'get off the hook' of a continued involvement in crime and to earn lenient treatment for past offences. By nature, therefore, an informant is unlikely to be among the most honourable or reliable of people, and may well be tempted to give false or exaggerated information to acquire merit; or the informant may fear that a former colleague might seek vengeance and may want to see that person locked up behind bars. Also, some police officers might be tempted to encourage this in order to secure a conviction.

Then there is the problem of monetary rewards. Because of the need to protect an informant's identity, the handling of money for rewards will be kept secret, with a minimum of recorded accounting for its disposal. This gives dangerous opportunities for corruption, embezzlement and other misuse.

Planting of evidence may also be a temptation. Among well over 100,000 police officers in Britain, there will inevitably be some dishonest ones. The measures needed to counter these hazards are dicussed later in this chapter and in Chapters 7 and 12.

Intelligence can be broadly divided into background intelligence and precise (or contact) intelligence. It may be acquired by technical means, such as by interception or sophisticated surveillance, or from human sources, including informers and informants; these are supplemented by routine perusal of public information in the media, specialist publications, trade associations or pressure groups.

The normal process of criminal intelligence is to acquire and study background intelligence, leading to the identification of individuals who are planning or have committed crimes. These potential or known criminals can then be targeted for specific intelligence, by surveillance and by building up information about them individually, with a view to acquiring evidence for arrest and conviction.

So the main purposes of background intelligence are: to prompt those seeking precise intelligence to look in the right direction; to provide a broad spectrum of knowledge against which that precise intelligence can be interpreted; and to select, target and recruit informants. All of these will be further examined later.

THE BRITISH INTELLIGENCE ORGANIZATION

Criminal intelligence involves separate processes of acquisition of information; analysis of it; and promulgation of the facts and of their analysis to those who need to know and act on them. There should be a clear demarcation between these processes. If those acquiring intelligence are also responsible for analysing it, they may instinctively seek or interpret new information to reinforce or justify their previous assessments or prejudices. Intelligence should be analysed objectively, not influenced by judgement of the use which may be made of it. Promulgation must balance the desire of operations officers to have all available information on which to act, against wasting or prejudicing delicate sources (informants) by using their information too early or in such a way as to compromise them. And the dangers of intelligence officers actually directing their own operations have often been demonstrated, notably by the US Central Intelligence Agency (CIA) in the disastrous Bay of Pigs invasion of Cuba in 1961.

Until 1992 the UK did not have a national *criminal* intelligence service, unlike the Germans (BKA), the Dutch (CRI) or the Americans (FBI). Each of the 50 or so English county, borough or city police forces had its own Criminal Investigation Department (CID) and, to deal with politically motivated violence and subversion, its own Special Branch (SB). The Metropolitan Police (New Scotland Yard) had a larger CID and SB which were available to reinforce local forces on request ('calling in the Yard' as in the detective stories) and which also carried out a good deal of research and investigation which was made available to local forces when relevant. In the mid-twentieth century Regional Crime Squads (RCSs) were formed with resources to deal with serious crime; there were initially nine RCSs, some later amalgamated to make five, each serving a number of county Chief Constables.

The two main non-police intelligence services were formed at around the turn of the century, primarily in response to the perceived external threat from Germany. The Secret Intelligence Service (SIS, colloquially referred to as 'MI6') acquires foreign intelligence, with the knowledge and where necessary the cooperation of the Foreign and Commonwealth Office (FCO) and the diplomatic service. The Security Service ('MI5') is concerned with domestic or counter-espionage intelligence. Its officers work closely with the police, but they do not have police powers and do not make arrests which, if needed, they ask the police to do.

Both services were originally formed as branches of military intelligence (hence the now outdated acronyms MI5 and MI6) in the run-up to the First World War. The role of the SIS has not changed, but the Security Service has more recently led the intelligence effort in protecting the UK from terrorist violence. Depending on whether IRA terrorism (suspended from August 1994 to February 1996) can be brought to a permanent end, the Security Service may be able to devote more of its resources to other forms of crime, including drug trafficking. It will also continue, as far as is necessary, its historic role of counter-espionage in the UK and countering subversion and terrorism by extremists (left, right, religious or other) who try to bring about change by any means other than democratic ones.

The Security Service has always worked closely with the police SB (which was originally formed in the nineteenth century to protect Britain from violence and subversion by the Fenians – the predecessors of Sinn Fein and the IRA). SB includes a number of officers trained in the use of firearms, which they carry only on specific assignments in which they may have to deal with terrorists and other armed criminals.

THE CENTRAL INTELLIGENCE MACHINERY

The National Criminal Intelligence Service (NCIS) was formed in April 1992, initially consisting of about 450 officers seconded from the Metropolitan and other police forces, officers from the Customs and Excise and civilian staff. It is financed 51 per cent by the Home Office and 49 per cent by local police authorities, in addition to which Customs and Excise supply staff out of their own budgets. The NCIS budget in 1993–94 was £24 million. Initially it gathered together various police functions such as the National Drugs Intelligence Unit (NDIU), and the Organized Crime, Counterfeit Currency, Financial Intelligence and Football Units. NCIS also houses the UK National Bureau for Interpol.[1]

From its foundation, NCIS was barred from acting as an operational executive; it would prepare intelligence packages and hand them over to Scotland Yard or the RCSs for action. NCIS recruited and handled its own informants (as Scotland Yard and the RCSs did) and these informants were paid, as informants should be, only for the successful results of their information, not for the information itself. NCIS surveillance, however, had to be passive and they were inhibited from following it up or developing it lest they overlap the Metropolitan or local police forces. In 1995 there was a move to broaden NCIS capability and authorize it to carry out mobile surveillance like its equivalent, the BKA, does in Germany. The Association of Chief Police Officers (ACPO) gave this proposal guarded support, with the proviso that the surveillance capacity of other police forces remained and that appropriate management steps were taken to avoid overlap.

At some time, the five RCSs are likely to be combined into a National Crime Squad. Up to 1995, there was a National Coordinator of the RCSs, located alongside NCIS, but he had no power to *direct* the work of the RCSs, who were responsible to the Chief Constables of the forces making up the region. If, however, the National Coordinator (perhaps with a new title of Director-General of the National Crime Squad) were given power to direct the RCSs, they would still be kept separate from NCIS, which would return to the wider remit of dealing with Interpol, Europol, Customs and Excise, the Immigration Service and the Bank of England, and would remain an intelligence gathering organization, not an operational police service acting on its own intelligence. It was proposed that the National Crime Squad should be accountable to a Board of Management whose executive directors would be drawn from Chief Constables, the Home Office and local authorities, with non-executive directors from special organizations and the business world, including financial institutions.[2] All of this reflected the growing importance of intelligence targeting of money laundering and the proceeds of crime, which are the lifeblood of organized criminal gangs (including drug traffickers) and often provide the best opportunities for acquiring intelligence leads into them.

At Cabinet Office level the intelligence services are coordinated by the Joint Intelligence Committee (JIC) which was originally established in 1936, reporting to the Chiefs of Staff of the Armed Forces. It was brought within the Cabinet Office in 1957 and the post of Intelligence Coordinator was established in 1968. This post was first held by Sir Dick White, the only person who had ever headed both MI5 and MI6 (in turn). The Intelligence Coordinator exercised his role through the Permanent Secretaries' Committee on the Intelligence Services (PSIS), comprising the professional heads of the Cabinet Office and of the FCO, the Home Office and the Defence Ministry – the departments which control the Police, MI5, MI6, GCHQ (radio intercept service) and the Defence Intelligence Service (DIS).[3]

In the Metropolitan Police, intelligence comes under the Assistant Commissioner for Special Operations (ACSO). He has four directorates – Special Branch, Criminal Intelligence, Operations and Fraud. In each of the 63 Metropolitan Police Divisions there is a Divisional Intelligence Unit, comprising a team of police officers and civilian intelligence analysts, which organizes acquisition of intelligence at working level. Once again, at every level, the gathering of intelligence is under separate direction from those who take operational action on it.

INTERNATIONAL COOPERATION

Interpol (the International Police Organization) has representatives from 176 countries. This inevitably means that it cannot pursue inquiries with a political flavour, and Article 3 of its Constitution bars its member countries from intervention in or investigation of military, political, religious or racial matters, although it has made provision for investigating international terrorism.

Interpol's main function is to maintain an enormous computerized international database of information about wanted persons or known criminals. Through the ASF (see p. 54), an enquiry from anywhere in the world can yield a reply from this database within two hours, compared with two weeks in 1987. As stated on p. 54, the originating country can specify which other countries may have access to its information.

This restriction in practice presents few problems. Since data with a political implication are in any case excluded, only data about ordinary crime and criminals (including terrorists) are on the database. Nearly all professional police forces share a common purpose of fighting crime, including terrorism and international crime such as drug trafficking and money laundering, and are happy that their colleagues from other countries have as many data as possible to help them to cooperate, regardless of politics.

Another valuable by-product of Interpol is that police officers get to know their opposite numbers in other forces; police officers are more accustomed than most people to deciding whether or not they can trust someone. Many good personal working relationships are developed between the most unlikely partners. Bilateral cooperation between police and intelligence agencies in Britain, France, Germany, the Netherlands and Spain, and between some of them and the USA, has yielded excellent results. There are examples of this cooperation every working day.

A hundred people were killed by terrorists in France between 1976 and 1988, over half of them by foreign terrorists, others by an extreme Marxist movement, *Action Directe* (AD), which cooperated with similar movements in Germany and Belgium and with various Arab terrorists. These killings reached a peak between 8 and 18 September 1986, when six bombs were set off in Paris, killing 10 people and wounding 170, in an attempt by an Arab terrorist movement to secure the release of their former leader, Georges Abdallah, who was in prison awaiting trial for murder. As a result of these Jacques Chirac, newly elected as Prime Minister, introduced laws remitting trial without jury for terrorist offences (see pp. 164–5) and for the police to require both French and foreign citizens to produce means of identification in the vicinity of a scene of crime (see pp. 186). Early in 1987 the French, German and Italian governments signed bilateral agreements for interchange of police liaison and of intelligence information about terrorism and other serious crimes. These institutionalized already thriving cooperation, largely as a result of the TREVI agreement of 1976, under which EU interior and justice ministers met regularly, authorizing similar meetings between officials, police and intelligence officers and facilitating bilateral cooperation between officers who had got to know and trust one another.[4]

A good example of this cooperation took place in 1987 in the wake of the 1986 bombings in Paris. On 16 January 1987 the German police at Frankfurt Airport arrested Mohammed Hamadei (later convicted of murder and participation in the hijacking of a US aircraft to Beirut in 1985) and, 10 days later, his brother Abbas Ali Hamadei. From material found in possession of the Hamadei brothers, the French were given the address of a Tunisian restaurant in France. The French Surveillance Service (DST) tapped the telephone of this restaurant and were able to arrest three terrorists red handed in possession of 12 litres of liquid explosive (methyl nitrate, the same type as found in Mohammed Hamadei's baggage in Frankfurt) and they later arrested five more terrorists. Some of these gave information with incentives under the French 'repentance laws' (see Chapter 7) leading to capture of members of a second network. These two Arab networks were believed to be those which had carried out the Paris bombings in September 1986 aimed at the release of Georges Abdallah; the arrests presumably accounted for the lack of the expected violent response to Abdallah's conviction and life imprisonment in February 1987. The information from the Germans is also believed to have assisted in the arrest of virtually all the leaders of AD and of many other AD members, also in 1987. So these arrests and the concurrent French legislation, by virtually wiping out both the Arab and AD networks which had killed so many people in the preceding few years, will have saved a great many more French lives.[5]

Europol (the European Police Office) has brought together the police forces of the EU and has a well-equipped headquarters in the Hague. It formally came into being in January 1994, having had an active European Drugs Unit (EDU) operating as a pilot scheme since 1992. Europol is not an operational body and has no police executive role. In essence it is a team for exchange and analysis of intelligence but, unlike Interpol, Europol does not record personal data, for which it relies on national police databases. Of its total staff of 90 in 1995, 30 were national European Liaison Officers (ELOs) – at least one officer from each of the 15 EU countries and several each from larger countries such as Germany and France. Its mode of operation is for one national police force to ask another for help or information through their respective ELOs at the Hague. In the case of the UK, the British ELOs then deal directly with NCIS, which has direct access to the Police National Computer (PNC) so answers can be provided very quickly – much more so than by going through government channels. Again, the ELOs are a body of professionals who get to know and trust each other. Europol is financed by the 15 EU countries at a rate based on their GNP.[6]

ACQUIRING BACKGROUND INTELLIGENCE

Much background intelligence can be acquired from published material such as telephone directories and official lists held by local offices such as electoral rolls. In interests of civil liberties, care is needed to ensure that official lists are kept secure and accessible only to those with bona fide reasons for consulting them. Citizens have the right to exclude their address and telephone number from the telephone directory for security reasons or to avoid harassment arising from public prominence in, for example, politics, business, sport, entertainment, modelling or the media. This privacy would be lost if any member of the public could get the address or telephone number by uncontrolled access to official lists.

Some background intelligence is received by the police from members of the public, prompted by wanted posters or by media reports, or when people see something which arouses their suspicion; for example, suspicion that a house, garage or vehicle might be being used for criminal or terrorist purposes. The police can quickly check this and must naturally respect the confidentiality of the source.

The most useful background intelligence comes from individual police officers themselves keeping their eyes open, especially in connection with people or premises about which they are already suspicious. A note of who talks to whom or who lives in or visits which café or bar, can lead to precise intelligence (see Chapter 7). Police officers should, in fact, be trained to observe things in such a way that they can convert background intelligence into precise intelligence.

In 1995, the Hertfordshire Police took an initiative in harnessing public assistance by recruiting 'intelligence developers' – often retired police officers. Their salaries (£15,000–16,000 a year) were comparable to those of a junior constable, but this was acceptable on top of a pension. They were trained to observe and report; also in the use of video cameras and other surveillance equipment. They did not have powers of arrest (other than a 'citizen's arrest'); their information could, however, help the police to look in the right direction in order to pursue specific intelligence and to make arrests; and the intelligence developers could, of course, give evidence.

Background intelligence often leads to identification of people on the fringes of criminal or terrorist organizations, who are then targeted to obtain precise intelligence about people in or associating with the hard core. Occasionally, however, background intelligence can lead directly to the arrest of members of this hard core or even of the leader. (There is a good example of this – from Peru – in the case studies in Chapter 8.)

TECHNOLOGY AND INTELLIGENCE

The power which emerging computer technology could place in the hands of the police is phenomenal but such power, unrestrained, could pose the severest threat to civil liberties. The speed of computer development is equally phenomenal. The aim of the computer scientist is to match the power of the human brain, which can recognize a human face or voice – among a babel of others – in a fraction of a second; this is the time it takes the brain cells to go through up to 100 separate steps, similar to the 'program steps' in a computer but much more selective. The computer still has a long way to go; its 'brain' is currently running about level with that of a fairly intelligent slug.

Alan Turing, whose first gigantic computer helped to break the German Enigma code in 1941–42, forecast that, 'within 50 years a machine may be able to fool people that they are talking to a human being.' He was not all that far out.

One of the most rapid fields of development is miniaturization. The human brain contains about 1000 billion cells (neurones) linked through cell junctions (synapses). With Turing's 1940s technology, relying on thermionic valves and metal grids, a system with 1000 billion electrical contacts capable of taking binary decisions ('yes/no') would have required industrial premises the size of Greater London. When the transistor replaced the valve in the 1960s, this mighty complex could have been fitted into the Albert Hall. By 1980 the microchip could have assembled these 1000 billion in a small room. Soon after the millennium, 'Risc' (reduced instruction set computers), otherwise known as neural computers, could reduce this to the size of the human brain itself. Computer systems can, however, make complex logical inferences within a fraction of a second, but when and whether they will be able to make judgements based on emotion or hunches is uncertain.

As a further measure of the speed of progress, the Californian-based firm Intel invented microprocessors in the early 1970s with 2300 transistors on a single microprocessor. Their Pentium model, launched in March 1993, had 3.2 million transistors. Their P7, launched in 1996, has 15 million.[7]

There are many ways in which computer science has already revolutionized police intelligence. Police National Computers (PNCs) can process information and reveal linkages far more quickly than human brains or any other data processing systems. If, for example, a witness recalls only three or four letters or figures on the number plate of a getaway car (E..87.J..) and, say, the make and colour of the car, there is a good chance that the computer will identify the car within a few seconds, or at least narrow it down to half a dozen, most of which can be quickly checked and eliminated. This would have taken many hours of sifting traditional documentary or card index systems. The Automatic Fingerprint Recognition (AFR) system can link every police force in Britain to a central fingerprint collection.

Machine readable passports, perhaps later also visas, benefit cards and ID cards (see Chapter 15), will enable police officers with portable terminals to confirm the identity of people leaving the area of a crime. And portable 'expert systems' can give police patrols instant access to a mass of data, and can prompt them to pursue a line of questioning ('ask Question A; if Yes then ask B, if No ask C', and so on) about complex subjects which they could not hope to carry all in their heads. A laptop computer in a police car could give access to a quantity of data comparable with that in the *Encyclopaedia Britannica*. All of these things are available now and are in regular use. Others are coming onstream faster than they can be tested and put into operation.[8]

The civil liberties implications cut both ways. The potential damage by misuse of personal data held in computers was mentioned at the start of this chapter. It will be important to have strict control of access to it, including the recording of every occasion on which any item of data is called up, when, and by whom. With modern systems this can be automatic, with no extra workload on the user. The vast majority of these records will never have to be examined unless there is a complaint of harassment. It will also be important to delete any data about a person as soon as they are no longer required.

There remains, however, one intractable problem; the human brain has no such facility for removal of data; there will therefore be a risk of unscrupulous officials misusing knowledge retained in their own memories.

Faster elimination of innocent people from inquiries is, however, a positive contribution by police computers to civil liberties; many people may be stopped, searched and questioned after a crime but computers, properly used, will be able to clear most of them far more quickly than is possible without them.

Video cameras (CCTV) are widely used to deter and detect shoplifting and help to identify bank robbers. These and cameras at traffic bottlenecks have been a valuable aid to the arrest and conviction of other criminals. At the same time, they can provide a great deal of useful background intelligence. (The technology of surveillance and its civil liberties implications are discussed more fully in Chapter 16.)

Police in most countries (including the UK) can apply to the courts for approval for tapping a particular telephone if there is reasonable ground for suspecting that it may be being used in connection with criminal activities such as drug trafficking, smuggling, money laundering or planning burlary or robbery. To prevent abuse or harassment, however, judicial approval is initially given for only a limited period and will not be renewed unless the police can make a case that it is achieving or is likely to achieve beneficial results. Other kinds of bugging devices could be authorized by Chief Constables for intelligence purposes without reference to the courts up till 1995, though this is likely to be put on a proper statutory footing by new legislation.[9]

Surveillance techniques are, however, still more significant in acquiring precise or contact intelligence when the background intelligence has enabled the surveillance to be targeted on a specific suspect or accessory, so it will be further discussed in Chapter 7.

7 Informants and Precise Intelligence

FROM BACKGROUND TO PRECISE INFORMATION

Precise or contact information enables the police to arrest a suspect in circumstances likely to lead to a conviction. Background information – who lives where, who does what and who talks to whom – is designed to lead to precise information.

In addition to informers and informants as described in Chapter 6, there is another category which falls in between the two. These are people whose work or other activities puts them in a position to give valuable information about suspected criminals to the police; examples are bank managers, security guards, caretakers, social workers, pub landlords or proprietors of 'corner shops'. They may do so of their own accord or they may be approached by the police and asked to watch out for comings and goings of particular people, use of cars or premises, and anything which arouses suspicion. These are sometimes referred to as 'contacts' – which must not be confused with 'contact information' (though they may on occasions be able to provide it); they may also sometimes develop into informants by being able to make personal contact with the criminals without being involved in the crime themselves.

These sources are supplemented by surveillance with cameras, observation posts, telephone tapping or bugging where authorized. But most of the best precise information still comes from informants who are or have been themselves within the criminal gang. So this chapter will focus primarily on how such informants are recruited and handled and on the measures necessary to protect their identity while at the same time guarding against corruption or abuse, such as planting evidence.

INFORMANTS

Some informants are already in custody (under arrest or serving sentences in prison), and are willing to identify, give evidence and provide intelligence about their fellow criminals in the hope of getting lenient treatment, rewards or remission. If they have not yet faced trial, they anticipate that the court will give them a reduced sentence, but care must be taken not to make promises without being sure that they can be honoured. In such cases it is usual for the police to consult with the Crown Prosecution Service (CPS) and/or the trial judge. They are commonly described as 'resident informers' and, if they are serving or likely to serve long custodial sentences they may, unlike clandestine informants, be able and willing to give evidence in court – though the future threat of retribution must always be taken into account, and protection or relocation may have to be considered when they are released. The decision as to whether informants, resident or clandestine, should appear in court, and whether their evidence can be used at all, is discussed in Chapter 13. One answer may be to use their information only as a guide to finding someone else who can safely appear as a witness and provide the necessary evidence for conviction.

On occasions, arrested persons may be released under discreet supervision to re-establish contact with their criminal associates, participating in conspiracy to commit further crimes themselves, under strict limitations as to what they may and may not do; they will be warned that their immunity from being prosecuted for participation will not apply to actions outside these limitations, for example, by acts with the intent of acquiring criminal gain for themselves.

Many participating informants, however, have not been in custody or, if they have, their accomplices are not aware of it. They are on very delicate ground; they will be told that they are strictly barred from acting as *agents provocateurs,* that is inciting people to commit crimes which they might otherwise not have committed. On the other hand, if the crime has already been laid on, they are not barred from taking part in its preparation or execution (again subject to specific limitations). In these circumstances, a great deal will depend on the personal relationship between the informant and the police handler, as will be discussed on pp. 82–4.

DOUBLE AGENTS

An informant is sometimes referred to as an agent. This carries an implication of a rather longer term involvement, perhaps serving as a sleeper or mole most of the time, rather than risking a continuous flow of information. Agents can be the most valuable of all in the long run because of the depth of their knowledge of the organization being targeted; they can also be used positively by their police handlers to feed in false information; but it also makes them particularly vulnerable to recruitment as a double agent if they run into trouble.

Double agents appear most often in international espionage or political terrorism, but they may also appear in the battle against organized crime, especially in dealing with drug trafficking gangs or money laundering. This can sometimes arise unintentionally. If a participating informant, continuing to take part in a criminal conspiracy, is suspected by the gang of having been in touch with the police, one of the ways in which he can bargain for his life is to give his gang information about police intelligence, the identity of undercover officers or their plans and techniques. The gang may then tell him to continue his contacts with the police and to prove his loyalty by acquiring specified information, or even giving a tip-off resulting in an undercover officer being murdered. He is then faced with the dilemma of trying to keep both sides happy, usually with the knowledge of one, but sometimes with the knowledge of both, each thinking that he is 'their man'.

This tightrope has successfully been walked in a wide variety of circumstances. During the Second World War, virtually every spy working in Britain for the Germans had by 1942 been 'turned' (the normal intelligence term for converted) into an agent for the British. Once detected, the only other alternative was death and, of course, most spies of German nationality did not choose to betray their country. Many spies, however, were East European refugees who had entered Britain in the 1930s and had been offered large rewards by the Germans – or perhaps the removal of a threat to their families – if they agreed to spy for them. They had no reason to die for Germany, so eventually all those who remained alive were secretly working for the British, who provided them with enough information to retain the confidence of their German handlers. They were also used with enormous effect to feed false information to the Germans, for example, before the D-Day landings in 1944. One brilliant spy – who never had to face this choice because he was working for both Britain and Germany in neutral Lisbon – was awarded the Iron Cross and the MBE, each unknown to the other side, in the same year.

The psychology of the double agent can best be understood by analysing the actions of some of the more notorious politically motivated spies. Moles or sleepers may spend many years gaining the trust of their future victims before they take any action at all. Philby worked for seven years (1933–40) under secret Soviet guidance, establishing himself as a right-wing journalist. In 1936–37 he was a war correspondent attached to General Franco's army in the Spanish Civil War and the supportive tone of his reports was such that it occurred to no one that he was acting under Soviet control all the time. Franco personally honoured him with a decoration. As a result of the reputation he built up and the friends he made in British establishment circles, he was in 1940 recruited to the staff of SIS (MI6). Starting in a fairly humdrum job, he rose rapidly in the ranks, reaching his peak as head of the Soviet section, directing British espionage against the USSR. Throughout the 1940s and early 1950s he was able to give the NKVD (later the KGB) priceless information about both British and US intelligence and espionage.

After the defection of his fellow spies, Burgess and Maclean, in 1951, Philby came under suspicion but survived investigation. SIS continued to use him, no longer at the centre, but in field assignments with cover as a journalist in the Eastern Mediterranean, until he defected to Moscow in 1963, after 30 years in the Soviet Communist Party.

Some people think that the SIS suspicions were overridden by their belief that, on balance, what they were getting from Philby (no doubt provided by his Soviet handlers to maintain his cover) was more valuable than anything he was then able to tell the KGB. Others believe that SIS decided that it was better to risk giving him this limited scope rather than arrest him and fuel CIA suspicions of ongoing unreliability in SIS. Perhaps they were confident that he would not wish to exchange his cultured and comfortable Western lifestyle for a drab retirement in Moscow. It has even been suggested that, when they realized the full extent of his treachery and that he had probably already told the KGB everything likely to be of value, they may have tried to frighten him into defecting rather than reveal this failure of British intelligence in a sensational trial.[1] Who knows?

By contrast, an outstanding British intelligence success was the recruiting of Lai Tek, Secretary-General of the Malayan Communist Party (MCP) as a Special Branch agent from 1934 to 1947, at which point he realized that the MCP suspected him and escaped (with the Party funds) allegedly to Hong Kong or Thailand, where he was reported to be still alive and well in the late 1960s. From 1942 to 1945 he was a triple agent, still Secretary-General, still reporting to the British, but also working for the Japanese who had detected his Communist role but, presumably, not his British connection. The Japanese used him to wipe out almost the entire hierarchy of the MCP, who still did not suspect him.[2]

The most bizarre double agent in history was probably Azev who, as Commander of the Fighting Section of the Social Revolutionary Party in Tsarist Russia, was also the highest paid agent of the secret police (the *Okhrana*). In 1904 his Party ordered him to assassinate the Minister of the Interior (Plehve). He felt that he must refer this to *Okhrana* since Plehve was their boss; *Okhrana* decided that his cover in the Party was more important than the life of the minister, so they told him to go ahead, which he did.[3] Avev died in 1917, in comfortable retirement in Switzerland.

To which side were these agents or informants ultimately loyal? Philby, certainly, to Moscow. Of Lai Tek and Azev, no one can be sure. Their final loyalty, faced with a life or death choice, would probably have been to themselves; they would, as Lai Tek did with the Japanese, follow the path of survival.

This is probably the wisest assumption to make in handling informants – or even undercover police officers – if there are serious grounds for suspicion that they may have been coerced, bribed or persuaded (turned) by the other side. If they detect a police officer or an agent, the leaders of a drug-related or other organized criminal gang or a money laundering syndicate will have the resources to offer huge financial incentives as an alternative to a grisly fate. One must assume that most human beings, faced with such a choice, will be sorely tempted to choose life. In the case of someone devious enough to have become an agent or informant in the first place, they almost certainly will.

RECRUITING AND HANDLING INFORMANTS

The recruiting of a resident informant is often a by-product of the process of interview and interrogation in custody. Great care and integrity is needed to keep on the right side of the lines between discussion, persuasion, inducement and incitement. Clever criminals or their lawyers may handle these discussions in such a way that if, in the event, they are not granted immunity from prosecution, but are tried with an implied promise of lenient treatment, they may be able to gain a not guilty verdict by claiming that admissions which they made were obtained by improper inducements, or that they were incited to commit further crimes with a view to trapping their colleagues. They may alternatively withhold such claims at their trial and keep them in readiness as grounds for appeal to get their convictions quashed, which can be even more effective, as it is rare for the Appeal Courts to order a retrial. The best way for the police to guard against this is to conduct all such interrogations in front of a video camera (see pp. 141–2), but this may be inhibiting if the police are hoping to get the person to take risks on their behalf.

Most informants, however, are not in custody. They are targeted for possible recruitment as informants as a result of background information leading to detection that they are involved in crimes. A typical example of this is a street drug dealer who has been identified by surveillance (observation,

CCTV, intercepting phone or mobile phone calls); or the dealer may have been detected by a client giving information, or by an undercover police officer posing as a customer. Police intelligence may decide to use the dealer at once or they may prefer to wait for bigger fish. In that case they would not make an arrest but maintain surveillance in the hope that the street dealer will unwittingly lead them to a distributor or importer.

The first step in recruiting informants will be to identify likely candidates for turning and build up a dossier of evidence against them. In the case of a drug dealer or distributor, this may include one or more test purchases by an undercover detective, and the subsequent proposition for recruitment may be done by that same detective or by another. With other types of criminals, the dossier may comprise evidence of involvement in robbery, counterfeiting, and so on. The recruiter (who will probably become the handler) will confront him with a list of crimes or suspicious acts which have been detected, with dates and places. The criminal will try to deny them at first but he himself will know that they are true. It is put to him that there is enough evidence to convict him and send him down for a long-time. He knows that if he continues doing the same he will undoubtedly be caught and convicted. He may try to brazen it out, denying the charges and hoping to branch into something else, but the detective may remind him that his gang may decide that he knows too much and guess that the police are on to him, with possibly dangerous consequences for him.

If the candidate has been well chosen, the recruiter will know that he is worried about the police closing in on him and would be glad to get off the hook. So, assuming that he does not want to go to prison, he has two other alternatives: to give information and, if it is judged safe, to give evidence in court in exchange for lenient treatment for his own crimes; or to continue to participate in the gang's future activities (within limits as described earlier) – but keeping his handler informed.

The aim, in the end, is to detect, arrest and convict the gang leaders. If the candidate agrees to become an informant, the handler may be authorized to offer substantial rewards to be paid on the arrest of certain wanted criminals if the arrest results from the informant's information. The handler may also be able to indicate the kind of protection that will be provided and the possibility of relocation, with his family, under a new name, with enough capital from his reward to start a new life.

Virtually every country makes provision in its laws to offer leniency, rewards and, if need be, protection to persons who give state's evidence. This has been particularly applied to tackling large organizations such as terrorist movements, Mafia style organized crime and international drug traffickers. In Italy, *pentitismo* has been hugely successful since 1981. This initially involved recruiting 'penitents' (better described as defectors) from right- and left-wing terrorist groups, and later against the Mafia, to act as informants and witnesses. The terrorist leader with whom the scheme began had been personally involved in nine murders and he went free, after a token period of 'protective custody' to start a new life with a new identity, in return for information leading directly to 84 arrests. This led to a total of 700 arrests, mainly based on information from the first 84. The same technique was started against the Mafia in 1984, based largely on the evidence of a senior Mafia leader who turned state's evidence, resulting in a mass trial in 1986–87 in which there were 361 convictions. In both cases there was ample corroboration by other witnesses. (These examples are examined further in the context of trial procedure and security of witnesses in Chapter 13.)

The British police grade information and its source to indicate its reliability. The sources are graded as follows:

A. Where there is no doubt about the integrity of the source or if the source has in the past invariably been reliable.
B. Where the source has proved reliable in most cases.
C. Where the source has in most cases proved unreliable.
D. Where the source is previously untried.

and the information is graded:

1. Where it is known to be true without reservation.
2. Where it is known personally to the source but not to the handler.

3. Where it is not known personally to the source but corroborated by other information received.
4. Where it is not known personally to the source and cannot be corroborated.[4]

PREVENTION OF ABUSE

A strong personal relationship often grows up between an informant and his handler. Once committed to the task, the informant's fate is totally in the hands of his handler. The handler, knowing this, may guard his dependant's interests with passion and react very strongly if anyone suggests using his information in a way which could put the informant or his family at risk.

The anonymity of an informant must be safeguarded, as his life may depend upon it. Normally, only three people should know – and must know – his identity: the handler; his controller, usually a detective inspector in the case of the British police; and the head of department. The head of department will be an assistant commissioner of the Metropolitan Police, the senior detective officer of other police forces, or the Regional Coordinator in the case of Regional Crime Squads.

The true identity and particulars of all informants must be registered with the highest security. Trust and frankness are essential between the handler, the controller and the head of department. All references to informants or their information, other than between these three, must be by pseudonym. With rare exceptions, all communications should be oral rather than in writing.

The Crown Prosecutor should always be informed, orally and using a pseudonym, of the involvement of an informant in any case in which the Crown Prosecutor is involved. If the defendant has been an informant, or if an informant has been authorized to participate in the crime, it is essential for the Crown Prosecutor to be aware of this. The police are strictly forbidden to mislead the court, and the prosecutor must know in advance whether the case is to be dropped in the event of the judge ruling that the informant must be called as a witness or that his or her identity must be revealed. (The security of informants and of witnesses under threat is further discussed in the context of trials procedure in Chapter 13.)

The control of money for rewards and so on can cause difficult problems owing to the need for secrecy. The money is provided from a fund administered by the head of department and dispensed and accounted for by the detective inspector acting as controller of the handler. The integrity of handlers is crucial as they will be subject to unlimited temptations. In the 1970s, there was evidence of considerable corruption in the Metropolitan Police CID, and that some officers of detective superintendent and inspector rank were turning a blind eye to corrupt deals – which sometimes helped to secure convictions. This was firmly tackled by the newly appointed Commissioner, Sir Robert Mark (see pp. 155–6).

The worst temptations probably come from bribery by criminals rather than misuse of police funds. For example, an undercover officer might be spotted by the organizer of a drug or prostitution gang operating from a pub or nightclub. The proprietor would then get the detective constable into conversation; he would indicate that he had an idea what was going on and that if the constable were to turn a blind eye it would be rewarded very generously. If the young constable were having trouble with a mortgage or was saving up to buy a second car, to get that kind of money simply by looking the other way and not reporting any suspicions would be quite a temptation.

The same might apply at a lower level if the detective were talking to someone suspected of being a drug dealer. A street dealer can make £1000 or even £3000 a week, and a distributor supplying a small team of dealers around £20,000 a week. They could make it seem worthwhile to the detective to take a slice of this to ignore what has been seen, perhaps with an implied threat to the officer's family if the bribe is declined.

There is, however, also scope for embezzlement of part of the money from a CID allocation for paying a reward. In 1994 a very senior civilian accountant at New Scotland Yard was convicted of embezzling huge sums of money which he had recorded as payments to informants over a period of some years.

In the early stages of an intelligence operation the demands for cash will be small, as rewards should not be paid to informants until their information has been evaluated, and the big rewards will be paid only when the target criminals have been arrested as a result of this information. Before that, however, small disbursements may be made for the informants' expenses. Also, undercover officers posing as gang leaders will need to look the part of someone making £10,000 a week, so they may have to turn up in smart clothes, driving a BMW rather than a worn out Metro.

When the time comes to pay out the big rewards it may be wise to counsel informants fairly firmly not to be seen spending too lavishly; sometimes the police may come to an agreement with informants to get the money banked in accounts not traceable to them, to be released later in controlled quantities in their own interest. Most often, however, informants will either remain for a time under police protection or possibly relocated to start a new life.

Handling informants is a high-risk business but, if an informant produces reliable information leading to the breakup of a dangerous criminal gang, it could be cheap at the price – cheaper than, say, another helicopter and probably much more cost-effective.

8 Case Studies – Intelligence

HUMAN AND TECHNICAL INTELLIGENCE

British criminal intelligence has always depended mainly on information from people rather than equipment. In recent years computers, long-range cameras and CCTV have played an increasing part, and there is no doubt that the issue of machine readable ID cards and visas would greatly assist the police and immigration service in spotting illegal immigrants, terrorists and criminals, including drug traffickers. Improved techniques for detecting explosives and drugs are also paying dividends. (The technology of all these and their potential are discussed in Chapters 15, 16 and 17.) Telephone and radio intercepts have also been valuable for military intelligence, such as ULTRA and the Y Service in the Second World War, and political intelligence (for example, by GCHQ). Some of these techniques have also been applied to criminal intelligence and investigation.

In this chapter, Dutch and British intelligence against drug trafficking will be examined; then some examples of British intelligence in Malaya, where much of the current expertise was developed; and finally a very successful intelligence operation in Peru.

ANTI-DRUG INTELLIGENCE

In most forms of crime (burglary, robbery, rape, mugging and murder) the victim or the victim's family will notify the police, providing a starting point for the search for background intelligence, some of which can then be developed into precise intelligence by targeting known or suspected criminals for surveillance.

This, however, is more difficult in the case of drug trafficking because there are no 'victims'. The buyers of drugs will not come forward voluntarily with information about the dealers who supplied them. It is therefore necessary for the police to break in by patiently building up background information, mounting surveillance of suspected venues for drug dealing and following individuals seen to be involved.

The Dutch police have been particularly successful in this respect. They have been criticized for the open sale of cannabis at hundreds of approved cafés, especially in Amsterdam, but this does release their surveillance resources to concentrate on hard drugs. Only slightly less controversial is their policy of not prosecuting consumers of hard drugs like heroin and cocaine, including crack, or of others found in possession of drugs in quantities small enough for a presumption that they were for their personal use. In practice, the Dutch seldom prosecute low-level street dealers either, finding it more expedient to use them as leads to distributors and importers higher up the chain. Because the dealers feel reasonably confident that they will not be arrested, they often operate openly in a particular bar, brothel or alley so that their regular and potential clients get to know where to find them.

As well as drugs being more freely available, a large percentage of Europe's drugs are smuggled through Rotterdam and manufacturers of synthetic narcotics abound in the Netherlands. Despite these circumstances, however, the proportion of the Dutch population regularly abusing Class A hard drugs and synthetics is lower than in Italy or the UK.

Up till the mid-1980s, the British approach to acquiring background drug intelligence was by police raids and sweeps through estates in which drug abuse was known to be rife. These were in the nature of fishing trips and they usually did find some people in possession of drugs, but they seldom led to the arrest of distributors higher up the chain, and they often caused resentment and sometimes riots, for example, in Bristol and Brixton in 1981. Thereafter, the approach became more like that of the Dutch.

In some areas, such as Moss Side in Manchester, the growth of drug abuse coincided with the growth of large criminal gangs, 30 to 60 strong, mostly aged between 18 and 25, some with links to big drug trafficking gangs in Jamaica. By the late 1980s, teams of teenagers sold crack and heroin freely in open spaces like shopping centres or through the windows of cars in public car parks. In 1989, the Greater Manchester Police mounted video cameras covering these areas (Operation Corkscrew) and then followed the street dealers to locate some of the distributors, who were buying drugs by the kilogram (at about £25,000) which they diluted and split into thousands of 100 mg or 250 mg doses. A number of these distributors were arrested and convicted, receiving sentences of up to 10 years.[1]

In June 1987, the Metropolitan Police used similar tactics in Notting Hill (Operation Trident). They mounted 4 video cameras and arrested 17 dealers, 11 of whom were convicted. In the course of these operations they identified many hidey holes, such as doorways, in which deals took place; they were able to mobilize a multi-agency approach (with local authorities and voluntary groups) to get these renovated to remove the cover. The police were pleasantly surprised to find that this was welcomed by 95 per cent of the residents, who wanted to be rid of the curse of drug trafficking in their community.[2] Operation Mint followed in October and November 1989; the police recorded 123 deals, mainly in cannabis and cocaine, including crack, in three weeks, during which they made no arrests; they then simultaneously arrested 85 dealers and buyers, mainly in their homes, in a dawn raid. For the next few years at least, the area (All Saints Road) was free of any significant drug trafficking.[3]

Operation Dalehouse in Brixton was on a much larger scale. In 16 months (August 1991 to November 1992) the police built up a database of 3500 dealers and buyers, including a number of gang leaders from Jamaica, who were organizing the import of drugs. This traffic was closely linked to other forms of serious crime. In all, 247 arrests were made, though all but about 20 refused to answer any questions because of fear of reprisals. Some of them were illegal immigrants, one of whom had been deported eight times in the year, returning each time with a different forged passport. Despite the fear of talking, many were identified by cross-checking with other evidence, including the perpetrators of four murders, ten attempted murders (four of which were against police officers) and one kidnap. Many of them, however, were never caught because of the ease with which they could move in and out of the country.[4] This demonstrates some of the weaknesses in the British immigration, identification and judicial systems which, despite good intelligence and evidence, result in such a dismally low rate of conviction in fighting organized crime. (That is the subject of Parts IV and V of this book.)

Meanwhile in Moss Side, reacting to the success of Operation Corkscrew in 1989, the traffickers changed their tactics, no longer selling openly, but arranging distribution and sales through a mobile phone network. Potential buyers obtained the number of one of the dealers and arranged a venue for the sale from a public telephone box. Again, the Greater Manchester Police responded with video cameras. Over a five-week period in 1991 they recorded 37 deals (36 for heroin and 1 for crack) and early one morning they arrested 23 dealers, some of whom were making £3000 a week. Drug consumers were usually dismissed with a caution but their diaries were valuable for piecing together the numbers on the mobile phone networks and the street names of the dealers. A further operation (Miracle) followed in 1992–93, based on these networks.[5]

A 'BUY BUST'

An example of another type of anti-drug operation, a 'buy bust', took place in North London in March 1991. This was based on background information leading to precise intelligence in which an individual distributor (Sammy Lewis) was targeted. Lewis, aged 23 at the time, was a West Indian born in England. He was buying pure cocaine, approximately 2 kg per fortnight, through a partner from a broker for about £30,000 per kg. He diluted it and converted it into crack. This is a simple process of dissolving the cut cocaine powder in water and heating it with an alkali such as bicarbonate of soda; it dries into hard toffee-like off-white slabs, which can be cut into raisin-sized quarter-gm 'rocks'; these, when smoked, give a very quick high, intense but shortlived, giving rise to an immediate craving for more. He sold the rocks to a team of three dealers whom he knew and trusted. He was making a profit of about £10,000 a week (half a million a year if he kept it up) and each of his dealers was making about £1500 a week.[6]

Lewis had been watched by the police since 1989, when they suspected him of involvement with a Dutch heroin dealer, but he was careful and, when he was stopped and searched, he never had anything incriminating on him. He did most of his business with a mobile phone and normally used runners to handle the crack. The police, however, remained suspicious because of his lifestyle; he lived in a two-storey flat – very expensive in London – and drove a red BMW, quite a change from his previous job in a pizza bar! They arranged for him to be approached by an informant, 'Ricky', with whom Lewis had worked in the past and trusted. 'Ricky' told him of an acquaintance, 'Andy', who he said wanted to buy crack to open up a regular team of dealers in Handsworth, Birmingham. Lewis, scenting big and regular profits, agreed to meet him.

'Andy' looked the part, but he was in fact an undercover policeman. At their first meeting, he bought 7 g of crack for £320, and said he would want 100–150 g a week. Lewis tapped a number onto the memory of Andy's mobile phone and three days later Andy made another 7 g purchase. They then arranged a third meeting, at which Andy agreed to buy his first full consignment of just over 100 g for £7000, at a rendezvous in Taylors Lane, London NW10.

For this third meeting, the police deployed a snatch team of five unarmed plain-clothes policemen, hiding in the back of an apparently empty van which had earlier parked on the roadside near the rendezvous. Andy drew up in his car, a new Daimler Jaguar, as would have befitted a successful drug distributor. After a call on the mobile phone Lewis, accompanied by two minders nearby in the shadows, came to the window of the car, checked that Andy had the money, went back into the shadows and returned with the slabs of crack. At this point, two of the plain-clothes snatch squad walked along the pavement pretending to be a pair of rowdies returning from a party. One, trained in judo, jumped on Lewis, who produced a gun and managed to shoot and severely wound the second policeman. Lewis broke away but was pursued and caught by the remainder of the snatch squad, who were following up on the pavement. He got 5 years for possessing 100 grams of a Class A drug and 17 years for attempted murder.[7]

RECRUITING AND HANDLING INFORMANTS IN MALAYA

Many of the British techniques for recruiting and handling informants were first developed in Malaya in the 1950s. The principles remain relevant for dealing with any large organized criminal gangs. Though they were varied and adapted to suit the circumstances and opportunities in each individual case, most of the successes came from identifying people on the fringes of the organization, on whom it needed to rely. In Malaya, most of these were suppliers of food and clothing from the Chinese villages to the guerrillas in the jungle. The art lay in picking out the ones who seemed likely to respond to persuasion to become informants with the prospect of earning very large rewards. When enough of these had been recruited and were continuing to supply the guerrillas, a concerted operation would be mounted. This was based on a patient build-up of background information. The tactics were to arrest simultaneously all other known or suspected suppliers from those villages so that the guerrillas were forced to rely entirely on the few who had not been arrested – and these few would include the ones who had been recruited as informants.

The method of identifying the suppliers, both those who were to be targeted as informants and those who were later to be arrested, was through meticulous searches of people leaving the villages each morning for work. Most would work in the rubber estates, where each covered a large isolated area of rubber trees from which they had to tap the latex, so it was easy for the guerrillas to contact them at gun point, and awkward for them to explain if they had failed to bring the supplies they had been ordered to bring.

If the police Special Branch (SB) spotted a supplier who they thought could be a candidate for turning, they might pretend not to have seen what he was smuggling (say, a false bottom in his latex tin concealing food) but simply take a note of it. Then, when the time was ripe, the SB detective would discreetly contact and question the supplier, not in the police station but where no one would see them. The proposition would be similar to those put to potential informants anywhere (as described in Chapter 7). The detective would confront him with the evidence: 'On 15 June you did this, on 20 June you did that', and so on. The supplier would of course deny it, but he would himself know that it was true and that if he continued to smuggle he would certainly be caught and face a heavy sentence. He also knew that it might be dangerous to stop as the guerrillas would guess why. He might hope that the police would arrest him and lock him up safely but they would decline to do that. The detective would then advise him to continue to supply the guerrillas but to keep the police informed. If that were to result in the capture of the gang of five guerrillas to whom he worked, the reward might amount to more than he could earn as a rubber tapper in ten years. And he could be relocated with his family in the Chinese community in another country, such as Hong Kong. If the SB man had chosen his target well, he would know that the supplier would be glad to get away from it all, so the proposition was hard to refuse.

His opportunities for providing information would be considerable. Since most of the other known suppliers had been arrested, he would have plenty of contacts with the guerrillas. If they required him to leave his supplies in hidden dumps among the trees, he could tell the police where, so that the army could mount an ambush.

Information provided by captured or surrendered guerrillas could be even more valuable, and they too were eligible for rewards. Those who surrendered voluntarily knew this well and had usually already decided to earn their freedom by giving information. Most of those who did not surrender but were captured also cooperated in the end. As a measure of the success of these techniques, out of 4000 guerrillas who were captured or surrendered during the 12-year Emergency (1948–60) all but 400 cooperated and were quickly rehabilitated into the community. Most of them felt confident enough to waive the option of relocation and remained in Malaya.[8]

HOR LUNG

One of the most successful intelligence operations in Malaya resulted from the surrender of Hor Lung, the guerrilla commander for the whole of southern Malaya in 1958. No one except a very small number of police officers knew of his surrender and his guerrillas thought he must be dead. He was persuaded to keep it secret and to visit his branches one by one in the jungle, giving them his authority to surrender, saying that the Party had decided to suspend the armed struggle and pursue their aims by political means. Most of the guerrillas needed little persuasion as they realized that the war was lost and that the only alternative was eventually to be captured, killed or die of malnutrition in the jungle.

Over a period of six months, Hor Lung lived in tight security in the home of a senior British SB officer (one of the many British officers asked by the Malayans to remain after the country had become independent the previous year). Periodically, Hor Lung would re-enter the jungle in his uniform, discreetly escorted by an army patrol. Communist security was such that guerrilla units repeatedly moved their camps and relied for communications on 'dead letter boxes', which remained fixed. A courier from a branch headquarters would call at the letter box (in a cleft tree or under a rock) on, say, each Tuesday, when he would leave and pick up messages. The courier from the superior district headquarters would call at the box each Thursday to pick these messages up and leave his own. The couriers would never meet, nor would either of them know the location of any unit other than his own. And no one except the couriers would know where the letter boxes were – except for certain senior officers who needed to know so that they could visit their units or, in emergency, re-establish the system if it were compromised or if a courier was killed. These, of course, included Hor Lung.

So he would go to a letter box, meet the courier and order him to lead him to his unit's camp. The army escort would follow, out of sight. On arrival, Hor Lung would convince the guerrillas that he had negotiated a deal whereby they would spend a short time in a rehabilitation camp and then be released to rejoin their families. Alternatively, dedicated Communists had the option, if they chose, to be deported to China, without interrogation.

Very few chose that option. Hor Lung knew, however, that some of the hardline guerrilla leaders were so fanatical that they would shoot him dead if he suggested surrender, so he told SB that he dare not risk visiting their units at all. He would meet the courier and order him to lead him to the unit with a larger army escort than usual in attendance, but he would not enter the camp, leaving it to the army to call on the unit to surrender. Those who could would do so but sometimes the hard-core leaders would fight to the death.

For others a different technique had to be used. Assisted by Hor Lung and others who had surrendered, including the couriers, SB might discover the location of the unit, or possibly use the normal informant techniques to lead it into a trap, so that the army could mount an ambush. If any of those who had already surrendered came from the hardline leader's unit, they were often very ready to cooperate in getting him caught or killed, because they knew that he would certainly kill them for having surrendered if ever he set eyes on them, even if that were ten years later.

During the six months May to October 1958 Hor Lung brought in 160 guerrillas who, with those who were killed or captured, comprised the entire MCP regional, district and branch organization for southern Malaya. Part way through this time the Malayan Prime Minister, Tunku Abdul Rahman, realized that, at some stage, an investigative journalist would inevitably discover that something was afoot and, wittingly or unwittingly, compromise the operation by public speculation. He therefore called all the editors together, briefed them and bound them to secrecy, promising to give them the full story when it was safe to do so, all at the same time (no scoops). They all respected this. The Emergency Regulations were such that they would have incurred severe penalties had they not complied but they would probably have cooperated in any case, as they knew that the vast majority of the public were heartily sick of the war and wanted it to end.

Arising from this experience, the British police, during the subsequent 38 years, have repeatedly followed this same technique of requesting voluntary media blackouts when lives have been at risk, such as in a kidnap, in the UK. Provided that all the editors (now including radio and TV) are present at the briefing together, they have invariably honoured the request. So this proved to be yet another British technique developed in Malaya.

Hor Lung qualified for rewards for each of the 160 wanted guerrillas he brought in. He received 247,000 Malayan dollars, roughly equivalent to £300,000 (US$450,000) at 1996 prices. Since virtually all his adult life had been spent as a guerrilla in the jungle, he had initially little idea of money or business. A retired SB officer (Chinese), aided by accountants and other advisers, helped him to start a timber yard and he became a prosperous businessman. He chose to remain in his home state (Johore) in south Malaysia, where the author spent two evenings with him and his retired SB minder nine years later, in 1967. He clearly had no anxieties about his personal security; the people in the villages around respected him, did not resent his prosperity and seemed to be grateful for the part he had played in ending the war.[9]

Not all informants or collaborators end up as happy as Hor Lung, but his story does provide an example of sensible handling, rewarding and aftercare of an agent in an intelligence operation which saved hundreds of lives.

PERU: AN INTELLIGENCE SUCCESS

An impressive example of background intelligence leading to the targeting and capture of a terrorist leader comes from Peru in 1992. The founder and leader of *Sendero Luminoso* (SL – 'The Shining Path'), Dr Abimael Guzman, had been operating underground since 1979, shortly before SL carried out its first terrorist attacks in 1980 in the Andean highlands. By 1988, after more than 10,000 people had been killed, there was evidence that Guzman had moved his headquarters into Lima, both for strategic reasons and because he was suffering from a painful skin disease, psoriasis. A video tape, seized by police in a raid in June 1990 on a house which had been used by SL, showed a party at which

Guzman was seen dancing. Other people were identifiable in the background, and this confirmed the suspicion that he was being accommodated by friends in the radical chic community in Lima.

One of the friends recognized on the video was Nelly Evans, a member of a rich family who had formerly been a nun and had become dedicated to liberation theology. She was suspected by the police of involvement with SL, possibly acting as their accountant. The police put her under surveillance and one day in January 1991 she became aware that the police were following her. Guzman was, in fact, living in her house, so she diverted her route and played for time. She had made an arrangement that if she failed to return within a specified time he should assume that there was some trouble and leave the house – which he did. When she arrived home, the police followed her in, found evidence of Guzman's recent presence and arrested her.

The police then turned their attention to others believed to be friends of Nelly Evans in the radical chic community. One of these was her niece, Maritza Garrido Lecca, a ballet dancer, who was also from a well-to-do family. After a visit to Cuba in May 1986, Maritza had moved from classical ballet into contemporary dance, convinced of its power in revolutionary propaganda. By late 1991 she had married an architect, Carlos Inchaustegui, who was also a supporter of SL. They moved into a house in the middle-class suburb of Los Sauces, where they converted the ground floor into a school for contemporary dance and lived on the floor above.

At the end of 1991, General Antonio Ketin Vidal took command of the anti-terrorist police intelligence service, DINCOTE. He inherited a dangerous situation. From 1989 onwards more than 3000 people had been killed in the war every year and the total death toll by 1992 reached 25,000. SL had clearly shifted their priority to Lima, and in the summer of 1992 there were a number of massive car bombs in the heart of the main business district. Public and police morale was low and there was a very real risk of a collapse of democratic government. Vidal knew that SL, with its Central Committee in Lima and a 'people's organization' well established throughout the country, financed by the Colombian drug cartels, was fully capable of emerging as a de facto government – as the Sandinistas had done in Nicaragua in 1978. Since Guzman had been missed twice in raids on houses in which he had recently been living, Vidal realized that he must on no account risk another unsuccessful raid.

Having confirmed that Maritza lived there and was running the dance school, Vidal began comprehensive surveillance of the house in Los Sauces; a number of undercover police officers took jobs as street cleaners and as gardeners in a nearby park, and Maritza was followed on her shopping trips. Vidal's suspicions were aroused by a number of things.[10] The provisions she bought clearly catered for about six people but only two, Maritza and her husband, were ever seen to enter or leave the house, apart from young students attending the dance classes on the ground floor. This anomaly was heightened by indications of several more people living in the rooms above the dance studio: the curtains of one part were permanently drawn, day and night, and the shadows on them in the evenings suggested a lot of activity. Perhaps most suspicious of all was that a check with the telephone company revealed that there was no telephone in the house, which was most unusual for a house of that size in a prosperous suburb. Maritza and her husband made all their calls from public telephones, presumably to avoid them being tapped or taped. The surveillance team also observed Maritza buying large-size shirts and other garments. Her husband was small and Guzman big and fat.

In the final days before the police raided the house, they examined the contents of the refuse bins and found many stubs of Winston cigarettes – a brand which Guzman was seen to be smoking in blow-ups from the video seized in 1990; still more significant were a number of empty packets of Kennacourt E Cream for the treatment of psoriasis.

Vidal was now convinced that Guzman was in the house. He had not, however, confided his suspicions to ministers and senior intelligence officials because he feared that they might prejudice his delicate operation by trying to rush the pace, to get a share of the credit and orchestrate a public splash. He picked 12 September – four days after his precise confirmation of Guzman's presence from the analysis of the refuse – for his raid.

On this day, nearly all the senior ministers and officials were to be at a reception for a visiting British Cabinet minister, Kenneth Clarke, at the British Ambassador's residence. Vidal himself had declined the invitation. It was evident in retrospect that none of those at the reception were aware that at that moment Vidal and his men were poised outside Maritza's house. When she opened the door for a pair of visitors, they seized the opportunity to enter the house and surprised Guzman watching television upstairs with three others of his Central Committee. Six arrests were made and, on the additional information obtained from the premises, another 200 were arrested in the next few days.

Vidal was a cultured man and treated the captured Guzman with courtesy – to his great surprise, as he expected to be summarily shot. They talked for a long time, in the car and in Vidal's office. Within a few months, Guzman was sending out calls from prison for the 'armed struggle to be suspended' and was giving TV interviews to similar effect. The number of killings fell from 3101 in 1992 to 1692 in 1993 and 646 in 1994.[11] The majority of those still at large – and nearly all of those in prison – responded to his call and there were large-scale surrenders. Though a splinter group continued to operate, still financed by the Cali drug cartel, the threat of a collapse of democratic government and of an SL takeover was removed. In 1995 President Fujimori was re-elected with a large majority and – unexpectedly – his party and supporters also won a working majority in the Congress. This single intelligence triumph had been a decisive element in transforming Peru from a nation in crisis to a stable country embarked on an economic recovery.

Meanwhile in 1992, also on Vidal's advice, the government had introduced a 'Repentance Law' based on his study of the British experience in Malaya and the Italian *pentitismo* (see pp. 81, 90–4 and 162), which further accelerated the crumbling of terrorism in Peru.

In 1995, General Vidal became Inspector-General of the Peruvian Police.

Part IV
Criminal Justice

9 Prevention of Terrorism

THE EMERGENCY PROVISIONS ACT AND THE 'DIPLOCK COURTS'

In October 1972 the Heath government appointed a Royal Commission under a senior Lord of Appeal, Lord Diplock, to consider legal procedures to deal with terrorist activities in Northern Ireland. At this time, the Special Powers Act had been in force for 50 years, and Lord Diplock's Report,[1] presented to Parliament in December 1972, proposed measures which resulted in the Northern Ireland (Emergency Provisions) Act (NI(EP)A) 1973. The Diplock Report noted that the main obstacle to dealing effectively with terrorist crime was the intimidation of witnesses and juries; that the fear of intimidation was well founded; and that it was unfair and unrealistic to expect witnesses to give evidence at risk of their own lives or the lives of their families. He gave as an example a bus driver who had been shot dead when answering the door at his home when he was due to give evidence for the prosecution at a terrorist trial the next day.[2]

Lord Diplock also proposed that 55 offences, mainly connected with terrorism, firearms, explosives, and so on, should be listed as Scheduled Offences,[3] and should be tried without a jury by a single High Court or County Court Judge. (This system is further discussed in Chapter 13.) Lord Diplock also recommended that the onus of proof should be altered so as to require a person found in possession of firearms or explosives to prove on the balance of probabilities that the person did not know and had no reason to suspect that the arms or explosives were where they found.[4] He proposed that a confession made by the accused in cases of scheduled offences should be admissible as evidence unless it was obtained by torture or inhuman or degrading treatment; also that a signed written statement made to anyone investigating a scheduled offence should be admissible if the person who made it could not be produced in court for specific reasons.

The NI(EP)A 1973 enacted all of these provisions.[5] The 'specific reasons' for being unable to produce a person making a written statement were: that he was dead, or unfit by reason of his bodily or mental condition to attend as a witness; or if he were outside Northern Ireland and it was not reasonably practical to secure his attendance; or if all reasonable steps had been taken to find him but that he could not be found.[6]

The Act also gave special powers of entry, search and seizure in relation to arms or explosives or to the suspected holding of a hostage;[7] also powers to stop, question and search people or vehicles.[8] It created an offence of belonging or contributing to a proscribed organization, to dress or behave in public so as to suggest that he was a member, or to spy in aid of terrorism.[9] All of these 1973 provisions were later reiterated or renewed in subsequent Acts of Parliament (as described in Chapters 10–14).

THE NORTHERN IRELAND CIVIL RIGHTS ASSOCIATION (NICRA)

The case against the Act was put in 1974 by the Northern Ireland Civil Rights Association (NICRA) in a leaflet. NICRA was alleged to have had links with the IRA in the late 1960s and their leaflet demanded the repeal of the NI(EP)A 1973.[10] It described the Act as a useful piece of British propaganda to claim that the Special Powers Act had been repealed. NICRA claimed that written statements accepted as evidence 'are normally from paid informers or army personnel moved to Germany' (out of range of revenge attacks), adding that 'this is an invitation to perjury'. It commented that the use of torture, brutality, degrading or inhuman treatment were almost impossible to prove. It said that the finding of arms or explosives gave the Royal Ulster Constabulary (RUC) every opportunity to indulge in blackmail and malice. Admissions could be obtained by threats to charge every member of a family with the offence, each one having the onus of proving that he or she was unaware that the arms or explosives were there – which was almost impossible to prove. A man might therefore confess to save his wife or mother from being charged. NICRA concluded that

> the worst feature of this section of the Emergency Provisions Act is the number of people being sentenced to long prison sentences solely on the basis of an admission they made to the police, which they were unable to prove was taken under duress.

NICRA also accused the authorities of abuse of the powers of arrest, detention, search and seizure, saying that

> any stranger in the area, particularly at night and if they are young, will be questioned about their identity and what they are doing there. Individuals and families whose political opinions are suspect are continually stopped and taken off for four hours screening and occasionally for 72 hours detention. Their homes are constantly raided and searched. People can be stopped and searched as often as four times per night, by the same patrol. We have records of houses searched eight times in two weeks. Compensation for damage in a search is only paid if nothing incriminating is found. Houses have been utterly wrecked, and an incriminating find made, a length of fuse planted so obviously that no charge is made but no compensation is paid.[11]

THE GARDINER REPORT

After the NI(EP)A 1973 had been in force for about a year, in June 1974, the newly elected Labour government convened a Committee headed by a law lord who had been Lord Chancellor in the previous Labour government in the 1960s

> to consider, in the context of civil liberties and human rights, measures to deal with terrorism in Northern Ireland.

Their report, 'The Gardiner Report', was presented to Parliament in January 1975.[12]

The Gardiner Report considered British legislation in the context of the European Convention for the Protection of

Human Rights and Freedoms, which specified in its Article 6 that, *inter alia*

> (1) Everyone is entitled to a fair and public hearing . . . by an independent and impartial tribunal . . . but the press and public may be excluded from all or part of the trial in the interests of morals, public order in a democratic society . . . or to the extent strictly necessary in the opinion of the court in special circumstances where publicity would prejudice the interests of justice.
> (2) Everyone charged with a criminal offence shall be presumed innocent until proved guilty according to law.
> (3) Everyone charged with a criminal offence has the following minimum rights . . .
> . . .
> (d) to examine or have examined witnesses against him and to obtain the attendance of witnesses on his behalf under the same conditions as witnesses against him.[13]

The Diplock Report had barred itself from recommending any changes which would not comply with the minimum requirements of Article 6, but commented that

> (15) The minimum requirements are based upon the assumption that witnesses to a crime will be able to give evidence in a court of law without risk to their lives, their families and their property. Unless the state can ensure their safety, then it would be unreasonable to expect them to testify voluntarily and morally wrong to try to compel them to do so.
> (16) This assumption, basic to the very functioning of courts of law, cannot be made today as respects most of those who would be able, if they dared, to give evidence in court in the trial of offences committed by members of terrorist organizations.[14]

Lord Diplock drew attention to Article 15 of the European Convention which

> permits derogation from these requirements in time of public emergency threatening the life of the nation – a condition which we consider unquestionably fulfilled in Northern Ireland at the present time.[15]

This view was endorsed by Lord Gardiner, who recorded that the UK had given due notice of derogation necessary to deal with terrorism in Northern Ireland. He concluded that 'the 1973 Act is therefore not in breach of international agreement', and commented:

> The suspension of normal legal safeguards for the liberty of the subject may sometimes be essential, in a society faced by terrorism, to counter greater evils. But if continued for any period of time it exacts a social cost from the community: and the price may have to be paid over several generations. It is one of the aims of terrorists to evoke from the authorities an over-reaction to the violence, for which terrorists are responsible, with the consequence that the authorities lose the support of those who would otherwise be on the side of government.[16]

Gardiner further commented:

> The continued existence of emergency powers should be limited, both in scope and duration. . . . A solution to the problem of Northern Ireland should be worked out in political terms, and must include further measures to promote social justice between classes and communities.[17]

and urged that consideration be given to the enactment of a Bill of Rights.

The Report recommended that jury trial should be continued as soon as possible. It re-examined the question of whether non-jury trial for scheduled offences should be conducted by a panel of judges rather than by a single judge. This issue had also been examined by Lord Diplock in his Report. Diplock had concluded that the size of the judiciary in Northern Ireland (a total of fourteen Appeal, High Court and County Court Judges) was insufficient to provide for six courts of three judges each. Gardiner agreed and added that to find twelve more judges would take away more than half the strength of Queen's Counsel from the Northern Ireland Bar, which would unacceptably weaken the Bar at a time when it was already overstretched.

Gardiner also considered another proposal made by various contributors to his Committee – that the court should consist of a judge with two lay assessors. He rejected this on the grounds that qualified assessors would be difficult to find and that they would be subject to the same intimidatory pressures which had made jury trial inappropriate for the scheduled offences. The 1973 Act allowed the right of appeal without leave against the finding or sentence of a single judge court, and Gardiner considered that this provided sufficient safeguard.[18]

Now that the 'Diplock Courts' have been operating for over 20 years, there is greater than ever reason for re-examining whether a single judge without a jury is a satisfactory method of overcoming intimidation of witnesses and juries. A judge sitting with assessors has worked successfully in many other countries, including the Republic of Ireland. In the Netherlands, juries are not used at all, and courts consist of a senior judge presiding over between two and six junior judges. This is quite practicable under the continental inquisitorial system, in which young lawyers can become examining magistrates. (This question is further discussed in a wider setting in Chapter 13.)

One of the practical problems, however, is that any judge who has passed sentence on a person convicted of terrorist offences in Northern Ireland has to have a 24-hour police guard for an indefinite period thereafter, and that the necessary security precautions inflict a blight on his life and on that of his family. The same would presumably apply to any additional judges or assessors who had sat on any but the most uncontroversial cases. The absolute minimum protection, one police personal protection officer round the clock, would tie up five of these highly trained officers and, with their equipment, transport, communications and back-up, the cost would be of the order of £3000 a week.

THE PREVENTION OF TERRORISM ACT

Although it was not presented to Parliament until January 1975, the Gardiner Report had already gone to press before the climate of the terrorist war was changed overnight by the Birmingham bombs in November 1974 – at the time of writing still the worst of all the atrocities committed by the IRA. This did not affect the Gardiner Report or the

NI(EP)A 1973, which apply only to Northern Ireland. Since Birmingham is on the British mainland, this atrocity led to the rapid enactment of additional anti-terrorist legislation applying to the whole of the UK – The Prevention of Terrorism (Temporary Provisions) Act 1974 – required to be renewed every year and periodically reviewed and revised. The current version quoted in this book is that of 1989, and none of the minor amendments since then has been significant, including those at its renewal in March and April 1996. Hereafter its short title will be used – PTA 1989.

On the evening of Thursday 21 November 1974, large IRA bombs were detonated in the crowded basement bars of two pubs in Birmingham, killing 21 people and injuring 162, many having their lives permanently shattered by the loss of arms and legs, by blindness or by brain damage. This caused particular public outrage as Thursday was weekly pay day, so everyone would have known, including the IRA cell operating on the mainland, that the two pubs would be packed with young people, predominantly weekly wage-earners and their friends; also because the 'warning', which did not specify the location of the bombs, was telephoned only seven minutes before the bombs went off. This may have been due to IRA incompetence rather than diabolical intent, but it was interpreted by British and world public opinion as a cynical act to inflict maximum casualties while claiming that warning was given. The public anger was such that Parliament rushed the legislation through all stages including the Royal Assent within one week, which suggests that the Act was held ready in draft as part of contingency planning. The anger remains, however, and none of the subsequent British governments, Conservative or Labour, has shown any serious intent of repealing it.

The essential provisions have remained the same. Despite the Peace Process initiated by the governments in London and Dublin in 1993 and the cease-fire in 1994–96, the PTA was renewed by Parliament every year. After the IRA broke the cease-fire with a gigantic bomb in London on 9 February 1996, it was renewed again on 14 March 1996, with only 20 votes against it. It was further strengthened by the Prevention of Terrorism (Additional Powers) Bill (PT(AP)B) 1996 on 2 April 1996, authorizing the search of pedestrians on the streets without the previous requirement for 'reasonable grounds for suspicion', to meet a further threat of IRA bombs.[19]

When Ireland was partitioned in 1922, the citizens of the Republic and of the UK, including Northern Ireland, remained free to move across each other's frontiers, to work in each other's countries without the need for permits, and even to register to vote in each other's elections. This freedom of movement survived for more than half a century – until the Birmingham bombs in 1974.

The PTA proscribed the IRA (and later a number of other terrorist organizations) and made it an offence to be a member, to profess to belong or to display support.[20] It gave the Secretary of State for Home Affairs the power to exclude people from entering or remaining in Great Britain if he was satisfied that they had been concerned in the commission, preparation or instigation of acts of terrorism, or were entering Britain with the intention of doing so. It also became an offence to secure or facilitate the entry of or to harbour someone known, or with reasonable grounds to suspect, to be an excluded person.[21]

Furthermore, it became an offence to give, lend or otherwise make available, or to accept, any money or property, knowing or having reasonable cause to suspect that it was intended for use or in connection with commission or furtherance of acts of terrorism. Repeating Diplock's departure from normal British jurisprudence, the onus was on accused persons to prove that they did not know or have reasonable cause to suspect this. It was also an offence to solicit, invite, give, lend or receive contributions to a proscribed organization or to assist in retaining or controlling terrorist funds – again with the onus of proof on accused persons to prove that they did not know or have reasonable cause to suspect that the contributions or funds were intended for any of these purposes.[22] It also became an offence to fail to disclose information, suspicion or belief that the money or property was so intended.[23] On conviction for any of these offences, the court had power to order the forfeiture of the funds or property concerned.[24]

This reversal of the traditional onus of proof – already in force in Northern Ireland since 1973 under the NI(EP) Act

– is now applied in Britain and most other countries to other assets acquired illegally or intended for financing illegal activities. It applies, for example, under the Drug Trafficking Offences Act (DTOA) 1986, and to money laundering generally under the Criminal Justice Act (CJA) 1988. In all these cases the police have the right, given a court order, to require a bank or other place of deposit to freeze assets pending investigation and, on conviction, they can be confiscated unless the owner can prove a legitimate source (see Chapter 5).

EXTENDED DETENTION

A person arrested under the PTA for any of the offences concerning membership or financing a proscribed organization or of terrorism could be detained without charge for up to 48 hours, and this could be extended for a maximum of five more days, up to a total of seven days in all, by the Home Secretary.[25] The purpose of this was to give time for questioning of other people who might have knowledge, not only in the UK, but also in the Republic of Ireland and in other countries in which the IRA operated (such as in Western Europe) or took refuge or raised funds (as in the USA), and in which the police or intelligence authorities were willing to cooperate against them. In particular, the extra extension (up to seven days) gave time for consulting informants (see Chapter 7). When a suspected IRA member or supporter was detained at a seaport or airport, some of the informants might be able to give information with which the detained person could be confronted in interrogation. Such an operation might take some days of careful preparation in checking which informants had relevant knowledge and then assembling the information and, in practice, such confrontation with new facts sometimes brought a swift end to several days of silence and non-cooperation.[26]

Because it proved so effective, this provision aroused much adverse comment from Sinn Fein and IRA sympathizers. It has also been criticized by human rights campaigners in Britain, who regard it as the thin end of a wedge whose application could be extended to other dissidents. Sinn Fein have expanded their campaign against it to the courts and Human Rights Commission in Europe on the grounds that a seven day period of detention before charge is higher than anywhere else in the EU (except for a period in Spain when ETA terrorists could be held incommunicado for up to ten days). Successive British governments, however, have consistently maintained their right to apply these measures (first introduced by a Labour government in 1974) pointing out that IRA terrorists have inflicted a far higher percentage rate of killing and wounding on the population than terrorists in any other West European country.

People campaigning against these powers of exclusion and detention drew attention to the small percentage of those detained under the PTA who were in the event charged and convicted. Parliament ordered periodic reviews for consideration in its annual debate on renewal of the Act.

In the first full year of the operation of the PTA (1975), a total of 1067 people were detained, 630 of these at airports or seaports and 437 elsewhere. Of these, detention was extended beyond 48 hours for 137 (13 per cent), exclusion orders were made against 46 (4 per cent) charges made against 63 (6 per cent), and 958 (90 per cent) were neither excluded nor charged. By 1982, the total detained had fallen to 220, of whom 37 (17 per cent) were extended beyond 48 hours; of the total detained, 5 per cent were excluded, 8 per cent charged and 87 per cent neither excluded nor charged.[27]

There was a close co-relation between the number whose detention was extended beyond 48 hours (13.5 per cent average 1974–82) and those excluded or charged (11.8 per cent average). Of those not extended the majority were set free in much less than 48 hours. The numbers were not unreasonable. Armed with wanted lists and photographs, backed by their own hunches, the SB police officers watched arrivals at seaports and airports, mostly those handling ships or flights direct from Ireland, North or South, but including in some cases passengers from Germany, Belgium or the Netherlands (where the IRA have frequently attacked British service personnel and their families) or from the USA. The numbers initially detained can be compared with the number of apples turned over by a greengrocer trying to pick out any in a box which may be rotten. The greengrocer would certainly expect to check more than 100 for every 10 found to be blemished.

Any doubts among the British public about continuing these powers were regularly dispelled by the IRA themselves by, for example, the murder of two young children by a bomb in a shopping precinct in Warrington in March 1993 and by the periodic giant bombs in the City of London.

The 1994–96 cease-fire aroused widespread hopes that the PTA might soon have had its day, but the detonation of a bomb in London on 9 February 1996 only a few hours after Sinn Fein had publicly stated that the cease-fire was 'total and permanent' shattered any prospect of the IRA's word being trusted. If there were to be a genuine repudiation of violence, perhaps after a change of IRA leadership, the powers of detention and exclusion would no doubt be suspended, but the power to reimpose them will probably always be retained in case the threat of terrorism (IRA or otherwise), organized crime or illegal immigration makes them necessary. (These and other options for the future are discussed at the end of this chapter.)

POWERS OF SEARCH

The PTA gave police, immigration and customs officers powers of search of people entering Great Britain or Northern Ireland at airports and seaports, or by train, or found within a mile of the Irish North–South border, for the purpose of determining whether there were reasonable grounds for detention or for application for exclusion. Those being checked could be required to produce a passport with a photograph or some other document to establish identity, which had not before been required of citizens of the UK or the Republic of Ireland. They could also be required to declare and produce any documents in their possession of a kind described by the officer.[28]

It became an offence for any person, knowing or having reasonable cause to suspect that an investigation was taking place under the PTA, to make disclosures (say, to warn others) or to falsify, conceal or destroy material likely to be relevant to the investigation. The onus lay on persons accused of such an offence to prove that they did not know or have reasonable cause to suspect that an investigation was in progress.[29]

WITHHOLDING INFORMATION

One of the provisions which has most often been questioned in the periodic reviews of the Act and in Parliament is the section making it an offence for persons to withhold information which they know or believe might be of material assistance in preventing an act of terrorism or in securing the apprehension, prosecution and conviction of any person involved in commission, preparation or instigation of such an act.[30] This clause was not in the original PTA in 1974 but was inserted as Section 11 in 1976. Lord Shackleton's Review of the PTA in 1978 recommended that it be allowed to lapse, but Parliament voted for it to continue.[31] The Jellicoe Review of 1983 recommended that it should remain, and it has become Section 18 of the PTA of 1989.

The obligation to provide information at pain of prosecution has not been a traditional provision of English law. It has been argued that it is not consistent with the principle that suspected persons are not obliged to give information which may incriminate themselves; also that a person may reasonably be wary of giving information based on suspicion (rather than sure knowledge) which could incriminate someone who might be innocent. It has also been alleged that it has been used by police to bring pressure to bear on people in detention by threatening that, unless they give certain information, they might be charged under Section 11 (now Section 18) of the PTA. These were Lord Shackleton's reasons for recommending in his 1978 Review that the clause should lapse, pointing out also that it had been rarely used in the two years for which it had been in existence – twice in Great Britain (one of those ending in acquittal) and 17 times in Northern Ireland – but Parliament did not accept this recommendation.[32]

In re-examining the question of retention of this offence in his review of 1983, Earl Jellicoe evaluated three factors:

the value of the offence, its effect on civil liberties and the right of silence, and the risk of abuse.

Regarding the value of the offence, he noted that charges for it had been rare. In the 7 years since it was introduced, it had been used 14 times in Great Britain with 9 convictions, only 2 of these resulting in custodial sentences, both of them for less than a year. In Northern Ireland, 62 people had been charged and, of the 46 completed at the time of his Review, 22 had been convicted, only 3 receiving custodial sentences. On the other hand, there was evidence that the existence of the offence had resulted in a larger number of people coming forward with information, leading to the prevention of acts of terrorism or the conviction of dangerous criminals. For example, if a car were hijacked to assist in a terrorist offence, a well-founded fear of reprisals had sometimes deterred car owners from reporting the hijack; the realization that failure to do so could result in prosecution had persuaded some of them to provide the relevant details and help to prevent the terrorist act or to catch its perpetrators.

Regarding civil liberties, Jellicoe argued that most anti-criminal and anti-terrorist legislation involved provisions which could have some unwelcome effects on civil liberties, but that extraordinary legislation was needed to deal with an extraordinary situation. In this case, the purpose of Section 11 was to prevent terrorist acts which involved murder or to assist in apprehending those responsible, and the reality of the threat justified it. Regarding the right to silence, Jellicoe considered that this applied only to the right of accused persons not to give information which could incriminate themselves, and that the information referred to in Section 11 was not in this category. He did, however, recommend that the Section should be amended to make it clear that the information that it was an offence to withhold related only to the conduct of third parties, and not to that of the person being questioned. This has been made clear by the words 'any other person' in the new Section 18 of PTA 1989.

Regarding the potential for abuse, Jellicoe argued that the risk applied to the interrogation rather than the prosecution phase. The procedures for prosecution ensure that 'victims of circumstance' (unwilling recipients of information about acts of terrorism) are not prosecuted. Regarding interrogations, however, Jellicoe identified three risks: the first was of unfair pressure being placed on the relative of a terrorist who, without involvement, became aware of information covered under Section 11, thereby facing a conflict between loyalty and risking prosecution. The Section does, however, restrict the action to acts of terrorism and apprehension of perpetrators of such acts which by definition involve a threat to life, and Jellicoe recommended that police throughout the UK should be reminded by circular that it should be applied only in such circumstances. Second, he recommended that the prolonged detention (48 hours extendable to 7 days) should apply only to detainees suspected of commission or intention of commission of acts of terrorism, not merely of withholding of information, for which normal limits of detention should apply. Third was the possibility of Section 11 being used to put pressure on people under interrogation to make statements incriminating themselves, and this has now been covered in the revised wording of the new Section 18 which replaced it.[33]

THE FUTURE

In January 1996 a Lord of Appeal, Lord Lloyd, was appointed to carry out an inquiry into the need for counter-terrorism legislation in the UK if there were a lasting peace in Northern Ireland. His inquiry was unlikely to be completed before late 1996 or early 1997, and had hardly begun when the IRA blew the Peace Process apart with the bomb in London's Docklands on 9 February 1996. Yet it is still worthwhile to be ready for an end to the violence, however unlikely that seems at the time of writing.

The IRA threat is, in fact, unlikely to go away. Government and Opposition parties in the Republic of Ireland have reiterated in the Anglo-Irish Treaty of 1985, and in the initiation of the Peace Process in 1993, that they do not want Northern Ireland to join the Republic unless the majority of the Northern Ireland population wish to do so; there is no possibility of this until the Catholic population in the North increases to parity with the Unionist majority, which is ruled out demographically until well into the twenty-first century.

The IRA and its political wing, Sinn Fein (who have never in the past 60 years achieved as much as 3 per cent of the vote in the Republic of Ireland), know this very well. Unification would raise the Protestant population to over 25 per cent of the population of the united Ireland. The Dublin government, while maintaining a long-term hope, certainly has no wish to bring a million thoroughly aroused Unionists into the Republic against their will. This could result only in a bloody civil war, in which the IRA would no doubt continue to participate. Yet, despite talk of peace by Sinn Fein, the IRA have in effect made it clear that nothing short of unification would lead them to abandon the armed struggle. Only a change of leadership is likely to change this.

Even if they were to do a token 'decommissioning' of arms, placing, say, 100 guns in the care of the Dublin government or of a neutral authority, they would still have the huge arsenal provided by Colonel Gadafi of Libya in the 1980s. This comprises several tons of Semtex explosives, several hundred guns and thousands of rounds of ammunition, buried in small secret dumps dispersed all over the Republic. When Gerry Adams, President of Sinn Fein, said in March 1996 that the IRA had the resources to continue the war for another 25 years, the threat was valid, regardless of any 'decommissioning'.

Nevertheless, if the IRA were to decide to resume an avowedly 'permanent' cease-fire, as in 1994–95, holding Gadafi's armoury in reserve, it is still wise to consider whether repeal, suspension or modification of NI(EP)A 1973 and PTA 1989 might be desirable. The experience of the 1994–95 cease-fire gave indications of the shape of possible modifications, and some of these were discussed in the debate in Parliament on renewal of the PTA on 14 March 1996.

The use made of the PTA has greatly declined. Of the 27,000 arrests under the PTA in 1974–96, only 15 per cent were charged, and very few of those still remain in prison. Of the 483 exclusion orders made from 1974–96, only 33 remained in place in March 1996.[34]

In considering amendment of the NI(EP)A and the PTA and future counter-terrorist legislation, it would be wise to take account of other terrorist movements likely to operate in the UK. Islamic terrorists are the most likely and are both murderous and suicidal; they have already operated in France and the USA as well as in Algeria and Israel, and may decide also to fight their battles on British streets, as Palestinians, Libyans and Iranians have in the past. Suicide bombers are hard to guard against in a free society. Other extreme religious cults can be almost as fanatical, as they showed in Tokyo in 1995, and are the likeliest to use chemical and biological weapons and possibly nuclear devices, for bombs, contamination or radiation. Right-wing racist terrorists have operated in Germany and the USA, though at present seem unlikely to do so in the UK. The terrorism of single issue groups, environmental or animal rights, if lethal at all, is likely to be on a small scale. But the overlap between political terrorism, the Mafia and organized criminal gangs must be taken into account.

With or without the NI(EP)A and the PTA, provision for proscribing terrorist movements must remain and if necessary also of organized criminal gangs. The power to restrict fund raising to finance violence by legitimate or criminal means, such as racketeering, will still be needed.

Consideration should be given to criminalizing fund raising and other activities in UK when they are part of a conspiracy to support acts of violence in other countries, normally by nationals of these countries or of their neighbours. There have been complaints of this from several countries, including India, Israel and Sri Lanka. If it is proved to the satisfaction of a British court that the actions they are conspiring to support in that country would be criminal if carried out in the UK, they should be liable for extradition, overriding any claim that their motives are political. Such extradition should be reciprocal.

Whether or not terrorism continues in Northern Ireland, the Diplock Courts should be replaced by trial before a jury which is protected by anonymity, sitting in a separate building, watching the accused, witnesses, judge and counsel on video cameras. This is explored more fully in Chapter 13 in the wider context also of trials involving organized crime. The possibility of extending this anonymity to witnesses – to be seen, through video cameras, only by the judge and jury – is also discussed in that chapter. So are the implications for a fair trial and for civil liberties.

There must be provision for declaring a State of Emergency, which already exists in the Emergency Powers Acts of 1920 and 1964 (though these have generally been used only for industrial disputes). The power to declare a State of Emergency, and the extent of the powers derived from it to deal with terrorism and other violent crime, should be permanently included in the relevant legislation.

Other powers (of arrest, detention, supporting terrorist acts or proscribed movements) should, where possible, be incorporated in the Police and Criminal Evidence Act (PACE) 1984 and the various Criminal Justice Acts (CJAs). Many of them are already included. The PTA, however, revised to apply to a flexible range of proscribed criminal and terrorist organizations as and when they are proscribed, should always be kept in draft, updated and in readiness to be instantly activated under the provisions of a State of Emergency.

Finally – as is applicable to every part of this book – intelligence is the key. The patient process of maintaining background intelligence, targeting known or suspected criminals and terrorists for surveillance, and recruiting and running good informants are the best of all safeguards and the best base from which to handle a crisis when it occurs. (Intelligence was discussed in Chapters 6, 7 and 8.)

10 Public Order

THE RIGHT OF ASSEMBLY

> The freedom to demonstrate peacefully under the law is, in a democracy, essential to the health of the community as a whole. But in order to realize that principle in practice, the law needs to balance the freedom to demonstrate with the sometimes conflicting interests of those who do not wish to do so.
>
> (Foreword to the Green Paper *Review of the Public Order Act 1936 and Related Legislation*, 28 April 1980)

It is no fluke that Britain has the world's longest record of continuity of government. Since 1688 (more than 300 years) there has been no change of monarch or of government by revolution, *coup d'état*, violence or any other unconstitutional means, in breach of the laws of the day. Only the USA (220 years) comes anywhere near that record – and that only at the price of a bloody civil war in 1861–65. Decisive ingredients in both countries have been freedom of speech and freedom of assembly, and the readiness of their governments not only to tolerate protest but also to respond to it, for example, the US withdrawal from Vietnam in 1972.

A dangerous new dimension arose in Britain in the 1930s, when demonstrations were not only against the government or employers, but also by rival political factions against each other – by thousands of Communists and members of Sir Oswald Mosley's British Union of Fascists fighting on the streets to deny each other the right to demonstrate. This led to the Public Order Act (POA) 1936 which included, among other things, the power to ban a demonstration if it was judged likely to result in serious public disorder, disruption or damage. This Act remained the basis of British public order legislation, with only minor amendments, for 50 years.

The Public Order Act 1986 was similarly prompted by a spate of violence by demonstrators on the streets in the 1970s – one of the most turbulent decades in British social history.[1] Some of this violence arose from mass picketing, starting at the Saltley Coke Depot in 1972, where 30 people were injured and 76 arrested. The worst example of this was the year-long strike at Grunwick in 1976–77, in which more than 300 were injured, mostly police (243), though no one was killed. On some days as many as 4500 police were deployed.[2]

Five of the biggest breakdowns of public order, however, like those in the 1930s, arose from clashes between right- and left-wing demonstrators, the National Front (NF) on the right and various Trotskyists on the left, including the International Marxist Group (IMG), the Socialist Workers' Party (SWP) and the Anti-Nazi League (ANL). In June 1974 in Red Lion Square, 54 were injured (including 46 police) and 1 killed – the first death in England in a public order context for 55 years. In August 1977, 2750 police were deployed in Lewisham (south London) and 327 people injured, again mostly police (270).[3] There were similar clashes in August 1977 at a by-election at Ladywood (Birmingham) in which NF and SWP candidates were standing, and in April 1979 in Leicester. These were largely contained, with fewer casualties, though at Ladywood 57 of the 400 police deployed were injured. One of the worst incidents was in Southall (west London) on 23 April 1979, in which 1 man was killed and 160 injured, including 97 police.[4]

The cost of policing these demonstrations, in addition to the disruption, damage and judicial expenses, was considerable. In London alone, the police costs of demonstrations involving 100 or more police in 1979 was £5.75 million, which would be £16 million at 1996 prices.[5]

The Southall incident again arose from clashes between NF and Trotskyist supporters, in this case in the run-up to the general election in May 1979 in which Mrs Thatcher came to power. On 27 June the new Home Secretary, William Whitelaw, announced a Review of the Public Order Act 1936, which was published as a Green Paper in April 1980.

This Green Paper was exhaustively discussed by interested parties over the next few years, and the conclusions (41 of them) were published as a White Paper in May 1985.[6] During this discussion period there were a number of serious public order incidents, including clashes between mainly black rioters and police in Brixton (London), Toxteth (Liverpool) and many other cities in 1981, and between police and mass pickets during the miners' strike in 1984–85. The new Public Order Act was passed in 1986,[7] and remains in force, though there have been some additions and amendments resulting from other legislation.[8]

RIOT, VIOLENT DISORDER AND AFFRAY

The POA 1986 abolished the common law offence of unlawful assembly, which could best be described as an incipient riot. Since the sixteenth century, this had been the bedrock of the discretionary power of a magistrate to order an assembly to disperse before any harm was done. Historically it was defined as an assembly of three or more persons with intent to commit a crime by open force. More recently it was defined as an assembly of three or more persons with a common purpose either to commit a crime of violence or to achieve any other object, lawful or not, in such a way as to cause reasonable men to apprehend a breach of the peace. As well as abolishing the offence of unlawful assembly, the 1986 Act also replaced the common law offences of riot, rout and affray, whose outdated wording was such that people were seldom charged with them. They were replaced by three new statutory offences – riot, violent disorder and affray.[9] Section 1 of POA 1986 defines **riot** as follows:

> Where 12 or more persons who are present together use or threaten unlawful violence for a common purpose and the conduct of them (taken together) is such as would cause a person of reasonable firmness present at the scene to fear for his personal safety, each of the persons using unlawful violence for the common purpose is guilty of riot.

It is immaterial whether the people concerned use or threaten the violence simultaneously and the common purpose may be inferred from their conduct. No person of reasonable firmness need actually be (or be likely to be) present, and riot may be committed in private as well as in public places. It carries a maximum sentence of ten years' imprisonment or a fine or both.

When the number of persons as defined above is between three and eleven, the offence is **violent disorder** (Section 2) and carries a sentence of up to five years or a fine or both.

Persons are guilty of **affray** if they use or threaten unlawful violence towards another and their conduct is such as would cause people of reasonable firmness present at the scene to fear for their personal safety. The threat or use of such violence is judged by the person's conduct or, if made by two or more, by their conduct together, and a threat made by the use of words alone does not constitute this offence. It carries a sentence of up to three years or a fine or both.

PROVOCATION, HARASSMENT AND INCITEMENT OF RACIAL HATRED

It is an offence under Section 4 of POA 1986 to use **threatening, abusive or insulting words or behaviour** against another person, or to display any visible representation which is threatening, abusive or insulting with intent to cause that person to believe that immediate, unlawful violence will be used against him, or to provoke him to use such violence. This carries a sentence of up to six months or a fine or both.

A further offence (Section 4A of POA 1986) was added by the Criminal Justice and Public Order Act (CJPOA) 1994 Section 154, under which it is an offence if the words or behaviour described above are used or visibly represented with **intent to cause harassment, alarm or distress** and it carries a similar penalty. Section 5 of POA 1986 is a lesser offence of using or displaying the words or behaviour within hearing or sight of a person likely to be caused harassment, alarm or distress thereby, and carries only a fine.

In all of these sections, 'violence' or the threat of it includes **violence against property** as well as against persons.

Sections 18 to 28 of POA 1986 create offences similar to those in Sections 4, 4A and 5, but specify more severe penalties if the offence is intended or likely to **stir up racial hatred**. These offences include words, behaviour, publication, presenting a play or broadcast or possessing inflammatory material intended or likely to stir up racial hatred. Sentences are up to two years or a fine or both.

PROCESSIONS AND ASSEMBLIES

Since their foundation in 1829, the British police had the **power to control the routes of processions**. When 30,000 Chartists gathered in south London in 1848 with the intention of marching on Parliament, for example, they were prevented by the police from crossing Westminster Bridge, and only their leaders (in three cabs) were escorted across the bridge to hand in their petition. It is an indication of the London public's attitude to public order in 1848 that, when the Commissioner of the Metropolitan Police invited Londoners to enrol for the day as Special Constables, 200,000 did so and escorted the march – six to every marcher. Britain was one of the few European countries which did not have an attempted revolution in 1848, the 'Year of Revolutions'.

The Act of 1936 had for the first time introduced the **power to ban processions**. The purpose of this was to prevent serious public disorder by the Communists and Fascists rather than have to deal with it after it had begun. Chief police officers could impose conditions on marches (such as their route) or, if they felt that this would not suffice, they could apply for a ban to the Home Secretary (in the Metropolis) or the local council (elsewhere).[10]

POA 1986 retained these ideas in principle but was more specific. It requires (Section 11) **written notice** to the police at least six days before the intended date or as soon as reasonably practicable. (Certain specified religious, educational or ceremonial processions were exempted from this requirement for notice.) Senior police officers then have the **power to impose conditions** if they reasonably believe that

(a) it may result in serious public disorder, serious damage to property or serious disruption to the life of the community, or

(b) the purpose of the persons organizing it is the intimidation of others with a view to compelling them not

> to do an act they have a right to do or to do an act they have a right not to do.
>
> (Section 12 (1) POA 1986)

Failure to comply with the conditions imposed carries a maximum sentence of three months or a fine or both.

Under Section 13, if they believe that the powers under Section 12 are not sufficient, chief police officers can apply through the Home Secretary or local council (as under the 1936 Act) for a **ban** on all **processions** or on specified classes of procession, for up to three months, at pain of the same penalties as under Section 12.

Under Section 14 of POA 1986, senior police officers have similar powers in relation to **public assemblies** if they consider that the assemblies may result in serious public disorder, damage or disruption to the life of the community, or intimidation as defined in Section 12 (1) (a) and (b) as quoted above. The officer may in these circumstances **impose conditions** as to

> the place at which the assembly may be (or continue to be) held, its maximum duration or the number of persons who may constitute it, as appears to him necessary to prevent such disorder, damage, disruption or intimidation.
>
> (Section 14 (1) POA 1986)

This Section has been applied to picketing and animal rights protests.

In addition to the powers under POA 1986, there are a number of other statutory offences in the general criminal law which can be applied to people organizing or taking part in processions or assemblies. These include

Obstructing the highway (Section 137 of the Highways Act 1980).

Obstructing a police constable (Section 51 (3) of the Police Act 1964).

Assaulting a police constable (Section 51 (1) of the Police Act 1964).

Committing criminal damage (Section 1 (1) of the Criminal Damage Act 1971).

or their Scottish equivalents. These and similar laws may also be applied, for example, to animal rights protesters or football hooligans (as will be discussed on pp. 126–7) and to industrial picketing.

TRESPASSORY ASSEMBLIES

A new set of police powers was inserted into POA 1986 by Sections 70 and 71 of CJPOA 1994 and became Sections 14A, 14B and 14C of POA 1986, to meet the controversial problem of **trespassory assemblies**, defined in Section 14A as follows:

> (1) If at any time the chief officer of police reasonably believes that an assembly is intended to be held in any district to which the public has no right of access or only a limited right of access and that the assembly
>
> (a) is likely to be held without the permission of the occupier of the land or to conduct itself in such a way as to exceed the limits of any permission of his or the limits of the public right of access and
>
> (b) may result
>
> (i) in serious disruption to the life of the community or
>
> (ii) where the land, or a building or monument on it is of historical, architectural, archeological or scientific importance, in significant damage to the land, building or monument,
>
> he may apply to the council of the district for an order prohibiting for a specified period the holding of all trespassory assemblies in the district, or part of it, as specified.[11]

On receiving such an application, a council may, subject to the consent of the Home Secretary, make an order either in the terms of the applications or with such modifications as may be approved by the Home Secretary. In the case of London, the Commissioner of the City or Metropolitan Police applies directly to the Home Secretary.

Section 14B laid down penalties for anyone organizing or participating in such a prohibited assembly. Under Section 14C, where constables in uniform reasonably believe that a person is going to an assembly which they reasonably believe to be one prohibited under Section 14A, they may stop that person and direct him or her not to proceed in the direction of the assembly. A person who fails to comply with this direction may be arrested without a warrant and, if convicted, is subject to a fine.

These powers have been used against animal rights protesters, hunt saboteurs, persons obstructing work such as construction of new roads, and 'new age travellers' (often wrongly described as 'gypsies').

CJPOA 1994 also gave power (Sections 61 and 77–80) to local authorities to remove **unauthorized campers** or **trespassers** from land forming part of a highway, from other unoccupied land or from private land entered without the consent of the occupier. The authorities can give notice of a direction to leave the land and to remove any vehicles or property they have with them. This can be addressed to all unauthorized persons on the specified land, including occupants of vehicles, without naming them. Any failing to leave or to remove their vehicles or property, or re-entering the land within three months, are subject to arrest and a fine. The authority may be empowered by a magistrate to take such steps as are reasonably necessary to ensure compliance.

If persons trespassing on land in the open air attempt to obstruct or disrupt any lawful activity on that land or to intimidate anyone from engaging in it, they commit the offence of **aggravated trespass** and are liable to imprisonment for up to three months or a fine or both. If the senior police officer present reasonably believes that people have committed or intend to commit such an offence, the officer may direct them to leave the land and, if they do not do so, or re-enter the land as trespassers within three months, they may be arrested without a warrant.

The most familiar use of this power has been against hunt saboteurs, but it can also be applied to attempts to disrupt any other lawful activity or to obstruct or intimidate those engaging in it. Its purpose is to prevent situations arising which are likely to result in serious disorder.

Sections 63–67 of CJPOA 1994 refer to **raves**, which are defined as

> a gathering on land in the open air of 100 or more persons . . . at which amplified music is played during the night . . . and is such that, by reason of its loudness and duration and the time at which it is played, is likely to cause serious distress to the inhabitants of the locality.

If a senior police officer believes that two or more people are preparing for a rave and ten or more are waiting to attend it, the officer may order them to leave the land and to remove any vehicles or equipment they have with them. If any fail to do so or re-enter within seven days, they can be arrested and imprisoned for up to three months.

If constables in uniform reasonably believe that people are going to such a gathering they may stop them, direct them not to proceed in the direction of the gathering and, if they fail to comply, arrest them without a warrant.

The courts also have power to confiscate any sound equipment if they are satisfied that it has been used at the gathering.

PICKETING

The laws on **picketing** were developed from the nineteenth century onwards and updated in Mrs Thatcher's Employment Acts of 1980, 1982 and 1984. The law does not specifically authorize a right to picket but gives **immunity from prosecution or civil damages** provided that certain conditions are met. Since 1906, this immunity has been provided for workers or their trade union representatives in dispute with their employers who picket the entrance to the workplace to **peacefully persuade** their fellow workers not to work. There is no immunity for criminal offences such as obstruction, intimidation, assault or malicious damage. As with demonstrations, the police have considerable discretion in enforcing the law.

In the 1970s, especially in the 1972 and 1974 miners' strikes, and in the dispute at Grunwick in 1976–77, there were repeated incidents of violence, obstruction and intimidation by mass pickets running into thousands trying to block the entrance, and these extended to **secondary picketing** of installations not involved in the dispute in order to apply political or economic pressure. Mrs Thatcher's Employment Acts restricted the immunities to picketing the workplace of those involved in the dispute and to their 'first suppliers' or 'first customers'. For example, strikers at a factory making components for a motor manufacturer could claim immunity for picketing a factory providing rubber tubing for incorporation in those components (a 'first supplier') or a factory which used their components in vehicle assembly plants (a 'first customer'); but their immunity would not extend to picketing a car sales showroom or a power station.

The law also restricted the numbers on the picket line to what the police considered reasonable for the purpose of peaceful persuasion, but not so many as to obstruct the highway or to intimidate people who wished to pass through, that is **mass pickets** had no immunity and could be prosecuted for obstruction or intimidation. Normally a reasonable level would be about six for any one channel of entry. The law was repeatedly broken by mass pickets in the miners' strike of 1984–85 and many arrests were made.

FOOTBALL HOOLIGANISM

Sections 30–37 of POA 1986 give the courts the power to exclude persons from any prescribed football matches if they have been convicted of offences at or on the way to or from a previous football match. The exclusion order can be made by the court only in addition to any sentence, probation order or discharge for an offence of which the court has found the person guilty. The offences to which this power applies include the use or threat of violence towards a person or property; also using threatening, abusive or insulting words or behaviour intended or likely to cause harassment, alarm or distress or to stir up racial hatred.

PRODUCT CONTAMINATION

In the early 1980s there was a rash of **malicious contamination** of food, drink and pharmaceutical products, some by criminals to extort a ransom, and some by animal rights activists in order to frighten customers away from manufacturers or retailers who practised or paid for the testing of products on live animals (vivisection). One case in 1984, the contamination of Mars Bars and a warning that other bars had been contaminated by the Animal Liberation Front (ALF), caused considerable alarm to children and aroused much public indignation. This prompted increased police surveillance which led to the imprisonment of many of the leaders of the ALF in the next few years (see p. 205).

One of the consequences was the inclusion of Section 38 in POA 1986, which made it an offence for a person

> with the intention
> (a) of causing public alarm or anxiety
> (b) of causing injury to members of the public using the goods, or
> (c) of causing economic loss to any person by reason of the goods being shunned by members of the public, or
> (d) of causing economic loss to any person by reason of steps taken to avoid such alarm or anxiety, injury or loss
>
> to contaminate or interfere with goods, or make it appear that such goods have been contaminated or interfered with, or to place goods which have been contaminated or interfered with, or which appear to have been comtaminated or interfered with, in places where goods of that description are consumed, used, sold or otherwise supplied.

Section 38 goes on to make it an offence, with this intent, to threaten that any of these things have been done or will be done; also to be in possession, with a view to committing an offence, of contaminated goods or of apparently contaminated goods or of materials to be used in making them so. (This was to deter or punish hoaxes, which could cause not only alarm, but also enormous economic loss due to the destruction of goods, especially if the threat seemed to be to children.) Offences under Section 38 carry a maximum sentence of ten years or a fine or both.

STRIKING THE BALANCE

> Total freedom is anarchy. Total order is tyranny.
> (Sir Robert Mark, Commissioner, Metropolitan Police 1972–77)

> This Inquiry has been concerned to discover where the balance should be struck and the role of the police in maintaining it. Indiscipline amongst demonstrators, heavy-handed police reaction to disorder are equally mischievous: for each can upset the balance. Violent demonstrations by creating public disorder infringe a fundamental human right which belongs to the rest of us: excessively violent police reaction to public disorder infringes the rights of the protesters. The one and the other are an affront to civilised living.
> (Lord Scarman, *The Red Lion Square Disorders of 15 June 1974*, Cmnd 5919, London, HMSO, 1975, p. 2)

The police in Britain have always had considerable discretion as to when and how strictly to apply the law. It is, for example, an offence to obstruct the highway; any demonstration is bound to obstruct it to some extent; but if the real purpose of the demonstration is to prevent use of the highway altogether (say, to prevent fuel from getting to a power station or trucks from driving onto a ferry) then the police have a legal obligation to keep the highway open. If they do not do their best to do so, people who suffer loss from the obstruction can sue the police for damages.

Though some demonstrators may have ulterior motives, for example, obstruction, damage or discrediting the police, the great majority have the lawful aim of demonstrating their view and arousing public support for it. In the second half of the twentieth century, demonstrators have become aware that the most effective way of doing this is to ensure that the demonstration is reported on the main TV news bulletins. The first stage in achieving this is to get the TV crews to attend, and they might seem unlikely to do so unless there is an expectation of a violent confrontation. The organizers may therefore deliberately arouse this expectation, for example, of a confrontation with police trying to keep the road open, or between people with opposing views, or of mass pickets against independent truck drivers who are paid for each load they deliver. Once the cameras are there, some of the demonstrators may 'act up' in front of them to make sure that they get into the news, and some journalists may encourage them to do so.

The organizers of demonstrations will, where possible, pick issues on which they can hope for public sympathy; others may join in to exploit the opportunity for ulterior motives. The demonstrations in 1995 against the transport of live calves to be reared for veal by barbarous methods in mainland Europe were primarily organized by sincere and non-violent campaigners for animal welfare (not to be confused with animal rights) but the confrontations at the docks were used by political activists to induce the police to use force in an unfavourable light.

Among the more controversial areas covered in CJPOA 1994 are offences related to trespass. Half a million young people attended raves each week in 1993 and spent £700 million in that year on Ecstasy.[12] Since one of the main purposes in attending raves is the excitement generated by drug taking, they are regarded as undesirable and the noise and nuisance they cause are widely resented by other people.

The same generally applies to 'travellers', of whom only a tiny proportion are gypsy families who have traditionally sought a nomadic lifestyle and have been tolerated, if not welcomed, by the rest of the population. Gypsies provide a mobile workforce which has a place in the rural economy for such times as harvesting. Many of the 'new age travellers', however, are not seeking work, and intend merely to live an economical lifestyle easily affordable on social security benefits. Some discredit the others by using their mobility to evade detection for petty crime. Fairly or unfairly, they are not welcomed by the rural population and their intrusion on farm land can cause public disorder. Although there is some anxiety that a conventional way of life is being forced on a minority who do not want it, the majority of the taxpayers, especially in rural areas, resent trespassers and welcome legislation against them.

Football hooligans earn nothing but disgust from the public, who almost universally approve when they are locked up. Long-range cameras are increasingly used to spot known hooligans, viewed from the opposite side of the pitch, or while entering or leaving the ground. There are many people who resent damage to Britain's reputation by hooligans at matches in other European countries, which are usually glad enough to get rid of them without punishment. There are suggestions that legislation should be introduced to enable these hooligans to be charged and punished in Britain on the strength of photographic evidence and the testimony of witnesses brought over from the country in which the offence was committed. This, with reciprocal legislation, should be possible in the EU, and would be popular with the EU public.

Product contaminators have few friends and there have been no significant objections to Section 38 of POA 1986. Contamination by criminals for extortion is resented because the public are put indiscriminately at risk. Animal rights activists claim that they have deterred firms from testing their products on live animals by inflicting financial loss, but again the public are put at risk and the ALF have paid a heavy price in the loss of public sympathy for their cause.

In striking the balance between tolerating disruption and stifling the right to protest, the ultimate consideration must be for the victims of the disruption. Even when it does not cause injury or damage, disruption will cause an unpredictable number of ordinary people to suffer loss or anxiety: for example, by being unable to get a sick or injured child to hospital; or to lose the chance of a job by missing an appointment. The skill in policing lies in controlling protest in a way that allows people to go about their business; this may be in direct conflict with the aims of demonstrators, whose chance of getting into the news may depend on confrontation or disruption. The right to protest certainly does not include a right to kill or injure or to damage property nor, in the words of the Public Order Acts, to cause 'violent disruption' or 'serious disruption to the life of the community'. But can it be effective without doing so? Is the right to demonstrate only if there is no damage to the public an empty right? Ultimately, the right of people not involved in the dispute to tranquillity must tip the scale.

11 Arrest and Interrogation

SPOT CHECKS, SEARCH AND SEIZURE

When the Single European Act (SEA, signed in 1986) is fully implemented, all of the EU's internal borders will be open for the free movement of people, capital, goods and services except for emergency controls to deal with specific threats to national security. It is estimated that this will save the people of the EU, and their manufacturers and traders something like 5 per cent of GNP previously wasted by the time spent by heavy goods vehicles and cars waiting at the checkpoints at three or four frontiers between, say, Rotterdam and Milan.

The economic advantages of the SEA should be similar to those enjoyed throughout its history by the USA, where raw materials acquired in the sub-tropical south can be transported to factories in Michigan to make goods consigned for sale in California, all done by labour which can move freely to wherever there is work to be done, financed by capital which can be swung equally freely through the New York Stock Exchange. If Kansas and Missouri and all the other states had had frontiers like those between France and Germany in the nineteenth century, the USA would not have been the richest country in the world for over a century.

Part of the price of such freedom of movement within the EU would be that criminals, terrorists and illegal immigrants could dodge freely between the jurisdictions of, say, the German, Dutch and Belgian police and law courts whenever they felt that there was a risk of them being spotted and arrested. It has therefore become more important for all the EU police, customs and immigration services to have the power to stop and search people and vehicles – with safeguards against abuse – anywhere, any time, at spot checks. They will need legal provision to refer to each other's records and to have the technology to do this effectively.

In Britain, the Police and Criminal Evidence Act (PACE) 1984 empowers police constables to search any person or vehicle if they have reasonable grounds for suspecting that they may find stolen or prohibited articles; these include anything made, adapted or intended for use in theft or burglary or for obtaining property by deception; also offensive weapons, including anything made, adapted or intended for use to cause injury.[1]

In 1994 these powers of search were extended. If police officers of superintendent or higher rank reasonably believe that incidents involving serious violence may take place in their area and that it is expedient to prevent this, they may authorize constables to stop and search any person or vehicle 'whether or not he has any grounds for suspecting that the person or vehicle is carrying weapons or articles of that kind'. This authority is limited to 24 hours (extendable to 30 hours in certain circumstances). These extensions made sense in view of the IRA bombing campaign in England in 1993–94 and of their renewed bombings in 1996, for immediate response to intelligence or tip-offs. As well as the 24 or 30 hour limit, a further safeguard against abuse is that drivers are entitled to obtain, if required, a written statement that their vehicle had been stopped.[2]

IDENTIFICATION

A harmonized EU identity (ID) card system would greatly improve the chances of catching criminals, including terrorists, drug traffickers, other smugglers and illegal immigrants at police spot checks, especially as border checks are further eased under the SEA. The French have for many years empowered their police to demand proof of identity of citizens and foreigners near the scene of a crime (see p. 186) and their voluntary ID cards provide a use- ful way of doing that. In 1995–96 the French, like the British, were plagued with terrorists, in their case from Algeria, living both inside and outside France, and President Chirac began to have second thoughts about lifting border checks.

In Britain, 75 per cent of the public favour the issue of ID cards, according to a public opinion poll published by the *Daily Telegraph* in 1995, but there remains some anxiety about their possible abuse, not only by police harassing minority groups by persistently demanding proof of identity, but also by commercial organizations, particularly if they were able to get their hands on confidential data on such things as financial, medical or police records.

If Britain does introduce ID cards, they should certainly not contain any such data, however these might be coded, and there is no need for them to do so. They should also have adequate safeguards against impersonation by including biometric data unique to the holder; and the system should ensure the prevention or detection of any misuse of the card. (The characteristics of such a system, including its technology and the civil liberties implications, are discussed in Chapter 15.)

DETECTING DRUGS AND EXPLOSIVES

Detection of drugs or explosives can be one of the most positive clues leading to an arrest. Great strides have been made in recent years in this science; the most promising technologies are enhanced X-ray, which can detect explosives as well as metal, and vapour detectors (including dogs). Vapour or particle detectors sensitive enough to find plastic explosives, such as Semtex, are expensive, and rely on taking and analysing samples, which is likely to take a minute or more. Instant hand-held detectors are also widely used but are less sensitive. Dogs have been remarkably successful, especially in detecting drugs, but their senses can get fatigued, unlike machines. (All of these techniques are discussed more fully in Chapter 17.)

ARREST

The fear of arbitrary arrest and disappearance is a key characteristic which differentiates an authoritarian state from a liberal one, and in Britain and other democracies there are strict rules for the duration of detention before being charged and brought before a magistrate, and for families and legal advisers to be informed.

In Britain, constables have the power to arrest a person who they reasonably believe is committing, has committed or may be about to commit an 'arrestable offence'. Arrestable offences include those for which a sentence is laid down by law, and other offences under Customs and Excise or Official Secrets Acts, sexual offences, taking a vehicle without authority, going equipped for stealing and corrupt practices; conspiring to commit such offences; and inciting, aiding, abetting or procuring their commission (PACE 1984 (24)).

For non-arrestable offences, constables will normally arrange for a summons to be served on persons whom they suspect of committing or attempting to commit the offence; but constables may arrest them if they cannot obtain these persons' names and addresses or if they reasonably believe that the names and addresses they have given may be false or unsatisfactory for service of a summons (PACE 1984 (25)).

Constables may also arrest people when they have reasonable grounds for believing that an arrest is necessary to prevent them from causing injury, loss or damage to property or unlawful obstruction of the highway; or from committing an offence against public decency; or in order to protect a child or other vulnerable person (PACE 1984 (25)).

Constables may search arrested persons if they have reasonable grounds for believing that these persons may present a danger to themselves or others; or for suspecting that these persons may possess anything which they might use to assist them to escape from lawful custody or which might be evidence relating to an offence. Constables also have power to search any premises in which the persons were at the time or immediately before they were arrested (PACE 1984 (32)).

The civil liberties implications of these powers depend on the interpretation of whether the grounds for the constable's beliefs were 'reasonable' and this would ultimately have to be adjudicated by the courts.

BAIL AND REMAND IN CUSTODY

Bail causes more controversy than most of the other laws affecting arrest and detention. There is an understandable outcry against the courts when someone given bail on a serious charge takes advantage of it to commit another offence, especially if it involves violence, rape or child abuse: and young offenders on bail, confident that most thefts and burglaries are undetected, often think it worth the risk to make the best use of their remaining weeks or months of freedom to build up and hide away a comfortable nest egg, ready for when they complete their sentences after trial. This causes anger and frustration among the police, who know that a large percentage of offences are committed by detected criminals on bail.

On the other hand, if the accused are remanded in custody, there is a serious ethical problem about locking up people who are innocent until proved guilty; and if they are then acquitted, they and their friends will do their utmost to arouse public opinion against the courts and the police.

Remand in custody also incurs heavy public expense. Custody before trial must not be punitive, so prisoners are given as much latitude as possible in the remand prison. On the other hand, they are held there only because the courts consider that they would put the public at risk or attempt to abscond if released on bail, so their security is no less important than that of convicted prisoners and their custody probably costs more.

The risk of their reoffending would be reduced by more stringent enforcement of their surety, for example by requiring the money or assets to be lodged in full in advance and forfeited in full if they fail to surrender to custody. Also, before being released on bail, they should be warned by the court that, should they commit another offence on bail, their sentences on conviction for both the original offences and those committed on bail would be greatly increased. As a guide, quadrupling such sentences should have a deterrent effect. This would also be fair, since an offence committed on bail would confirm their criminal intent beyond doubt.

In CJPOA 1994 (25), Parliament legislated that people who had previously been convicted of murder, attempted murder, manslaughter, rape or attempted rape would not be granted bail if charged a second time with any of those offences. This certainly reflected public opinion.

Generally, the public are more often critical of leniency

in granting bail than of perceived injustice in holding people in custody before they have been convicted of any offence. Ultimately the decision lies with the judge or magistrate, who take into account the impression made on them by the accused, which the public cannot see. The judge gets little credit for being kind but faces angry criticism if the person does commit another offence while on bail. The growing concern about the suffering of the victims of crime will probably tip the balance towards custody rather than bail. All political parties, dependent on popular votes, will be influenced by this.

POLICE DETENTION

The case of a person arrested and held in police custody must be reviewed not later than six hours after detention was authorized and thereafter at intervals of not more than nine hours. There is provision for delaying these reviews, for example if the person is being questioned and the review officer judges that interruption would prejudice investigation. If the person has been charged, this review may be carried out by the custody officer, but if the person has not been charged, it must be carried out by an officer not below the rank of inspector who has not been directly involved in the negotiation (PACE 1984 (40)).

Subject to some exceptions mentioned later, a person may not be kept in police detention for more than 24 hours without charge (PACE 1984 (41)). Officers of the rank of superintendent or above have power to extend this to 36 hours if they have reasonable grounds for believing that this is necessary to secure or preserve the evidence relating to the offence or to obtain such evidence by questioning, and thereafter for a further 36 hours if they consider that these reasons still apply (PACE 1984 (42)). In certain circumstances a magistrate's court has power to extend this to a maximum of 96 hours after detention was first authorized (PACE 1984 (43) and (44)). In cases falling under the provisions of the Prevention of Terrorism Act (PTA), the Home Secretary has power to extend this further to a maximum of seven days (see Chapter 9).

Persons in police custody after arrest are entitled, if they so request, to have one friend or relative or other person of their choice told as soon as possible that they have been arrested and where they are detained. If the detention is for a serious arrestable offence, officers not below the rank of superintendent can delay the exercise of that right up to a maximum of 36 hours if they have reasonable grounds for believing that informing the named person

(a) will lead to interference with or harm to the evidence or interference or injury to others; or
(b) will lead to alerting other persons suspected but not yet arrested; or
(c) will hinder recovery of property obtained as a result of such an offence.

(PACE 1984 (56))

This power of delay also applies to anyone detained under the terrorism provisions (such as the PTA) as well as those detained for a serious arrestable offence. As well as the reasons given under (a), (b) and (c) above, the delay may be imposed if the authorizing officer has reasonable grounds for believing that telling the named person

(d) will lead to interference with the gathering of information about the commission, preparation or instigation of acts of terrorism; or
(e) by alerting any person will make it more difficult
  (i) to prevent an act of terrorism; or
  (ii) to secure the apprehension, prosecution or conviction of any person in connection with the commission, preparation or instigation of an act of terrorism

and, instead of the maximum of 36 hours, the delay may be imposed up to the end of the period beyond which the person may no longer be held without the authority of the Home Secretary (PACE 1984 (58)).

Similar provisions apply to the right of access to legal advice. Persons in police custody after arrest or who are detained under the terrorist provisions are entitled, if they so request, to consult a solicitor privately. This can be delayed on the authority of an officer not below the rank of superintendent for the same conditions and reasons as were set out in (a), (b) and (c) above. In the case of persons detained under the terrorism provisions, officers not below the rank of Commander or Assistant Chief Constable additionally have the power, if they judge that these same conditions and reasons apply, to direct that the person may consult a solicitor only in the sight and hearing of a qualified uniformed officer of at least the rank of inspector and who has no connection with the case (PACE 1984 (58)).

INTERROGATION AND THE RIGHT TO SILENCE

When persons are arrested, the police have an immediate duty to investigate their case, to decide whether to release them, to hold them in detention for further questioning, to apply for their detention to be extended or to charge them and bring them before a magistrate.

Before starting to question arrested persons, the police are obliged to caution them. If they choose to remain silent, the police were until 1994 barred from bringing this to the attention of the court at their trial – in which, again, the accused did not have to give evidence or say anything if they did not wish to do so. These rights to silence remain but Parliament in 1994 enacted legislation that in future the prosecution would be empowered to draw attention to the failure of the accused to give evidence or answer questions and for the judge and jury to draw such inferences as might be proper from this failure.[3] This had already been the case in Northern Ireland since 1988.[4]

The rules prior to 1994 devolved from the anxiety of Parliament during and before the nineteenth century that most people accused of crimes were uneducated and illiterate, unaware of their rights and of the processes of law, and vulnerable to inducement or coercion to make statements without realizing that these might later be used against them at their trial. There was a fear that police officers would be able to persuade or intimidate such people into believing that it was in their interest to make admissions, even if those admissions were not true. Others might in desperation make false admissions in order to end the ordeal of being questioned or to protect members of their families from being questioned. These fears remain valid, as is proved by the number of cases in which the courts have declined to convict because they did not believe the admissions, or considered that they were obtained by unfair means. So any change must maintain effective safeguards against possible injustices.

In the twentieth century, however, a number of new factors developed which had to be taken into account in ensuring, not only that these safeguards remained but also that they were not abused by sophisticated terrorists or other criminals so that more victims would suffer from their future crimes if they were wrongly acquitted. From the mid-nineteenth century, universal education brought illiteracy down to a very small percentage of the population (see p. 25). Then the advent, in turn, of a popular press (late nineteenth century), radio and the cinema (early twentieth century) and television (mid-twentieth century) meant that people generally understood the processes of arrest, detention, investigation and trial. As a symptom of this, most members of terrorist movements (especially the IRA, Palestinian and Islamic terrorists) and of organized criminal gangs are specifically trained to refuse to answer any questions at all and, if possible, to trap the police officers arresting and interrogating them into some action which can later be used to overturn their conviction on a point of law on appeal.

Another technique was evolved by lawyers defending those accused of terrorist or criminal offences; having persuaded their client to answer no questions, they would do their best to conceal evidence from the prosecution and then to spring it on the court during the trial so that, whether true or false or partially false, it was difficult for the prosecuting counsel to refute it, bearing in mind that days or often weeks of police investigation are needed to establish or disprove evidence. By contrast, the prosecution are barred from presenting any evidence to the court which has not been made available during investigation – weighting the balance heavily in favour of the accused and contributing to the large percentage of acquittals of guilty defendants.

CJPOA 1994 did not apply the same rule of advance exposure of defence evidence as the law does to prosecution evidence. It did, however, authorize the court and the jury to 'draw such inferences . . . as appear proper' from failure of accused persons to mention any fact relied on in their defence which they could reasonably have been expected to mention, on being questioned under caution before they were charged, or from their failure to do so on being charged.[5]

At the same time, the wording of the caution to be given by the police before questioning an arrested person prior to being charged was changed. Previously it had been 'You are not obliged to say anything but anything you say may be taken down and used in evidence'. From November 1994 the caution added 'If you do not mention something which you later use in your defence, the court may decide that your failure to mention it now strengthens the case against you'. But there may be a case for further modification (see next section).

VIDEO TAPES OF INTERROGATION

There will always be controversy about the ethics of interrogation because there are conflicting risks, first, of police inducing the accused to make a false confession and, second, of guilty criminals being wrongly released to commit more crimes. The fairest answer to both of these would be the wider use of video tapes. Already, for some years, it has been normal for the police to record interrogations for serious offences on audio tapes. Video tapes are also sometimes used, for example, in response to allegations of maltreatment of suspects under interrogation in Northern Ireland. It would be best if all police interrogations prior to serious charges were conducted in front of a video camera, and identical copies of the tape given to the prosecution and to the accused or their lawyers immediately after each session is complete, to rule out tampering or accusations of tampering. When the case comes to trial, no evidence from these interrogations, oral or documentary, should be admissible unless backed by the video and subject to challenge by either side.

This procedure would be fairer to all sides: fairer to the accused because it would prevent or reveal any unlawful methods of interrogation, such as inducements, threats or verbal or physical bullying; fairer to the police because juries would be happier to accept video evidence in preference to the 'verbals' (oral accounts by police officers of what the accused said); fairer to the administration of justice in that the demeanour of the accused in face of questions (even if silent) could be seen on the video by the judge and jury, just as they see his or her demeanour in court, whether the accused elects to give evidence or not; and fairer to the public if more of the guilty were convicted – more than the present sad record of only 1 conviction for every 50 crimes committed.

In the police caution before an interrogation, in place of the warning about the effect of failure to mention evidence which is later presented as part of the defence in court, the following might be substituted:

> You are not obliged to say anything, but my questions and your answers, or failure to answer, will be recorded on this tape, of which you will receive a copy. You and the prosecution will be free to present any part of this tape in evidence at your trial.

In commending modification of the right to silence in response to interrogation after arrest, *The Justice of the Peace Review* wrote in November 1972:

> everything would turn (as with any other piece of evidence) upon what it is reasonable to expect from that particular person with that particular inquiry in those particular circumstances. To expect more would be oppressive to the accused. To expect less (as we do now) is to fetter justice to no good effect . . . the unjust acquittal of guilty men . . . is the foremost defect of our criminal procedure today.[6]

Perhaps the last word should be given to one of our great liberal philosophers, Jeremy Bentham, 200 years ago:

> If all the criminals of every class had assembled and framed a system after their own wishes, is not this rule (that suspects cannot be judicially interrogated) the very first which they would have established for their security? Innocence never takes advantage of it. Innocence claims a right of speaking as guilt invokes the privilege of silence.[7]

12 Trial

STATEMENTS, CONFESSIONS AND THE RIGHT TO SILENCE

Uncorroborated confessions are notoriously unreliable as the sole evidence for conviction. In the Soviet Union, it was common for prisoners awaiting trial to remain in custody until they had made a written or oral confession so comprehensive that the trial itself amounted to no more than acting a play with a script.

China has never in the past accepted most of the ideas of judicial procedures taken for granted in liberal democracies. The 'facts' were presented by the police and the accused persons had very limited rights to challenge them and, knowing that conviction was almost certain, frequently settled for a prospect of more lenient treatment in exchange for a confession, influenced by fear of what might happen to their families if they did otherwise – much as was the case in the USSR. Amnesty International reported that there were more executions in China than in all the rest of the world put together; the death penalty was imposed, not only for murder but also for armed robbery, drug trafficking, blackmail, organizing pornography or prostitution and numerous economic crimes such as selling counterfeit currency and tax evasion. Once in prison, the prisoner's date of release was largely dependent on 'repentance', usually made abjectly in public. After an exchange visit in 1996, however, the British Director of Public Prosecutions (DPP) reported that China, under worldwide criticism for its human rights record, was moving towards giving the accused more scope for defence and more access to lawyers for advice.[1]

Many other Asian countries claim strong justification for the 'Asian way' both of justice and of government on behalf of the people, such as Islamic, Marxist, tribal, feudal or various versions of democracy, some of which bear little resemblance to Western conceptions of that term; and they may well ask 'Why should they?'

Regarding justice, for example, once an accused person is sent for trial in Japan or Thailand, the chance of conviction is well over 90 per cent. These and other Asian countries claim that their system gives a fairer chance of justice for the victim as well as the accused, but it is important to strike a balance.

Chapter 11 considered the safeguards needed to prevent a person being bullied, coerced or tricked into making statements under interrogation while in custody which will prejudice the fairness of a trial before it begins. This chapter will examine the safeguards against unfair conviction in court, and against perverse acquittal of people who are guilty.

The essential rules for admissibility of confessions at a trial have remained substantially unchanged in English law for several centuries. The current version of these rules was laid down in the Police and Criminal Evidence Act 1984.[2] A confession is not admissible as evidence if the defence submits and the court agrees that it was obtained by 'oppression' or 'in consequence of anything said or done' which was likely to make the confession unreliable. The Act defined oppression as including 'torture, inhuman or degrading treatment and the use of threat of violence (whether or not amounting to torture)'.[3] Although the Act does not spell it out, 'anything said or done' presumably includes misleading or improper promises or incentives, false implications that it would be in the accused's interest to admit to the offence, warnings that otherwise the accused's family might have to face interrogation, and so on. The Act also makes a confession inadmissible if the accused is mentally handicapped unless it was made in the presence of an independent person (not a police officer or anyone employed or engaged on police purposes).[4]

PACE 1984 also lays down, however, that even if a confession is wholly or partly excluded as evidence, this does not preclude the admission of any facts discovered as a result of the confession, or 'where the confession is relevant as showing that the accused speaks, writes or expresses himself in a particular way, of so much of the confession as is necessary to show that he does so'.

The court also has a general power to exclude anything it considers to be 'unfair evidence' if it appears to the court that 'having regard to all the circumstances, including the circumstances in which the evidence was obtained, the admission of the evidence would have such an adverse effect on the fairness of the proceedings that the court ought not to admit it.'[5]

There are strong arguments for and against empowering the courts, in deciding on guilt or innocence, to make their own inferences from the silence of the accused; silence under police questioning (preferably as recorded on video tapes); and from the accused declining to give evidence and face cross-examination in court.

There is nothing new about interpreting silence. A small boy caught at the jam cupboard, licking his lips to remove the forensic evidence, is asked by his mother 'What are you doing?' If he folds his arms and exercises his right to silence, his mother puts her own interpretation on that. So throughout life; at school; at work; or being interviewed on television.

The basis of a normal trial under English law is that the individual jurors will base their judgement of the truth on conflicting evidence and on their interpretation of the demeanour of the accused and of witnesses throughout the trial. During cross-examination of a witness, the jury will be influenced by the attitude of counsel; a bullying cross-examiner may swing their sympathy to the witness. The same applies if the accused elects to give evidence and faces hostile cross-examination. If (as recommended in Chapter 11) police interrogation is recorded on video tape, and the tape shows the police interrogator bullying or offering improper incentives or diabolically leading the accused into a trap, the judge and jury will again draw their own conclusions.

If defence counsel consider that any part of the interrogation has been carried out unfairly, they may submit to the judge in advance that that part of the tape should not be shown to the jury at all; judges may decide this themselves when they see the video before the trial; or, if one counsel presents a selected clip from the tape, the opposing counsel may object and the judge may rule that it is misleading and that fuller extracts must be shown.

Most people agree that justice is best served by the presence of accused persons throughout their trial, in a position in which the jury can see their reaction to every piece of evidence. They will no doubt try to put on an expression that suits their case. The jury will interpret all these things according to their experience in dealing with honest, dishonest, clever, stupid, tough, sensitive or devious people in everyday life. Few would suggest that it is unfair on the accused to have to face this ordeal, and it is no less fair that the jury should see them under police questioning. (Having the trial broadcast on television, however, as in the USA, prejudices justice by encouraging histrionics.)

Of course witnesses should be seen and judged in the same way but this may be impossible if accomplices of the accused (members of a terrorist or organized criminal group) attempt to intimidate or corrupt any of the witnesses. It may then be necessary to protect their identity from the accused and the public. This inevitably lowers the quality of justice but is part of the price which must be paid when criminals or terrorists try to make the liberal system of law unworkable. (This problem is discussed in Chapter 13.)

It is a cardinal principle of the law that the accused has the right to decline to give evidence and to face cross-examination. This is essential, as some people, innocent or guilty, may be intensely nervous and afraid that a clever counsel may confuse them or trip them up into saying something they do not wish to say or do not mean. CJPOA 1994 does direct, however, that at the conclusion of the evidence for the prosecution, the judge must ensure that the accused are aware that, if they exercise their right not to give evidence or, having been sworn, without good cause refuse to answer any question, the court or jury may draw such inferences as appear proper.[6]

The right to silence is an essential safeguard against abuse and must always be maintained. There is no way, however, to prevent people drawing their own conclusions from silence. They will do this in any case, whether they are invited to do so or warned not to do so. It is unfair to the accused to lead them to think that jurors will not be influenced by it. In countries with universal education and reasonable availability of mass media of communication, justice for both the accused and the public will best be served by being honest about it. Judges and juries should be openly and lawfully entitled to draw their own inferences from silence, and the accused be made aware that they will do this and not deluded into believing that they will not.

CORROBORATION OF EVIDENCE

In some European countries, conviction on confessions alone, without corroboration evidence, is barred. This is not the case in the UK, but jurors may be reluctant to convict in such circumstances, or the Appeal Court may quash the conviction. The courts are similarly reluctant to convict on the uncorroborated evidence of a single witness, especially if that witness has a strong personal interest in giving such evidence, for example if the witness fears retribution unless the people being tried are locked up, or in expectation of a reward, or of lenient treatment for his or her own crimes if this evidence secures a conviction.

This particularly applied to the 'supergrass' trials in Northern Ireland in 1981–83, roughly coinciding with the similar use of 'repentant terrorists' (*pentiti*) in Italy (described in Chapter 7, p. 81). 'Supergrass' is English criminal slang for a star police informer. Using the existing legislation for leniency for prisoners giving evidence for the Crown, a number of people arrested for terrorist offences – some loyalist and some republican – agreed to give evidence for the prosecution in exchange for reduced sentences and then relocation with their families under a new name in a new country. Ten cases came to trial before single-judge 'Diplock Courts' (see Chapter 9). Of 217 people tried with supergrass evidence, 120 were convicted, but 67 of these convictions were quashed on appeal, on the ground that they were based on uncorroborated evidence from a single witness who had a personal interest in securing a conviction.[7] The chief reason for the success of the *pentiti* trials was that in Italy there were many more *pentiti* (389), so there was plenty of corroborating evidence.

LENIENCY FOLLOWING A PLEA OF GUILTY

There is special provision in English law for reducing the sentence for an offender who pleads guilty. CJPOA 1994 directs that, in determining what sentence to pass, the court should 'take into account the stage in the proceedings at which the accused indicated his intention to plead guilty and the circumstances in which this indication was given'. It also directs that if, as a result, the court imposes a less severe punishment than it would otherwise have imposed, 'it shall state in open court that it has done so'.[8]

In contrast to the USA, there is no formal process of plea bargaining, in which the defence counsel bargains with the judge and the prosecution for the accused to plead guilty to a lesser charge if the prosecution drops a more serious charge (for example, manslaughter instead of murder). It is, however, sometimes done more informally in Britain, when defence counsel advise their clients that it will be in their interest to plead guilty to a lesser charge.

MONEY LAUNDERING AND FRAUD

Much recent legislation has been concerned with money laundering and fraud. The Royal Commission on Criminal Justice (RCCJ) *Report* in July 1993,[9] and the House of Commons Home Affairs Committee (HAC) in its *Third Report on Organized Crime* published in July 1995,[10] both paid a lot of attention to it. Fraud is endemic in the financial world, mainly perpetrated in large corporations on a large scale, for example the alleged misappropriation by Robert Maxwell of £400 million from the Mirror Group Newspapers and the frauds by the Bank of Credit and Commerce International (BCCI) which came to light in 1988. In Britain, the Serious Fraud Office (SFO) expanded rapidly from 10 cases involving £50 million in 1991–92 to 500 cases involving £5000 million in 1993–94. Responses to a survey in 1993–94 revealed that, of British finance corporations questioned, 68 per cent had suffered from fraud, about half of it perpetrated by members of their own middle management. Relatively little of this was done by hacking, the fraudsters usually working from the inside.[11] To counter this, there is no substitute for firm and efficient middle management, which includes able and determined auditors who are given unimpeded access. The rapid development of the Internet will increase the opportunities for fraud.

Much of the international fraud with which the London finance houses get involved is with Third World countries in which the border between 'commission' and 'embezzlement' is not clearly defined; also with Russia and East Europe, where the chaos following the demise of their command economies has given exceptional opportunities for fraud, especially by former members of the *nomenklatura*, who are often the only people who know their way around, and have gained controlling positions in the newly privatized businesses. Counterfeit currency and counterfeit goods, with forged documents, are thriving businesses.

These subjects were discussed in earlier chapters, Chapter 5 being devoted entirely to money laundering and Chapter 4 to drug trafficking. Some of the matters discussed in the following pages (such as the advance disclosure of evidence by the prosecution and defence and confiscation of assets acquired by drug dealing or other criminal activity) are applicable to money laundering, but this chapter will focus mainly on trial for other types of criminal offences.

DISCLOSURE OF EVIDENCE BEFORE TRIAL

In the early 1990s, there were some sensational appeals against miscarriages of justice in certain convictions for terrorist-related offences which had been tried in the 1970s. Some of these convictions were quashed as 'unsafe' on account of one or more of four main aspects of the prosecutions some fifteen years earlier: irregularities by the police, especially in obtaining statements and confessions; forensic evidence techniques, since discredited, particularly regarding traces of explosives on people's hands and clothing; failure by the prosecution to disclose some bits of evidence which they did not intend to use at the trials, but which might have been used by the defence as part of their case if they had been aware of them, but which did not come to light until several years later; and the possible prejudicing of juries by events or statements outside the court during the trials (for example, ministerial statements about future criminal justice policies).

Possible injustices arising from interrogation and obtaining statements and confessions have been discussed in Chapter 11 and earlier in this chapter. The technology of identification and explosive detection will be examined in Chapters 15–17. The problems of disclosure of evidence, however, are cardinal to the effectiveness of the processes of law in convicting the guilty, but only with proof beyond reasonable doubt; and to their fairness, in ensuring that all evidence relevant to reaching a verdict is presented to the jury.

It was in the wake of these miscarriages of justice that the RCCJ was convened under Lord Runciman and reported in July 1993.[12] Evidence was put to the RCCJ that the present rules, based on the Attorney-General's guidelines of 1981 and elaborated by the courts, had extended too far the obligation of the prosecution to make available to the defence material gathered in the course of the investigation which it was not proposed to use in the prosecution case but which might have a bearing on the defence.[13] Interpreted too widely, this sometimes led to enormous quantities of documents having to be made available – amounting in some cases (especially of fraud) to several truckloads, irrespective of whether they had any significant bearing on the case. This led to a great waste of time and inflation of the costs of both prosecution and defence ploughing through it all. There were accusations that some defence lawyers were cynically demanding this time to delay the trial.

The RCCJ proposed that it should be the prosecution's initial duty to disclose all material *relevant to the case*, irrespective of whether they intended to use it, but that they need disclose other material, considered to be irrelevant, only in list form. To obtain this other material, the defence would have to establish its relevance to the case. The RCCJ added a majority recommendation that the defence would be under an obligation before the trial to disclose the substance of its own case.[14]

On 16 May 1995, the government announced its own proposals in a statement to Parliament accompanied by a consultative document.[15] It suggested that the burden of disclosure by the prosecution proposed by the RCCJ was still too onerous, and proposed that, in the first stage, the prosecution should be required to disclose only the material which it intended to use at the trial, plus any material which it did not intend to use but which might undermine the prosecution's case. (An example of this might be a statement by a witness giving the police a description of the perpetrator of the offence which did not resemble the person accused.) The defence, in turn, would be required to disclose sufficient particulars of their own case to identify the issues in dispute, after which the prosecution would have to disclose any additional material which appeared to assist that defence.[16] Disagreements on further disclosure would be resolved by the judge.

There could be problems for the defence in finding out whether there was any material held by the prosecution which should have been disclosed but had not been; if that came to light after a conviction, it might give the defence good grounds for having the conviction quashed on appeal. But it is important not to give professional criminals and their lawyers the opportunity to delay and frustrate the process of law by making unjustified use of power to demand irrelevant prosecution disclosure.[17]

EVIDENCE OF PREVIOUS CONVICTIONS

It has long been a principle of English law that it is inadmissible to present evidence of previous convictions of the accused such as would suggest that they had a disposition to commit the kind of offence with which they are charged.[18] On the other hand, there is little or no restraint imposed on defence counsel in the means they use to discredit witnesses for the prosecution. This may quite properly include past convictions of witnesses for offences (such as perjury) which can be regarded as relevant to this credibility.

In one case, a man was accused of violently assaulting and raping a girl; he had previous convictions for sex with violence, but the jury did not know this. The girl was naturally a prime prosecution witness; she was also evidently in some distress at having to relive her experience in open court. Though she had no previous convictions, the defence counsel conducted an aggressive cross-examination to discredit her, which could be regarded as part of his job. If, however, the accused had elected to give evidence, the prosecution counsel would have been barred from referring to his previous convictions or questioning him about them. If any mention had been made of them before the jury gave their verdict and he had been convicted, the conviction would probably have been quashed on appeal. In the end, the jury found him not guilty of both assault and rape.

He had, however, pleaded guilty to a minor offence (on which the evidence was not contested) so, after the jury had announced their verdict on the main charges, but before he was sentenced for the minor offence, his previous convictions were read out to the court. On hearing these, the jury (and the public) were appalled. Many of the jury were in tears at having, as they saw it, been misled into releasing a man who they were now convinced was guilty, and having failed in their duty to the girl and the community.

This does present a serious civil liberties dilemma. On the one hand, people who have committed an offence should not thereafter be condemned to be found guilty of everything they may be accused of in the future. On the other hand, it should be within the judge's discretion to have the jury apprised of the accused's previous record *if the judge believes it to be relevant*, at the same time warning the jury that any conviction must be based on evidence presented in court proving beyond reasonable doubt that the accused committed the offence with which he or she is charged. This would do something to correct the present imbalance between fairness to the accused and fairness to future potential victims, and the repeated failure of the system to convict so many of the guilty.

CROOKED LAWYERS AND BENT COPPERS

A large number of people arrested plead guilty, usually because there is no doubt about the evidence of their identification; they are advised by their lawyers that they have little chance of acquittal and that a guilty plea will get them a more lenient sentence. These, however, are usually not the professional criminals, who are confident that they can get off, and they all too often do. About half those who plead not guilty and are tried by jury do get off.

This may seem at first a fair proportion but many more than that escape prosecution altogether, because the DPP and CPS prosecute only if they consider that the evidence is so strong that it is probable that the accused is, and will be found, guilty. As quoted earlier (p. 3), in 49 out of every 50 crimes *actually committed* no one is convicted and the guilty go free. This cannot possibly be called justice.

Sir Robert Mark, then Commissioner of the Metropolitan Police, set the cat among the pigeons in 1973. He is widely regarded as the best British police officer of the twentieth century. He was in a strong position to criticize the criminal law and lawyers because, on taking over as Commissioner in 1972, he had already tackled the problem of corruption in the CID (see pp. 155–6).

He was invited to give the annual Dimbleby Memorial Lecture on BBC Television in November 1973, in which he drew attention both to crooked defence lawyers fabricating evidence and alibis and to corrupt and crooked police officers. He made it clear that he was referring only to a small minority in both cases but added that

> experienced and respected metropolitan detectives can identify lawyers in criminal practice who are more harmful to society than the clients they represent.[19]

The Dimbleby Lecture was probably watched by nearly 4 million TV viewers but the resulting furore from the legal profession, on TV and radio and in the press probably ensured that Sir Robert's views were brought to the attention of well over 10 million people. Among other things, he said:

> There is no point in catching criminals if the system of trial is so inefficient that it lets them go free. Savage punishments serve no purpose if very few offenders are actually caught and punished. Equally, Parliament and the police are wasting their time if penalties are so small that it pays people to go on offending.[20]

He referred to the rules governing the adversarial system of justice in which every advantage is given to the defence, dating from the time when most accused were ignorant and illiterate. He questioned whether these rules were suited to the trial of an experienced criminal, using skilled legal assistance, in the late twentieth century.

> The criminal and his lawyers take every advantage of these technical rules. Every effort is made to find some procedural mistake which will allow the wrongdoer to slip through the net. If the prosecution evidence is strong the defence frequently resorts to attacks on prosecution witnesses, particularly if they are policemen. They will be accused, as a matter of routine, of perjury, planting evidence, intimidation or violence. What other defence is there, when found in possession of drugs, explosives or firearms, than to say they were planted? Lies of this kind are a normal form of defence, but they are sure to be given extensive publicity. In many criminal trials the deciding factor is not the actual evidence but the contest between a skilled advocate and a policeman or other witness under this kind of attack, often part of what Lord Devlin calls 'The world of fantasy created by a defence counsel at a loss for anything better to do on behalf of his client.'
>
> The advocates are, for the most part, only doing their job. They are there to get their client off. . . . Whatever his personal feelings about the case, the lawyer must devote himself to the cause of his client. . . . At the same time he also owes a duty to the cause of justice and the ethics of his profession. He must not put forward a defence which he knows to be false.
>
> A minority of criminal lawyers do very well from the proceeds of crime. A reputation for success, achieved by persistent lack of scruple in the defence of the most disreputable, soon attracts other clients who see little hope of acquittal in any other way. . . .
>
> A conviction said to result from perjury or wrongdoing by the police rightly causes a public outcry. Acquittal, no matter how blatantly perverse, never does, even if brought about by highly paid forensic trickery.

Sir Robert quoted an example of an alibi which appeared

to have relied on forgery with the participation of a lawyer or his clerk.

> This was a case in which a hardened criminal burgled a flat and wounded one of the elderly occupants very badly. He was arrested and . . . remanded to prison. A month after committal for trial his solicitor disclosed an alibi defence which suggested that he was playing bingo on the night of the offence and had signed the visitors' book. Enquiry showed that the prisoner had actually signed the book at the foot of the relevant page but that unfortunately for him the two preceding and the two following signatures were those of people with different surnames who had visited the club in one group and had signed the book together. The signature could, therefore, only have been added later and, it would seem, must have been written in prison. The prosecution notified the defence of their findings. Defence counsel thereupon withdrew from the case, as indeed did the instructing solicitor. The prisoner, on the advice of his new solicitor and counsel, pleaded 'guilty'. It was not, of course, possible to prove who had taken the visitors' book to prison, although the prison authorities pointed out drily that only a visit by a lawyer or his clerk would be unsupervised and that such visits had occurred. There was, in fact, a painstaking attempt to establish a false alibi for a dangerous and persistent criminal.[21]

Sir Robert went on to condemn equally strongly the minority of detectives who also act dishonestly:

> The criminal trial has come to be regarded as a game of skill and chance on which the rules are binding on one side only. . . . Most detectives have a strong sense of commitment . . . and are sometimes outraged by the result. All are under occasional temptation to bend the rules to convict those whom they believe to be guilty. . . . A few may sometimes be tempted also to exploit the system for personal gain. . . . The next step may be to demand money for not opposing bail, for not preferring charges, for a share in stolen property, and so on. . . . In the past we have paid heavily and unnecessarily in loss of public

> confidence by trying to conceal or minimize the wrongdoing of a very few.[22]

Immediately after his promotion from Deputy Commissioner to Commissioner in April 1972, Sir Robert had tackled the problems of dishonesty and corruption. He reorganized the CID, warning that he would put an end to corruption, saying that he thought that bent detectives were a cancer in society, worse even than the criminals and some of the lawyers with whom they had to deal. He formed a new branch (A10) to deal with complaints against police officers, and in the following months there were about 50 suspensions from duty and well over 100 officers left the force. All of this was well known to the public; it had been very well received, in both Parliament and the press, so his comments about crooked lawyers in the Dimbleby lectures carried all the more weight.

The legal profession, however, was up in arms about the lecture. Lord Salmon said:

> I cannot think why Sir Robert thought it worthwhile to make an allusion to the small minority of criminal lawyers whom he vividly described as dishonestly inventing spurious defences and alibis for their clients, suborning witnesses and doing very well out of highly paid forensic trickery.

The Times replied in a leader: 'There is a very simple reason. It is true.'[23]

The public reaction was similar. Sir Robert received hundreds of letters, 99 per cent supporting him. The quality newspapers, liberal and conservative, reacted in the same way. *The Times*, for example, said that the rules governing police investigation and trial ultimately resulted in the acquittal of many defendants who are in fact guilty. It commended his proposal that, while he supported trial by jury, there should be impartial research into the deliberation of juries and that a literacy test for potential jurors might be worthwhile.[24] *The Observer* commented:

> The idea that the legal profession might nurture a number of black sheep may be outrageous to lawyers: to everyone else it will seem a perfectly reasonable proposition . . . any

system of justice worthy of the name must be even-handed; the conviction of the guilty being as important for justice to the victims of crime as the acquittal of the innocent is for those who are wrongly charged.

William Deedes wrote in the *Daily Telegraph*:

> He has been delivering this message with minor variations, to my knowledge for upwards of 10 years. His only innovation on this occasion was a relevant and well-merited attack on certain lawyers. Nearly everyone in the business knows they exist, and that what Mark says of them is true.

Writing five years later in his autobiography, *In the Office of Constable* (1978), Sir Robert commented:

> Nothing has really changed since [the lecture] was given. The same corrupt practices continue and no satisfactory machinery exists to prevent them. Only the police have made progress in preventing the wrongdoing of which the lecture accused them. The other participants in the criminal justice process are only too willing to let sleeping dogs lie.[25]

Today, over 20 years after the lecture, the same comment would apply.

13 Witnesses and Juries

INTIMIDATION OF WITNESSES

The House of Commons Home Affairs Committee (HAC) reported in July 1995 that there was evidence of a 'dramatic increase' in the number of cases of intimidation of witnesses by terrorists and organized criminal gangs, who had the means to carry out their threats.[1] The Metropolitan Police Criminal Justice Protection Unit (CJPU) had dealt with an average of 10 cases in each of the years 1988–92, rising to 14 in 1993 and 57 in the five-month period February to June 1994, in which protection was sought for 81 people. In addition to threats, there were many actual cases of homes being burnt, robbery, shooting and abduction. Threats were made, not only against potential witnesses but also against their families, including relatives living abroad. In the climate of terrorism and organized crime which has developed since 1972, police reported that 'many of those who give evidence are the subjects of contracts to kill them.'[2] Threats were also made against police officers and their families, including attacks on houses, death threats, a threat that an officer's wife would be raped, and persistent abuse leading to one officer and his family being rehoused 200 miles away.[3]

The government in 1993 introduced a new offence summarized as 'Intimidation etc of witnesses, jurors and others'. The offence covered both acts and threats 'intending thereby to cause the investigation or the course of justice to be obstructed, perverted or interfered with.'[4] This carried a maximum sentence of five years or a fine or both. The police reported that 'intimidation of jurors is seen by the determined criminal as a successful way in which to bring about an acquittal', and the Home Secretary made provision for retrial of a case where there had been a conviction for nobbling a jury.[5]

Since 1973, written evidence has been admitted by the courts in Northern Ireland if there are 'specific reasons' why the witness cannot be produced for oral examination in court.[6] (These reasons were set out in Chapter 9, pp. 101–2.) A similar provision was enacted for England and Wales in 1984,[7] with equivalent legislation in Scotland. In his report on Northern Ireland in 1972, Lord Diplock made it clear that these 'specific reasons' were designed to admit signed depositions from witnesses who had been murdered to prevent them giving evidence; also from witnesses who had fled from Northern Ireland or gone into hiding in fear for their own safety.[8] The Criminal Justice Act (CJA) 1988 ruled that a written statement made to a police officer could be admitted if the witness did not give evidence 'through fear or because he is kept out of the way'.[9]

Terrorism and international organized crime led the European Justice and Home Affairs Committee in June 1995 to pass a resolution calling for measures against intimidation of witnesses and others helping the police but these measures were all already in accord with UK law and practice. The HAC Report of July 1995 noted that in Germany and Italy, witness protection was now regarded as very important and added that 'intimidation of this nature, if allowed to succeed, amounts to a threat to the very principle of the rule of law and it is of the utmost importance that they are contained'.[10]

Other possible measures, such as dispensing with jury trial for certain offences (as in France) or for all trials (in the Netherlands) will be discussed later in this chapter, but first it is necessary to examine the particular problems relating to evidence from informants.

PROTECTED WITNESSES AND INFORMANTS

Pre-trial disclosure of the names and addresses of witnesses can present problems on both sides. Witnesses for the defence, especially if they themselves have criminal records, may be reluctant to agree in advance to give evidence if they fear that this will lead to over-zealous police inquiries.[11] It is quite proper in the interests of justice that counsel on either side should be able by questioning to challenge the reliability or integrity of witnesses in front of the jury, but there would be a potential injustice if fear of police investigation or harassment deterred them from giving evidence at all.

This probably applies even more to potential prosecution witnesses. If their names and addresses are given in advance to the defence, accomplices of an accused member of an organized criminal gang will have the opportunity of threatening them or offering them bribes. If the police perceive that witnesses are likely to be intimidated or corrupted, they can offer them police protection. This will be expensive, before, during and after the trial; the witnesses may prefer to keep out of it, and to say that they know nothing and have no evidence to offer.

A particularly delicate situation arises over trials in which informants have been involved in the police investigation of the case, especially 'participating informants' but also 'resident informants' who are already in police custody or prison.

This problem, from the viewpoint of the informant and the handler, was discussed in Chapter 7. The best way to handle informants is to have the aim, from the start, of not using their evidence at all, and certainly not putting them in the witness box, but to use their information simply to prompt the police as to where to look for other evidence (forensic, documentary – say, of a car hire – or circumstantial) or other witnesses who can be asked to appear in the witness box without risk to themselves.

It will probably be a wise precaution for the police to notify the CPS in the early stages of an investigation if they are employing an informant, who should be referred to only by a synonym. The actual name should be given to no one other than the handler, controller and head of CID (see pp. 82–3). If, as is usually the case, an appearance in court would put the informant or his or her family at unacceptable risk, the CPS should confidentially inform the judge of this and indicate that, if continuance would involve that risk, the prosecution would be dropped. The judge will then have to decide whether it will be fair to the accused to proceed with the trial without that witness or fair to the community to let the accused go free without facing trial at all.

The problem will be crucially affected by the precise terms of the legislation governing advance disclosure of evidence or information. If the law obliges the prosecution to disclose all the information in their possession, whether or not it is relevant to the case against the accused, this could severely hamper the use of informants at all. If the law is as proposed by the Home Secretary on 16 May 1995,[12] then there should be no need or obligation to disclose the existence of informants, since any evidence they might have been able to give, if it is given at all, will be given by another witness. Prosecuting counsel may decide to put the essentials of the dilemma in a pre-trial discussion with the judge. The law does make provision, if particularly delicate information is involved, for such a discussion to be *ex parte*,[13] and this will be at the discretion of the judge. If the judge decides that it would be improper not to mention this situation to the defence counsel, then, under the adversarial system, the defence counsel is likely to demand the right to see the information, hoping thereby to ensure that the case against the accused will be dropped. It must be stressed that none of the three, the judge nor the two counsel, will know the identity of the informant, nor need they know the precise details of the information, as it will not be presented as evidence. If, however, the defence counsel declares an intention to pursue the matter further, the police will almost certainly feel obliged to abandon the prosecution. If the other evidence against the accused is ample for a conviction and he or she is in fact guilty, the accused will be encouraged to commit other offences. This is not in the interests of justice at all.

This presents one of the greatest dilemmas between justice and civil liberties. Some will feel that the rights of accused persons (innocent until proved guilty) are being denied if they or their counsel are not privy to *all* the information discovered by the police since they began investigating the case. Others will feel that, if there is strong enough evidence which can be presented in court to lead a jury to convict, it is wrong to release the accused without trial simply because an informant told the police where to find this information. The public, as well as suffering from the accused's future crimes, will also suffer from those of others encouraged to believe that they, too, can get away with it. The rights of the public are severely infringed when so big a proportion of those guilty of crimes go free.

JUSTICE IN THE FACE OF INTIMIDATION AND CORRUPTION

The disturbing growth in the intimidation and corruption of juries and witnesses (as described earlier in this chapter) may increasingly demand round-the-clock protection. This is very expensive, even for a single witness; it ties up about five highly trained armed police bodyguards working in shifts; with their backup and equipment, they cost around £3000 a week for each person guarded. If an *average* of 50 jurors or witnesses were being guarded at any one time, this would add up to about £7.5 million ($11 million) every year from police funds. No doubt a cheap security firm could be found who would do it for less than half that amount, but their 'protection' would probably provide no more than a sense of false security.

Added to the threat to witnesses and jurors themselves, both terrorists and organized criminal gangs threaten the families and relatives of those they wish to intimidate, if necessary all over the world. Tommaso Buscetta, an old-style Sicilian Mafia chief, who was on the losing side in the internecine Mafia war in 1981–83, took refuge in Brazil. Unable to get at him, the Mafia murdered seven of his close relatives before he was extradited from Brazil back to Italy, where in 1984 he became a *pentito* and gave evidence leading to arrest warrants for 366 mafiosi. At the same time a Mafia footsoldier, Salvatore Contorno, also became a *pentito* after 30 of his relatives had been murdered, and his information led to 127 more arrest warrants. In the Mafia maxi-trials in 1986–87, 361 of the 475 defendants were convicted, largely on the evidence of *pentiti*. Both these *pentiti* and many others will presumably need to be guarded and/or relocated, with their families, for many years to come. But whatever the cost, the benefit that the Mafia *pentiti* have brought to the community has already made it more than worthwhile.

In many more mundane cases of bomb attacks, murders and robberies, witnesses and jurors may still need to be guarded during the trial and, in some cases, this may continue as an open-ended commitment. One of the civil liberties aspects of this is the effect on the lifestyle of the witnesses or jurors who may, as a result of serving the community, have to endure years of anxiety and inhibition, being deprived of privacy for their families with bodyguards always with them. Protection should be provided only when there is a real threat from the accomplices of an accused or convicted prisoner, but one has to ask if it is fair to ask innocent people to suffer these hardships to give people making this threat the benefit of jury trial with public examination of witnesses. The trial judge may have to take this into account when people on the jury panel ask to be excused from duty or when counsel tell the judge of witnesses who are reluctant to appear.

The alternative, if the law allowed and a judge so ruled, would be to dispense with jury trial where this threat is real, as has already been done for all terrorist trials in the Republic of Ireland (1962), Northern Ireland (1973) and France (1986). The Dutch have no jury trials at all.

In Northern Ireland (as described in Chapter 9) the single-judge Diplock Courts are widely criticized, especially as so many convictions have to rely on confessions and on witnesses who cannot be seen. Lord Diplock rejected the use of lay assessors (as in the Republic of Ireland) on the grounds that assessors would be no less vulnerable than jurors; and the use of second and third judges or barristers on the bench as the load on the two professions would be too great; the Gardiner Report supported this view (see Chapter 9). They could have added that the commitment to police protection, already open ended for every judge who has tried a terrorist case in Northern Ireland, would be more than doubled. Diplock concluded that, since those convicted by a single-judge court have an automatic right of appeal to a court of three Appeal Court Judges, this should be sufficient to prevent miscarriages of justice.[14]

In the event, however, the Appeal Courts have quashed numbers of convictions in cases where neither they nor the public can have had any doubt that the accused did commit the crimes. This may be good jurisprudence but it is unfair on the victims of further terrorist attacks, including attacks by other terrorists, encouraged that their comrades have got away with it. It indicates a failure of the judicial system.

To strike a balance, if terrorists and organized criminal gangs set out to make jury trial and the public examination of witnesses impossible, it may be necessary to substitute other processes of law to protect the public when the judiciary considers that the threat warrants it and is deliberate. Others have had to do this too.

France has for many years had trial without jury for offences involving secrets concerning national security and, in the 1950s and 1960s, for trials of right-wing terrorists of the 'Secret Army Organization' (OAS) opposing withdrawal from Algeria, who were using violence and intimidation to frustrate the course of justice. In 1984–86, France suffered a wave of horrific terrorist violence from the far left *Action Directe* (AD) and from a group of Arab terrorists led by Georges Abdallah (see p. 68). In December 1986 an AD terrorist, Regis Schleicher, set out quite blatantly to intimidate the jury from the dock with the 'spectre of proletarian vengeance' from AD if they were to find him guilty. Within five days, five members of the jury had absented themselves for 'health reasons' and the trial had to be postponed. The newly elected Prime Minister, Jacques Chirac, at once introduced trial without jury for terrorist offences. Both Schleicher and Abdallah were convicted without juries in 1987,[15] and 54 other members of AD in 1988–89. France thereafter had very little terrorism until suspected Algerian terrorists began a violent bombing campaign in Paris in 1995.

In France, the courts for trial without jury comprise a presiding judge, sometimes with a number of citizen assessors (equivalent to lay magistrates in England) and always two junior judges, most of whom are *juges d'instruction* (or examining magistrates). These are young lawyers, many of whom go into the judiciary direct from law school (though some may have spent a few years as advocates). The day-to-day duty of examining magistrates is to investigate cases, interview the accused and witnesses and recommend whether the accused should be charged. This is a feature of the inquisitorial system of law, based on Roman Law and on the *Code Napoleon* and used in almost all European countries other than Britain.

There is little doubt that examining magistrates would make better assessors than advocates do, since the experience of advocates has been in selecting and making the most of evidence to support their own side of the case, whereas the task of examining magistrates throughout their working lives has been to seek the truth, regardless of whether it suggests innocence or guilt.

The Dutch have never used juries in living memory. All their courts are similar to the French non-jury courts, except that the number of judges and assessors varies, from one or two for trying minor cases up to six for serious cases.

It is generally only Britain, the USA and former British colonies which use the adversarial system. As well as greater flexibility in providing for non-jury trials, there could be a great saving of police time if more of the investigation and interrogation were done by examining magistrates. Scotland has a system with elements of both the adversarial and inquisitorial traditions, with procurators fiscal to investigate cases before prosecution. A shift in their direction might have many advantages for English law, in fairness, in flexibility and in convicting more of the guilty; also in easier harmonization with other EU countries; but, sadly, it seems unlikely to happen, so, while hoping for gradual change, we probably have little option but to make the best of the system we have.

USE OF VIDEOS TO PROTECT JURORS AND WITNESSES

An alternative to non-jury trial would be to take reliable measures to guarantee the anonymity of jurors before, during and after the trial. This could be achieved, in cases where the judge saw fit to order it, by locating the jury in a separate room – preferably in a separate building – equipped with five closed circuit television (CCTV) screens, one each to show the accused, the witness giving evidence, the prosecuting and defence counsel and the judge; and perhaps a sixth to show the general setting in the court. There would, of course, be no camera in the jury room, which would be fully secured, including a means of selection and entry which would protect jurors from being spied upon by accomplices of the accused.

This would be as satisfactory as sitting in the court for the jury, perhaps more so, because the faces on all five screens would be close-ups. Viewers are now fully accustomed to judging expressions of people on TV screens. Whether they are politicians or pontificators, the viewers form their own opinions as to whether they are telling the truth.

Barristers would probably not welcome this, as they like to exploit their histrionic abilities before a live jury, judging their response by the expressions on the jurors' faces. But politicians, advertisers and campaigners are quite content to exercise persuasion through the TV camera without being able to see the faces of the viewers. The price, if any, would be small compared with that of the perversion of justice by the jurors being threatened with violence, and anxious about what might happen to them or their families after the trial. It would also protect jurors from attempted corruption.

There would be complaints that counsel would be denied their present right to object to jurors before a trial starts on grounds of bias and balance, for example of age, background, sex or race. This, however, has sometimes been abused, particularly in multiple trials where counsel have been able to object to six jurors for each defendant, and have used that power to go on objecting until they are satisfied that they have a jury sympathetic to their clients. The fairest way would be for juries to be selected by a panel headed by a known and trusted retired judge; alternatively by the trial judge, working to strict published guidelines. Again, the price would be small, bearing in mind that 'video juries' would be ordered only when the trial judge was convinced that there was a real threat of perversion of justice.

The video system could be extended to witnesses when they are considered vulnerable. In addition to the provisions of the NI(EP)A 1973 in Northern Ireland, steps may sometimes be needed in England to protect witnesses at risk, with screens, voice distortion, and so on, but videos might be a better alternative. In the case of such witnesses, the jurors should see them on their video screens, and the judge should also be able to see them on a personal screen.

Of the means considered in this chapter for protecting jurors and witnesses, the best is probably the remote video; failing that, to dispense with juries where necessary by using the French or Dutch systems of using legally qualified assessors, though the British adversarial system would make this less satisfactory.

THE ADVERSARIAL AND INQUISITORIAL SYSTEMS

This book has been dominated by the tiny percentage of crimes resulting in conviction under the British adversarial system, comparing badly with many other countries. There is, however, little likelihood of Britain, still less the USA, changing over to an inquisitorial system in the near future; it would involve an upheaval in the training and career pattern of lawyers, so it would take a long time. Nevertheless, the adversarial system, as well as its other shortcomings, is extremely expensive, enabling solicitors and counsel with a reputation for winning cases to command such high fees that the great majority of the population have little hope of employing them. So the justice system is heavily weighted in favour of the very rich and those poor enough to qualify for legal aid. Difficult as it would be to make the change, the time has come to examine whether it would be in the interests of the public (rather than lawyers or criminals) to make a start in trying to develop some of the advantages of an inquisitorial system.

Chapter 12 recorded the experience of Sir Robert Mark, which showed how the adversarial system can tempt some criminal lawyers to cross the line from making the most of the evidence to fabricating or deliberately distorting it.

Under the adversarial system, people cannot become judges without spending the first half (or nearly half) of their professional lives handling every case they deal with from the viewpoint of only one side – as a barrister or as a solicitor, selecting such evidence as helps their case and doing their best to minimize, or sometimes even to suppress or distort, evidence which is against it. This creates an attitude, in some judges, of an umpire, deciding the case 'on points' won by the competing counsel.

This philosophy was illustrated at a conference of forensic scientists at which one scientist described research into a forensic technique concerning explosives, and concluded: 'I think it is urgent to find the funds to pursue the research because this technique, if perfected, could be of enormous assistance to the courts in arriving at the truth'. A judge who was attending the conference intervened: 'I must remind you that it is not the function of the courts to arrive at the truth, but to decide whether the prosecution has made out a case'.

By contrast, in the Netherlands young lawyers, after completing their training, can choose between going into the advocacy or into the judiciary or one and then the other. If they go directly into the judiciary, they spend their late 20s and early 30s as examining magistrates with the task of investigating the evidence and interviewing the witnesses in order to recommend to their senior judge whether there is a case to answer. This is interspersed with assignments as an assessor under a presiding judge, here again seeking the truth. To many people, this would seem to be a more satisfactory background to becoming a senior judge.

It would be well worth making a start by providing opportunities for young lawyers in Britain to follow the Dutch path and to build up a new class of examining magistrates, gradually taking some of the load off the police and providing the necessary experience for a more balanced judiciary as well as a means of substituting a professional court for a jury in cases which merited this.

There is, however, another reason why this may be unlikely to happen in Britain. A large percentage of Members of Parliament are lawyers. Under the adversarial system lawyers can earn a lot of money. This enables them to supplement their salaries when on the back benches, and to keep in practice so that they can be sure of continued high earnings if they lose or resign their seats. So a vote by a majority in the House of Commons to start a move towards an inquisitorial system unfortunately seems to be almost inconceivable.

14 Prison and Alternatives

DETERRENCE, CUSTODY AND REHABILITATION

It is well proven that the likelihood of conviction is a stronger deterrent than the likelihood of a heavy sentence. This must be looked at in the context of three-quarters of crimes being unreported and only 1 in 50 leading to a conviction. The majority of crimes are committed by previous offenders and most of them believe that the prospect of conviction is so low that it is easier to commit another crime than to look for some other means of livelihood.

At what stage should custody for repeat offenders to protect the public take priority over rehabilitation? Have we anything to learn, positive or negative, from the 'three strikes and you're out' rule so widely applied in the USA?

CHILDREN AND YOUNG OFFENDERS

The problem of children (14 and under) and young offenders (15–17) is the biggest worry of all in the long term, because of the high proportion of teenagers who do commit crimes, the proportion this represents of total crime and its effect on the future lives of those teenagers.

The causes of juvenile crime were discussed in Chapter 3, starting with upbringing in early childhood, truancy leading to low literacy, the contagion of the disillusion of unemployed siblings, and the development of the idea that a rotten society has no use for them and will provide them with nothing other than what they take for themselves.

The punishment of children under 12 for serious crimes is extremely difficult. It is mercifully rare to find children like the two 10 year olds who tortured and murdered a 2-year-old toddler, James Bulger, in 1993, in the way that children sometimes torture cats and puppies for no apparent reason other than sadistic gratification. Whatever the medical and mental condition of such children, however, there must be provision for keeping them in custody, if necessary for ever, because they must not be released until qualified doctors are convinced beyond doubt that they will never do anything like it again. Their rehabilitation must take second place.

Decisions are more difficult in the case of children who discover that magistrates and judges are unlikely to lock them up, so they take a pride in 'one-boy crime waves' – burgling and especially putting the public at risk by 'joy riding' in fast cars. Custody is unlikely to do them much good but, once again, protection of the public must take priority. Mothers of young children and old people are often more in fear of teenagers than of any other criminals, and magistrates are failing in their duty when they discharge persistent young criminals after three or four offences to commit more crimes.

CJPOA 1994 (Sections 1–22) does now make provision for secure training orders for children who persistently commit crimes when they are aged 12 to 14. These orders must be for not less than six months and not more than two years; they can be given only if the child has already been convicted of three offences which would be punishable by imprisonment for a person aged 21 or over, and has been found by a court to be in breach of a supervision order for one of these or other crimes. The first of these secure training centres came into use in 1996. The interests of potential victims must be paramount in deciding whether to commit the offenders to a secure training centre and thereafter whether to keep them in long-term custody after the two year order has expired.

There can be only a limited capacity of detention centres for young offenders, so alternative means of punishment within the community (see pp. 178–81) should be used wherever possible. Also, detention centres (like the former Borstals) put young offenders together, and can encourage their urge to show off and take pride in their contempt for society, as well as enabling them to learn new tricks. But the dangerous crimes committed by some teenagers do make it essential that enough secure accommodation is available, even if the good it does to young criminals is doubtful. (This question is re-examined later in this chapter.)

ESCALATION OF SENTENCES

Most of Britain's crimes are committed by a very small proportion of the population, mostly between 15 and 25. Of the 15 and 16 year olds convicted of crimes, 90 per cent reoffend within four years.[1] Of criminals of all ages, more than half those sentenced offend again. Reasonably competent burglars soon develop the experience to judge which small items in a modest middle-class home can most easily be sold for a good price with little chance of being traced. Having established by surveillance that the house is empty, they can pick up enough to sell for one or two thousand pounds in two minutes and be out before anyone can respond to an alarm, even if there is one. After a few successes like that and little risk of being caught, why would they bother to look for a job or register for unemployment benefit?

A great deal of the crime is committed by professional criminals who may go in and out of prison five or six times. In 1994–95, the average sentence for burglary was 16.1 months for a first offence, 18.1 for a second and still only 19.4 months for a third offence.[2] This is no use at all. Targeting the professionals for surveillance and subjecting them to much heavier sentences if they reoffend will provide the best protection for potential victims of crime, by deterring those most likely to commit serious crimes and locking them away for longer if they do.

Many ordinary people live in fear, not only for themselves, but also for their families, especially the old and the young; they may have to restrict their lifestyles, at home and when travelling, to an extent that would have been inconceivable even half a century ago. Because of the vivid portrayal and reporting of violent crime on television (do not blame the media; that is what makes the viewers choose which channel to watch) the polls suggest that the fear of crime has risen faster than the amount of crime itself.

First offenders are usually treated leniently, as they should be. If a judge thinks that there is a good chance that a person convicted will respond to generosity and kindness, that person will be sentenced to probation, community service or to a suspended sentence. When first offenders do go to prison, a great deal of trouble will go towards rehabilitation, and training in skills to help them to earn a living after release; they will be encouraged to take part in discussion therapy under professional guidance, to help them to overcome personal weaknesses or problems with drugs or alcohol. No one who visits prisons regularly can fail to be moved by the dedication of people who devote their working lives to trying to help those who regret their failings and want to overcome their weaknesses. They accept, however, that many of those who apply for their therapeutic groups may prove incapable of learning to control or organize themselves or may have no serious intention of doing so, using the treatment either as a change from other prison routines or as a means of conning the authorities into believing that they intend to go straight. The therapists and trainers are well aware that their attempts at a cure will fail for 90 per cent of those who attend, and they are content if they can cure only one or two offenders in months of hard work. But they should not be asked to waste this dedication on people who have proved that they have no intention of going straight, that is if they have already reoffended several times before.

Responding to public exasperation with the failure to tackle repeat offenders, particularly those using violence or rape and persistent burglars, the government introduced a White Paper on 3 April 1996, proposing legislation for a Bill to be presented to Parliament in November 1996 to become law in April 1997.[3] This proposed automatic life sentences for a second conviction for attempted murder, threat or conspiracy to murder, manslaughter, wounding with intent to do grievous bodily harm (GBH), robbery involving use of a firearm, rape, attempted rape and unlawful sexual intercourse with a girl under 13. This sentence would be imposed even if the second offence was not the same as the first, which could include a relevant offence committed when under the age of 17 and before the new measures became law. Judges, however, would be able to decide a lesser term if they thought that there were genuinely exceptional circumstances. A judge would set the minimum term for 'deterrence and retribution', on completion of which the Parole Board, not a politician, would decide whether the person should be released.

A mandatory sentence of seven years was proposed for a third conviction for trafficking in heroin, cocaine, Ecstasy or other Class A drugs by anyone over 18 at the time of the third offence, even if the previous offences had been committed under the age of 17. For domestic burglary, a third conviction would carry a minimum sentence of three years for those over 18.

The White Paper stressed that the repeat offences must all be among those listed. This would avoid the anomalies in the 'three strikes and you're out' rule adopted in 23 states of the USA. In California, after two serious offences, a third conviction for any one of a list of 500 felonies, however minor, will trigger a sentence of 25 years or life. Since it was introduced in 1994, it had been applied in 1500 cases up to April 1996, generally with popular approval, though sometimes (such as the theft of a pizza from four boys eating at a café in 1995 constituting the third offence to send a man to prison for 25 years) it has earned some ridicule.[4]

The White Paper proposed abolishing automatic early release and parole. Prisoners would serve the full sentence ordered by the court, though they could earn remission up to six days a month in sentences of up to 12 months with a maximum of 2.5 months off a full 12 months' sentence. Prisoners serving more than 12 months could earn three days a month by cooperation and a further three days for 'positive good behaviour' up to a maximum of 20 per cent of the sentence, and they would remain under supervision after release for a minimum of three months or 15 per cent of the original sentence.

It was anticipated that these measures would increase the prison population from 54,000 to about 64,000. In addition to 135 existing prisons and six new ones already being built, a further 12 prisons each housing 800 inmates would be needed. The average cost of keeping a prisoner in 1996 was £23,000 a year.[5]

Many judges objected to mandatory sentences, arguing that each case must be treated on its merits in the light of the evidence presented in court and the attitudes, intentions and provocation, if any, at the time of the crime. They particularly opposed the statutory life sentence for second offences of rape, as this might encourage the rapist to kill his victim (usually the only witness) since it would seem to make no difference if the sentence was to be for life in any case. Some judges have for a long time opposed the existing statutory sentence of life imprisonment for murder.

Public opinion is strongly in favour of more severe punishment for persistent offenders and for this reason both the major parties support it, though they differ as to how it should be done. In the long term the most important factor must be the independence of the judiciary, whose members argue that neither ministers nor Parliament have any right to order a judge to impose any specific or minimum sentence. But the public is not happy with the failure of the judicial system to convict more than a tiny proportion of criminals.

Rather than mandatory sentences, it might be better to lay down guidelines for minimum and maximum sentences for certain crimes and to leave it to the Attorney-General to appeal against a sentence he considers too lenient. The Appeal Court could then adjudicate between the trial judge's reasons for sentencing below the guideline and the case put by the Attorney-General. The final decision would therefore remain throughout with the judiciary.

One of the advantages of publishing these guidelines would be the deterrent effect on criminals, knowing that, even if they managed to get the judge to pass a lower sentence, the Appeal Court had the power to increase it.

A sensible guideline for serious offences, especially those involving violence, might be that for a second offence of similar gravity, the sentence should be between twice and four times the guideline sentence for the first offence; and that for a third offence, four times the guideline for the second offence. Thus a person sentenced to four years for a first offence on a serious charge, on conviction for a second such offence could expect 8–16 years; and for a third offence 32–64 years, which would amount to life – which (as will be argued later) should be 'life meaning life'.

It would contribute to the deterrent effect if the judge were required, in passing sentence on each occasion, to warn prisoners of the guideline sentences in the event of them committing a further offence of similar gravity.

Prison governors should also be required to warn new

arrivals, at the beginning and end of their sentences, of these guidelines and of the provisions for escalation of sentences. They should, at the same time, warn prisoners that, in the event of their reoffending, they would face a much harsher regime, with fewer privileges and more stringent requirements to earn those privileges; also that they would not qualify for the rehabilitative efforts which would be made for a first offender – the education, training and therapy which, although regarded cynically by some inmates, is popular with others, including recidivists, who volunteer for it as a more agreeable element of prison life. During the closing months of their first and second sentences, inmates should be taken to visit a prison, or part of a prison, in which this harsher regime is enforced, and reminded that persistent offending may lead to imprisonment for 'life meaning life'.

CAPITAL PUNISHMENT

Is there a case for a return to the death penalty, especially for such people as serial killers, child murderers or criminals who murder a police officer in the course of committing a crime? In public opinion polls there has been strong majority support for this but Parliament regularly rejects it. Parliament is right to do so for at least three reasons. First, the death penalty is irrevocable and, during the final years before it was ended in 1965, there was at least one case in which an innocent man (Timothy Evans) was convicted and hanged. He was mentally subnormal and was convicted in 1950 for the murder of his own baby; later evidence emerged to show that another man had committed the crime. Second, the judicial taking of life in cold blood has a damaging effect on the moral values of a democratic society in which everyone has some responsibility for it. And third – a strictly practical reason – because the existence of the death penalty would make conviction less likely; people would be reluctant to give tip-offs to the police and still more reluctant to give evidence in court; juries would be reluctant to convict because they would not want to have it on their conscience or might fear revenge; and conviction is the real deterrent, not the punishment.

LIFE MEANING LIFE

So the most severe penalty should be life meaning life – which has already been carried out in the case of particularly bestial child murderers whose release the public and Parliament are unlikely to accept. For the reasons given earlier, there is a strong case for this sentence to be enforced on people who have proved by repeated serious offences that they should forfeit the right ever again to be free to make the public suffer. And persistent offenders should know that it will mean what it says.

Life meaning life sentences would, however, demand special measures to enable the prison service to handle them. If prisoners were in for life, with no prospect of remission, what deterrent would there be against them committing further offences while in prison, including murderous attacks on prison staff and other prisoners? With no death penalty, what would they have to lose?

The best solution would be to have three regimes in the high security prisons in which long-term prisoners are held – segregation, normal and privileged. Every high security prison has a segregation wing, under various names, for example a 'control unit'. Prisoners are put into this wing for one of two reasons: it may be at their own request, under 'Rule 43' to protect them from the threat of violence from other prisoners (those convicted of sexual offences or cruelty to children are frequently beaten up by 'ordinary criminals'); or they may be put in solitary confinement as recalcitrant prisoners who have used or threatened violence against other prisoners or prison officers, or who have persistently and deliberately defied orders and prison rules. As well as any necessary restraint, they are denied association with other prisoners and, after a time, they usually decide to cooperate in order to rejoin the others in the normal cell blocks. Once back there, they have an incentive to behave, so as not to return to solitary confinement.

In some prisons (for example, Barlinnie and Bullwood Hall) there have been successful experiments with a third, privileged, regime for selected long-term prisoners, sometimes known as a 'Special Security Unit'. This is located within the prison compound in a separate building from which there is no possibility of escape (with fully secured exercise areas on the roof and no occasion to leave the building for any purpose whatever). Within the unit, however, conditions are relaxed, sometimes with open cells or dormitories, continuous association and opportunities for keeping fit, and for study and recreation. The inmates in these units should know that any abuse of these privileges will mean immediate return to the cell blocks or, if necessary, direct to solitary confinement in the segregation unit.

Prisoners sentenced to life meaning life would initially be housed in normal cell blocks within what will in any case be a top security prison. Only by consistently good behaviour could they earn transfer to the Special Security Unit and, once there, the advantages would be such that they would have a strong incentive to stay there. The combination of the threat of solitary confinement and the incentive of the privileged unit would be the weapons available to the prison officers to enforce discipline. It must be stressed that this would be the sole purpose of the triple regime. Prisoners would not be there at all unless they had forfeited any entitlement to rehabilitation or release.

Most of these 'life-for-lifers', once they realized that there was no hope of escape, would resign themselves to a tolerable and, if they chose, purposeful existence, with opportunities for spending their time constructively, above all among friends – a mixture as good as any they would be likely to have (effectively barred from crime). Most human beings are adaptable when faced with the inevitable.

The chief drawbacks revealed by previous experiments, such as Barlinnie and Bullwood Hall, have been high cost and the risk of an evil and devious prisoner eventually taking advantage of the privileges and posing a threat to the prison staff. Regarding cost, the technology now available for surveillance and security within a specially designed unit is such that, properly applied, it could be operated with a low level of personnel and very little exposure of exposure of staff to physical contact with prisoners, minimizing the risk of personal attack. This would need to be combined with strict enforcement of the exclusion of prisoners proffering any risk of abuse of the privileged regime, and playing safe by sending them back to solitary confinement before they posed any threat. Again, the secure custody and safety of the staff would override any claim to 'rights' by prisoners whose record was bad enough to qualify them to be there at all. Though there have been some hazards (e.g. from hostage taking) in the experimental regimes so far tried, there are no recorded cases of escape.

Once criminals realized that, after one or two repeat offences, their prison life would become very bleak and that in the event of a third or fourth offence it would be for ever, this system would provide the best available deterrent to professional criminals and, should the deterrent fail, of ensuring that the public never had to put up with them again.

ALTERNATIVES TO PRISON

Community service as an alternative to prison has been pioneered and successfully developed in Scandinavia and is increasingly used in Britain. It has immense advantages: it costs far less than prison; convicted offenders can continue their normal lives, with their families, if they have them, being required to sacrifice only the time which would otherwise be available for leisure; some of the criminals may be influenced by ordinary people they might otherwise never meet, who may be very different, especially in the case of teen-agers, from the circle they have lived in before. If their community work includes repairing damage done by their crimes and if they come face to face with people who have suffered from what they have done, especially children, it may strike a chord on even the most depraved conscience.

Unfortunately, however, it is unrealistic to hope for this to succeed with many of those most likely to be among the 90 per cent of convicted teenagers who reoffend. Many may see it as a soft option to pass the time, or to acquire sympathy which might be useful if they were caught again.

Probation under supervision of a probation officer who builds a rapport with the offender can achieve a lot, especially if combined with professional group therapy. Frances Crook, of the Howard League for Penal Reform, has proposed a two-year experiment in which one city (she suggests Leeds) sends none of its juvenile offenders to prison at all, making available the money saved from prison costs to be spent on education, individual care and attention and getting them to repair the damage they have done.[6]

This is well worth trying and may well be better than much of what is done now, so long as it is combined with a realistic determination not to be conned. There will always be some teenagers who grow up in an environment which gives them little doubt that crime does pay. These – and many more honest ones who genuinely mean to keep out of trouble when their community service or probation is over – may be unable to resist the lure of acquiring £1000 a week from crime with every chance of getting away with it, when the alternatives seem hopelessly bleak. Why else do 90 per cent reoffend?

Generally, alternatives to prison do save money and, not surprisingly, are more likely to succeed with first offenders than with persistent criminals, young or old. In New York, there is the Court Employment Project for young men facing their first felony conviction; instead of prison, they undergo six months of supervision and evaluation, including drug treatment where necessary. It is claimed that arrest rates are lower than for those who go to prison, and it costs only half as much. Drug treatment also saves money in the end. A long-term study in California of people who had completed drug treatment programmes showed that every dollar spent yielded $7 in benefits, since they committed less than half as much crime as they did before treatment, and were less likely to be a load on the hospitals.

New York also pioneered a Community Service Sentencing Project for persistent petty criminals. They were ordered to perform 70 hours of community work, with a return to prison if they failed to complete it. In 1994, 70 per cent of those sentenced did complete their community work, which provided $370,000 in services and saved £2.5 million in prison costs, though the cost of supervision must be set against this. Schemes like this were usually most successful when tailored specifically for a narrowly defined group of offenders for whom similar treatment was likely to work.[7]

Another constructive approach, tried in Britain and many other countries, is to mobilize volunteers from within the community to mount unarmed, unaggressive patrols. These worked well in Birmingham, where they used their own initiative to drive pimps and prostitutes off the streets; they then, at police request, continued to patrol in sufficient strength to deter petty criminals, not least by photographing known trouble makers and convicted petty criminals on the streets. While this could have undesirable overtones if misused to harass minority groups and young people, it proved very effective if well controlled, with enough people of goodwill in the group to prevent such abuse. In Birmingham, it had the effect of driving the petty criminals away to other areas,[8] which is fine if the other areas are encouraged by the police to organize similar patrols, and if enough able and honourable leaders emerge among the volunteers.

Volunteer maintenance groups, subsidized by rebates from the Council Tax, can also do a great deal to improve the environment and can encourage other members of the community to also cooperate in preventing crime. Among other things, this can prevent the vicious circle which makes areas with bad housing and a high crime rate worse, where decent tenants leave, and are replaced by the council with 'problem families'.

The threat of this kind of drift was averted in the 1970s in Islington by a determined initiative by a group of volunteers who formed a cooperative independently of the council but with council approval. They managed to attract active participation from the residents in large and potentially declining blocks of council flats, installing lighting, front-door grilles and caretakers with means of communication. They opened a children's playground and a club and organized a rota for cleaning. In effect, the cooperative took on a maintenance contract for their council estate and received a rebate from the rents. The rubbish and the graffiti have gone. The crime rate is low, and they attract 'a different kind of resident' when vacancies arise, including private buyers. The only cloud on the horizon is that the private buyers tend to keep themselves to themselves and do not volunteer to work for the cooperative, but the quality of life and the attitude of the residents have reached levels from which they are unlikely to decline.[9]

In 1995, the Home Secretary, Michael Howard, proposed

a pilot scheme of military-style prisons for young offenders, based on the experience of about 50 'boot camps' in the USA. Schemes of this type have often had disappointing results in the past, but lessons learned from these failures may avoid them being repeated. Attendance would be voluntary, that is when the offender chooses this in preference to other forms of punishment. It might, however, have a better chance of success if the stress were on physical fitness rather than military discipline. Many young offenders pride themselves on physical strength and prowess and would welcome the chance of spending their sentence developing these, with access to facilities and professional instructors, especially if these included some former footballers and other athletes. Money would be better spent in giving these instructors generous salaries than on expensive prison custody. The offenders would be well aware of the self-discipline needed for success in top sports and this might be the best way of getting them to develop their own self-discipline. Offenders should, however, be offered this opportunity only once and this should be made clear to them at the start.

THE REAL DETERRENT: CONVICTION

Ultimately, however, a credible deterrent will be the only really effective way of inducing persistent offenders to resist the lucrative temptation of returning to crime. And the best deterrent is the belief that they are likely to be caught. Intelligence-led policing means that previous offenders should be watched and they should know that they will be; and it is not the odds on arrest but the odds on *conviction* which will count. The task of the legislature, the police, the intelligence services, the judiciary, the legal profession and members of the public who volunteer to assist the fight against crime is to ensure that loopholes are closed in the shamefully unsuccessful processes of law enforcement for convicting the guilty.

Part V
Technology and Civil Liberties

15 Identification and Impersonation

EXPERIENCE IN BRITAIN AND OTHER COUNTRIES

Do citizens in a democratic country have the right to be anonymous? If they feel threatened, have they a right to conceal their identity? What about someone with a spouse in one part of town and a lover in another? Does the right of assembly carry with it the right to wear a mask or balaclava, or should demonstrators 'stand up and be counted'? And when, if ever, should people be obliged to prove their identity?

Whatever the answers to these questions may be, few would defend the 'right' to *impersonate* someone else by stealing or forging that person's credit card or passport.

Britain has only twice issued compulsory identity (ID) cards – in the First and Second World Wars. These ID cards were, in fact, of little use as they contained only brief personal particulars with no photograph or other means of identification. They were really just registration cards to help the issue of ration books and so on, and were easy to forge.

ID cards with photographs are, however, used by the British armed forces, the police, the BBC, many other institutions, and by corporations whose work is in any way confidential; and most clubs issue membership cards. All passports carry certified photographs and personal particulars. When due for renewal, British passports now follow a standard EU format in which the personal particulars are machine readable. Driving licences, on renewal, will also now carry a photograph. In 1994, plans were announced for issue of benefit cards whose machine readable data can be checked with a central database through readers at Post Office counters, for issue of pensions and other benefits.

The British reluctance to have ID cards is surprising in view of the readiness to carry credit and debit cards, charge cards, cheque guarantee cards and automated teller machine (ATM) bank cards for cash withdrawal. The latter contain a personal identication number (PIN) recorded on a black magnetic stripe on the card. The holder has to key in the PIN (from memory) on the bank's cash dispenser ('the hole in the wall'). There are currently 83 million bank and building society plastic cards carried in the UK,[1] and most adults carry at least two, and often a dozen plastic cards in their wallets. A Gallup poll in the *Daily Telegraph* in January 1995 showed 75 per cent in favour of an ID card scheme, to reduce crime and especially fraud, though some people expressed anxiety that it might harm police relations with the public, especially with young people and minority ethnic groups. There was also some concern about how information provided for the cards might be misused, and about the possibility of criminals stealing or forging them.[2]

Of the 15 members of the EU all but 4 (Britain, Denmark, Ireland and Sweden) have ID cards; of these, Denmark and Sweden both allocate personal numbers which are recorded on passports and used in taxation, obtaining state benefits, opening bank accounts, and so on.

Six EU countries have compulsory ID cards: Belgium (from age 12), Germany (16), Greece (14), Luxembourg (15), Portugal (10) and Spain (14). Five others – Austria, Finland, France, Italy and the Netherlands – have voluntary ID cards but in France and Italy they are so widely used that they differ little from compulsory cards; in both countries, people may have to prove their identity on request by the police (for example, near the scene of a crime) and to support claims for state benefits or banking transactions. If they have no ID cards, they may pay the price of delay or inconvenience. The British Government in August 1996 announced a plan for voluntary ID cards combined with driving licences.

Switzerland also has voluntary ID cards. Norway does not (though personal numbers are used as in Denmark and Sweden). Australia, Canada and New Zealand have no ID cards, but photographic driving licences are used for informal identification for social security and banking transactions.

In the USA, driving licences contain photographs and, in some states, personal details such as height and colour of eyes. Similar cards are available for non-drivers and are headed 'identification card'. People over 21 have the photographs on the right side of their cards, while those of people under

21 are on the left, with 'under 21' printed on the card, which is used to enforce the strict law against sale of liquor to anyone under 21. It seems to work.

CARD TECHNOLOGY

The simplest 'ID card' (say, for membership of a club) carries just the club logo and a signature. Identification can be enhanced by addition of a photograph and further improved by the inclusion of a black **magnetic stripe**, which can contain a PIN, a digitalized photograph and a small amount of other data. The data can be revised as necessary, but can be easily forged. Such a card costs little, generally less than £1.

A **barcode** is more reliable and still cheap. The code can be read only by a scanner, but a criminal with sophisticated equipment could copy it. To overcome this it can be written in invisible ink, or covered all over in black so that it can be read only by an infra red scanner; or the data can be encrypted. The barcode can, like the magnetic stripe, contain a PIN, a digitalized photograph and personal data.

Optical Character Readable (OCR) lettering is the most acceptable form of providing machine readable data on a card. The lettering is readable both by the human eye and by the machine. All recently issued EU passports, including British ones, and many other types of cards, now contain personal particulars in this form – surname, first name, date of birth, country of birth, sex, number of passport (or of card or registration) and its date of expiry. There is only one person in whom all these particulars coincide. If desired, other recognition data can be added, such as height and colour of eyes. When the card is put in the slot at, say, a benefit agency, it will activate that person's benefit data on the DSS database. Similarly, a police checkpoint terminal could activate a police record, if the person had one.

OCR alone, however, cannot prove that the person presenting the card is the authorized holder of it. For this, biometric data unique to the cardholder (such as digital fingerprint or hand geometry) would also have to be recorded on a magnetic stripe or barcode on the card. This is not at present done, on passports, visas, ID cards, driving licences or benefit cards, but it should be. It could also be recorded, voluntarily, on, for example, bank ATM cards, to ensure that they do not release cash through the hole in the wall to someone who has stolen or forged the card and has obtained the PIN. (Biometric techniques are discussed in the next section of this chapter.)

OCR is now used for machine readable passports (**MRP**) and ID cards (**MRI**) and is increasingly likely to be used on visa cards (**MRV**). A machine readable zone (**MRZ**) can be incorporated on any kind of card for whatever information the issuer wishes to add.

Holograms are often added to the face of plastic cards such as credit and debit cards. These add considerably to the cost, but are difficult and expensive to forge.

Holomagnetic processing can lay the hologram over a magnetic stripe, which can still be read by machine. This provides higher security than a visual check but again adds to the cost.[3]

A **watermark** can be added to the magnetic stripe and can enhance the security of other data on the card through encryption, again at extra cost. The watermark magnetic stripe is currently used by many corporations to control access for authorized staff to high security areas.

A **smart card** contains a microprocessor with a memory; it may be passive (powered by the reader) or active (with its own battery – making it thicker and more expensive). The reader can instantly match the data on the card to a database and the card can record new data. It can keep records of the identity of staff members using the facility and of each time they enter and leave. This could be useful in detecting improper use, especially if there has been a leak. Shell petrol stations issue passive smart cards to customers to credit them with points for free benefits for each pound they spend, which shows how cheap they are when made in bulk.

An **optical card** has data recorded by laser in tiny pits and can be read only by laser. This is seldom worth the cost but its rarity may decrease the risk of forgery of cards giving access to high security areas. (An example of its use is given on p. 193.)

BIOMETRIC TECHNOLOGY

Biometrics – the digital recording of biometric features unique to an individual – has been in use since the early 1980s. It had some early successes in restricted situations with small databases, for example to check that a visitor leaving a prison was not a prisoner in disguise (using digital fingerprints) or to confirm the identity of a relatively small number of authorized staff to sensitive premises (using voice prints). It was not until 1991, however, that its wider use seemed likely to be economic, for example in air travel passes, and even for these it is still in the trial stage (see next section).

Digital fingerprints (FP) led the way. In a typical commercial situation, authorized staff enrol by placing the right index finger on a scanner, which records a number of characteristics. These are encoded in digital form on a database linked to the scanner. To gain entry, the enrolled member places the finger on the scanner and if it matches that on the database the gate opens. Enrolment takes 30 seconds, and entry 3 or 4 seconds. Alternatively, the data can be recorded on a card which can be matched to the finger on the scanner without the need for a database. This, of course, is easier to get round, by imposters recording their own data on a forged or stolen card.

Fingerprints are among the easier characteristics to forge. They can be copied onto a plastic 'finger' or on a plastic sheath which can be slipped over the imposter's finger. This was done by an enterprising journalist, who persuaded a card holder to give him a plaster cast of his finger and lend him his card, to get through one of the earliest air travel pass schemes in 1993, so a new system was introduced to prevent this (see next section).

The pattern of the **retina** is also unique and can be measured by an infra red reader. The pattern of the **iris** and the shape and contours of the **ear** can also be digitally recorded;[4] so can the **vein pattern** on the back of the hand or wrist. **Voice prints** are simple to use ('say good morning to open the gate') provided that the number on the database is not too large. **Signature dynamics** recorded digitally give more reliable results than matching a signature by eye. The **facial image** can be recorded thermally, the variations being measured by their infra red transmissions.[5] **Photographs digitally recorded** on a magnetic stripe or two dimensional (2D) barcode can also be reconstructed and projected on a screen for visual matching with the person in the flesh. These many varieties will enable multiple biometrics to be recorded on a database or card for a rapid second check in the event of a false rejection, which at present can cause considerable delay and irritation (see p. 192).

DNA – the unique genetic molecules found in all body fluids – are regularly used by the police to provide positive forensic evidence in rape or murder cases by matching traces of blood, saliva or semen found on the victim with the DNA characteristics of the person accused. This is equally valuable in providing incontrovertible proof of innocence of people wrongly suspected. The matching, however, currently involves time-consuming laboratory tests, so DNA is not suitable for immediate proof of identity at checkpoints.

Hand geometry (HG) is probably the most promising technique to have been comprehensively tested so far. This records the bone and knuckle structure of the hand, placed palm downwards on a scanning platen. Enrolment (30 seconds) and verification (2 or 3 seconds) is as quick as FP; the digital data are just as unique but require fewer bytes and can be recorded on a barcode or magnetic stripe. A new variant of HG, **Digi-2**, was developed in 1994 using just two fingers, needing a smaller platen and only 29 bytes on the database.

HG systems have been under test since 1993 at JFK, Newark and Toronto airports; these tests are analysed in the next section of this chapter.

A cardinal characteristic of any detection system, be it for identification or detecting drugs or explosives, is that the lower the rate of false acceptance the higher the rate of false rejection. The primary aim of all systems is to ensure that no unauthorized person, bomb, gun or drug gets through. Systems are therefore calibrated to reduce false acceptance to a minimum, hopefully nil, by demanding a very accurate match (or minuscule trace) which inevitably results in a higher percentage of false rejections.

This is the right way round but can cause a lot of delay and inconvenience; luckily, the speed and potential variety of tests available makes it easy to overcome in the case of identification. The AIT Corporation has developed a combined system of **multiple techniques** incorporating a choice of five different technologies. When the user is enrolled, the scanners record five different characteristics: right forefinger; left forefinger; hand geometry; facial image; and signature. If, say, the right forefinger gives a false rejection, the left forefinger is placed on the scanner; if this too is rejected, hand geometry, facial image and signature dynamics can each be tried in turn – each taking only a few seconds. The only extra costs are for the additional scanners, readers and staff and a larger database – all on the same installation with the same infrastructure (computer, barriers, gates, and so on). Added advantages would be the extra security from confirmation, and the cards would be much more difficult to forge. A limited application of this system is currently under test in Canada (CANPASS), not yet using the full range of options (see next section). Many more options are now available if required (see pp. 189–90).

There is reason to believe that there are many fewer false rejections when users become accustomed to the system, that is they place the hand or finger accurately on the scanner without moving it. This view is supported by the experience of a Middle Western university in the USA, which used an HG reader incorporating its own database (no cards) for students enrolled to use the cafeteria. Since every student used the cafeteria every day, false acceptances and false rejections were virtually unknown.

TRIALS OF BIOMETRIC TRAVEL CARDS

There has long been pressure in the airport and airline industries to speed up the processing of passengers through immigration since the projected growth of air travel will inevitably clog up the existing systems unless they are improved. The initial approach has been to offer voluntary advance screening to regular travellers, who are then issued with a travel card giving entry in about 15 seconds through a special automated fast-stream gate instead of joining the passport queue.

The first major trial began in Schiphol Airport. Amsterdam, in February 1991. Volunteer travellers were security screened and issued with a Schiphol Travel Pass (STP), a smart card on which a fingerprint was digitally recorded. The card also contained machine readable (OCR) personal data with the card number. The traveller passed through two gates. The slot at the first gate checked the validity of the card – that the person with those particulars was enrolled in the scheme – and the gate opened automatically. At the second gate, the traveller put a finger on a scanner and, provided that this matched the FP data on the microchip on the card, that gate also opened automatically. The whole process took about 15 seconds.

The problem was that there were too many false rejections, which recurred when the card was passed through again, and the consequent delays defeated the object, so that volunteers (who had paid for their cards) were alienated and few others joined. The tests were suspended in January 1994, but were resumed in 1996 with HG in place of FP technology.

In 1993 the German Border Guard (*Bundesgrenzschutz* – BGS) developed a system at Frankfurt Airport in which two types of biometric data – FP and HG – were recorded for enrolling volunteer regular travellers. These data were stored in a database on the second of the two gates, so the traveller did not have to carry a special card. The OCR personal particulars on the normal passport or ID card at the first gate confirmed that the traveller was enrolled in the scheme. At the second gate, the traveller merely put a hand on the screen (no card) and if that matched the biometric data linked to those personal particulars on the database, the second gate opened.

The intention was that, if the Frankfurt tests were successful, other airports in Germany and in some other cooperating countries (most EU countries, Australia, Canada, Singapore and the USA had shown an interest) would also be provided with the database or have on-line access to it. The ultimate aim was a worldwide system. Financial and political considerations, however, delayed the implementation of the Frankfurt scheme, and it was overtaken by the Future Automated Screening of Travellers (FAST) Trials.

The FAST Trials were initiated by the World Travel and Tourism Council (WTTC) in conjunction with the US Immigration and Naturalization Service (INS) with a core group of representatives from Australia, Canada, Germany, the Netherlands, the UK and the USA. The first trial began at JFK Airport, New York, in June 1993, with the issue of an INS travel pass (INSPASS) to regular travellers who volunteered for screening. The card contained HG data for the traveller. By January 1994, 8883 cards had been issued, using kiosk gate systems at five of the dedicated terminals at JFK (TWA, AA, UAL, Delta and the International Arrival Building). Within the next few months, similar schemes were introduced at Newark and Toronto airports. By January 1994, the total number of cards issued was 12,991 with 10,114 inspections and 417 (4.1 per cent) false rejections.[6] By August 1995 there had been 114,678 inspections in all, including 39,790 at Toronto, again with about 4 per cent false rejections.[7]

In October 1995 a pilot scheme was launched at Vancouver Airport to facilitate rapid clearance of Canadian and US travellers who volunteered for enrolment, paying an annual charge of C$50. The primary identification was by digitalized FP data, with HG scans also being taken at enrolment for later use if needed. The data was stored on an optical card (CANPASS). This has the advantage of high data storage capacity but is slower than other types to read; it is also less suitable for combination with other purposes and it would be more difficult to make it compatible with the systems being developed by other countries. The advantages of multiple biometric technologies, however, are considerable (see p. 191). It should not be impossible to change to another type of card if necessary.[8]

Australian Immigration are planning to introduce a border clearance trial using facial recognition biometrics, to be known as Advance Passenger Clearance (APC). This was introduced by Prime Minister John Keating at a conference in Osaka, Japan, in November 1995. This envisaged the issue of an Australian Arrival Card at the time of check-in for departure for Australia from another country, initially for those flying by the Australian QANTAS airline, but designed to allow linkage with other airlines later.

At the departure airport, the QANTAS check-in staff will transmit (electronically) the passport or visa number of any passenger who has enrolled in the scheme to the immigration computer, which will extract the biometric data and return these (electronically) to the airline, along with a unique 'passenger identifier' which is encoded on the magnetic stripe of the passenger's APC card, with the flight number. The data are also stored on the 'expected movement file' which is transmitted ahead to the destination airport where, on arrival, the card is swiped through a reader and, provided the data match, the passenger will pass through in about 20 seconds to baggage collection and exit.[9]

Meanwhile, the German Minister of the Interior in January 1996 approved a pilot scheme for Frankfurt Airport using HG biometrics and OCR. It was hoped that a private company would be found to develop and finance the scheme but, if not, the German government would sponsor it. The intention was that it would come into operation before the end of 1996.[10] Germany was also leading the way in research for standardization.

UK Immigration, British Airways (BA) and the British Airports Authority (BAA) are hoping to get a pilot scheme operating if funding can be obtained, and a new pilot scheme, using a smart card with HG and OCR, was planned at Schiphol Airport, Amsterdam, starting in the spring of 1996.[11]

PASSPORTS, VISAS AND ID CARDS

Most European passports now carry OCR data, which confirm that they are valid for the person described by those data. Impersonation, however, has proved all too easy, provided that the imposter bears a passing resemblance to the photograph or inserts his or her own.

It would greatly increase the reliability of passports if they also contained biometric data such as HG or FP. Criminals with access to a computer with an HG scanner could, however, add or substitute their own biometric data on a forged or stolen passport. It would therefore be necessary to store passport holders' biometric data, with their OCR data, on the database at the office at which they were enrolled. They would have had to attend at such an office personally in any case to have their biometric data recorded, so there would need to be a number of such offices distributed about the country, each with its own database. The first characters on the OCR data could therefore be a number or letter code for that office. Whenever the passport was checked, therefore, the machine could also feed in the HG data from the holder's hand on the reader to compare it. It would, however, take several years to renew all the millions of passports onto this system, just as it is currently taking ten years to renew UK passports onto the EU OCR format.

It is equally desirable for visas for visitors to the UK to carry OCR and biometric data to detect illegal immigrants, drug smugglers and other international criminals. The British Consulate issuing the visa would be responsible, as it is now, for whatever screening and validation is ordered by the FCO for people seeking entry from that country. Given the necessary enrolment machinery, the Consulate could record and enter the OCR and biometric data on a plastic visa card and dispatch these data by landline or satellite to a database in the UK to which immigration offices in air and sea ports would have access. Police and other checkpoints in Britain should also have access to this database if needed.

It must be hoped that, over the next 10 years, EU passports, visa cards and ID cards will be harmonized, with standard OCR and biometric data, so that all EU citizens will be able to establish their identity anywhere in the Union.

The issue of British ID cards will have many advantages and harmonization will almost certainly be needed in the future with the ID card systems of other EU states. Driving licences on plastic cards with photographs incorporating magnetic stripe or barcode technology are already being issued in the UK as in other EU states.[12] Though it is at present uncertain whether the personal data will be machine readable, this must undoubtedly come, so that suspected licences can be checked. The best way to start the issue of ID cards in the UK would be to expand the data on the driving licences, since the compulsory issue of a new type of ID card from scratch for the whole population would take many years and would probably cost about £600 million.[13]

In addition to making the personal particulars machine readable, two additional panels would be needed to enable the driving licence to double as an ID card – probably on the back to keep it small. The first panel should contain digitalized biometric templates (preferably two, say HG and FP). These could be recorded in 2D barcode form, ideally protected from forgery by a hologram, or covered over in black if the use of infra red readers is acceptable. The second panel would be available for optional additional information at the request of the holder; this could include blood group, allergies, ailments requiring special treatment (such as heart trouble, or diabetes), and could incorporate a donor card. It could also include entitlement to health care in other EU countries, as at present authorized by the E111 form. This voluntary information would not be sensitive so it could be in open OCR lettering. The issue of driving licences/ID cards with biometric data would necessitate the applicant calling at a local enrolment office to have the data recorded. As with passports, the OCR data would start with a code giving access direct to that office.

It will be wise to offer ID cards initially only to volunteers. The advantages to the volunteer will be sufficient to ensure that the number of applicants would exceed the capacity of the enrolment offices and eventually, as has happened in France and Italy, virtually the whole population would probably apply for them.

In whatever way ID cards are issued, separately or combined with driving licences, they need not and should not contain any confidential information – just the open OCR data and the holder's own biometric data to confirm who is the authorized holder of the card. Recording other data (for NHS, benefit entitlements, driving offences or other police records) would arouse anxiety that it might be accessible to people who have no right to see it, possibly prejudicing chances of getting credit or a job. And, as pointed out earlier, it is quite unnecessary. To activate the PNC for police records, all the police need is the open OCR personal particulars. Similarly for NHS, benefit agencies, and so on. So one card could serve all these purposes. Provided that these principles are followed there will be few if any civil liberties hazards inherent in the card.

SAFEGUARDING CIVIL LIBERTIES

The biggest advantage of the voluntary issue of ID cards (initially by adding extra OCR and barcode data to the new driving licences) would be to reduce the amount of crime, especially fraud. Card fraud is currently estimated at £100 million each year, plus another £150 million from fraudulent girocheques and orderbooks.[14] Every penny of this is ultimately paid by members of the public in terms of banking costs and taxes, so it is their civil liberties which are being infringed by fraud.

This is the main reason for the 75 per cent public support for the issue of ID cards. To use a stolen bank card to get money, all the thief has to do is to discover the card holder's PIN, usually thanks to the card holder's carelessness; the thief will, in fact, probably already have found this out before deciding which card to steal. If the holder had a government ID card with barcoded biometric data, the bank could incorporate on the magnetic stripe on the bank card an endorsement that no money was to be released without a barcoded ID card being produced or, better still, for the bank card itself to carry the barcoded biometric data, but the use of biometric technology will need to become more widespread before that can happen.

Smaller scams are perpetrated by a host of other criminal acts, such as multiple applications for social security benefits under a series of different names. Also, over a 12 month period, there were 700 bogus applications for student grants, for which £1.5 million were paid out.[15] Again it is the public who foot the bill.

ID cards would also be useful as proof of age, say by senior citizens entitled to concessionary fares. As in the USA (see pp. 186–7), people who appear to be under age could be required to produce proof of age before being sold alcohol or cigarettes.

The value of automation for speeding international travel was discussed on pp. 191–4. In the future, a single card with OCR and biometric data might serve as a passport, travel card, ID card and driving licence – and as an NHS card and benefit card for those entitled. The voluntary inclusion of non-sensitive medical data (blood group, allergies, heart pacemaker, for example) could save lives after an accident.

Perhaps one of the biggest benefits would come from the ability of the police to check people's identity quickly after a crime without the need for house-to-house inquiries; and the existence of ID cards would act as a further deterrent to criminals. There is little doubt that the police would welcome such cards for checking people leaving the scene of a bombing or other crime, or for checking those approaching seaports or airports when there is reason to believe that criminals may be attempting to leave the country. The civil liberties of innocent people are served by their rapid elimination from police inquiries as well as by prevention of crime and the conviction of criminals.

Restraints on the right to demand to see ID cards would be necessary to protect privacy and to prevent unnecessary harassment. For this reason, most advanced countries do now have data protection legislation, in the case of the UK the Data Protection Act 1984. Among other provisions, this requires that personal data may be held only for one or more specified and legal purposes; that it shall not be used or disclosed in any way incompatible with those purposes; that it must be relevant, accurate and kept up to date; that it shall not be kept for longer than is necessary for the specified purposes; that the individual must be informed that such data are recorded; and must have the right of access to it and, where appropriate, the right to have it corrected or erased; also, adequate security measures must be taken against unauthorized access, alteration, disclosure, destruction or accidental loss of personal data.[16]

Apart from the worries (whether justified or not) about unauthorized access and abuse of personal information, the biggest public anxiety about ID cards would be the fear of them being used by over-zealous police officers or other officials to harass young people or members of minority ethnic communities, by repeated and unnecessary demands to produce the card. The proposed single card system, however, should help to minimize the risk of such harassment. Every time the card is slotted into a computer terminal (police, NHS, DSS etc.) the database should automatically record the access code number of the official who checked it and the date and time of access – along with the OCR details of the person being checked. If that person were to complain of harassment within a specified number of weeks (say, six) it would be easy to call up onto the computer screen every occasion on which the person was checked, when, where and by whom. This would reveal any pattern of harassment if it had occurred. Modern computer systems have ample memory capacity to accommodate this, provided that the records of these checks are regularly washed off if not called for during the specified period. The vast majority would never need to be looked at before they were washed off, and would cost nothing.

Given these safeguards, the advantages should far outweigh any disadvantages or inconveniences, whether these arise from malice, incompetence or technical failure.

In a free society, citizens enjoying democratic rights should be prepared, if asked, to prove their entitlement to them by proving their identity. If the tools needed to do this might also make it more difficult for them to deceive their fellow citizens in other ways which they would be ashamed for them to know, an encroachment of those dubious freedoms is an acceptable price to pay.

About impersonation, however, there can be no controversy. There can be no honest justification for impersonating someone else, especially if this involves stealing or forging that person's proof of identity.

16 Surveillance and Access Control

INSIDE THE CASTLE WALLS: STAFF SELECTION

'The strongest castle walls are not proof against a traitor within'. To secure the safety of people lawfully within the perimeter of an airport, factory, office block, school, hospital or bank, the first line of defence is the selection and screening of staff who have regular access. This can raise civil liberties dilemmas. Some previous convictions, for example, are expunged from records after a specified period, and it could be judged defamatory to refer to them. On the other hand, the law does permit employers to check with the police for specified offences relevant to particular jobs, for example previous sexual or child abuse offences by people applying for jobs in schools or children's homes.

For safeguarding the public against crime, it is important that the law should not inhibit references to other relevant convictions, for example for theft or fraud where there is access to money or goods without close supervision. The 'greater good' must be on the side of public safety.

On the other hand (as was discussed in Chapter 3), if anyone, especially someone young, is branded indefinitely for a first offence and cannot get another job, this may well be adding another recruit to the alienated band who become persistent criminals.

PERIMETER SECURITY

No single line of defence is 100 per cent secure. Security must be planned in concentric rings, none of which must be regarded as impregnable, but each of which should provide deterrence, impose delay and, above all, give warning to alert those inside to staff the inner rings.

Procedural defences may be more important than physical obstacles. Staff selection and vetting have already been mentioned. Intelligence is equally essential and was discussed in Chapters 6, 7 and 8. Cooperation with the police and neighbouring institutions are also important.

Of the physical rings, the first is a secure outer perimeter. In the case of an airport, this may be up to 10 miles long, and for a large oil refinery, almost as much. Seaport landside premises may be more difficult to secure, as they are often located in old cities, with honeycombs of poor housing and derelict areas abutting onto them. In all external perimeters, radar, photoelectric beams, infra red lights, video cameras and other surveillance equipment will need to be supported by patrols, including guard dogs.[1] Some care may be needed to ensure that these do not give rise to an accusation of using more than the minimum necessary force. Examples of this would be obstacles which could cause injury without warning, or uncontrolled use of firearms or dogs. The courts have sometimes awarded damages to intruders, even those with unquestioned criminal intent, who suffered injury while breaking in.

Perhaps the most extreme example of a secure external perimeter, built by a government without regard for life or civil liberties, was on the frontier between East and West Germany in the Brezhnev era of the Cold War, especially that surrounding West Berlin to prevent the escape of East Germans into the City and thence to the West. Dividing East and West Berlin was the notorious Berlin Wall, on which anyone trying to climb out from the East was shot at sight. The Western perimeter of West Berlin, mainly through fields in the outer suburbs, comprised a 50 metre swathe, bulldozed clear of all vegetation and kept clear with herbicides. There were barbed wire entanglements along either side, and anti-personnel mines in the first few metres of soil within the barbed wire. Along the centre of the swathe, through the length of each countryside section, ran a steel wire mounted on posts some 3 metres high. Along the wire ran steel rings, each tethering a huge German Shepherd dog. There was one dog on its steel ring between each pair of posts, so that the dogs were able to run freely along the wire, ranging on either side, and to overlap the neighbouring dogs by the length of their leash beyond the post at each end of their pitch. The leashes were, of course, short enough to prevent them from reaching the mines up against the barbed wire on either side. At intervals were watch towers occupied by armed People's Police, 'Vopos'. At night, the whole of the swathe was floodlit throughout its length and breadth.

This must have been as far as security could go, but it would certainly not have been within the law in any democratic country, even around the most sensitive defence establishment or top security prison. Security police in other authoritarian countries will no doubt have studied this example.[2]

In more normal premises in the UK, within the external perimeters, there will be inner perimeters, with tighter protection around key points, such as control centres, pumping stations, generators, telephone exchanges, switch boards or computer centres. Robust perimeters round these facilities will need to be reinforced with surveillance equipment, such as buried line sensors. These comprise a pair of wires, buried a few feet apart (or incorporated in a fence) which create an electric field which sounds the alarm when any foreign body, human or animal, enters it.[3]

ACCESS CONTROL

Apart from staff vetting, the most vital security of all will be reliable control of the main entrances for pedestrians and vehicles. More intruders enter by outwitting the guards than by climbing the fences. For people on foot, control of entry to high security premises should be based on two stages, whereby an inner gate will be operated by someone inside it, with a good view of the outer reception area, and a procedure for ensuring that the reception staff are not signalling clearance for entry under coercion.

Apart from regular and authorized staff, security will also depend on strict control of visitors and of contract personnel, such as construction or repair workers. Visitors' badges should be issued, showing the date, and coloured to show whether the visitor must be accompanied or not. Accompanied visitors should be picked up by their hosts or escorts in the outer reception area, and responsibility for their security and supervision must be allocated without any room for doubt from the time they arrive until they leave.

Access control of the main pedestrian entrance, in addition to secure barriers and automated or card operated locks, depends on reliable means of identification and prevention of impersonation (as described in Chapter 15) and upon surveillance equipment (see next section) to detect anyone in an unauthorized area.

A valuable security measure within the premises is to equip the entrances to particularly sensitive premises with automated locks which are opened by swiping with a coded card issued only to authorized persons, but which also record the time at which each individual enters and leaves the facility (as described in Chapter 15). This is especially valuable in investigating any leakage or other misuse, and the pattern of activity of an individual may give early warning of unreliability or potential treachery. He or she will, of course, be aware of these measures so they are also valuable as a deterrent. This must be seen in the context that the majority of corporate fraud is carried out in house by middle management (see pp. 148–9).

Vehicle access to premises liable to be targeted is very important in view of the enormous damage and loss of life which can be inflicted by car and truck bombs. (For example, 241 killed by a suicide truck bomb which penetrated the courtyard of the US Marine Corps Base in Lebanon in 1983.[4]) The first essential (especially in city centre premises) is to erect barriers or bollards to ensure that vehicles with access from public streets or car parks cannot park close up to the walls of buildings liable to be targets. A gap of a few metres can enormously reduce the damage and casualties.

Entrance to the premises themselves and to their reserved vehicle parks (especially in basements) should be controlled in a similar way to pedestrian entrances. Coded ID cards pushed into a slot are simplest. Coded tags on the windscreen read by surveillance beams or tags under the vehicle read by a coil buried in the roadway are also commonly used. These can operate gates or (better) can lower robust roadblocks normally kept raised from the road surface. But these automated checks are of only limited value unless monitored, preferably by a security guard in person, or at least by a video camera watched by an operator who has the means to overrule the opening of the barrier if necessary.

SURVEILLANCE AND CIVIL LIBERTIES

The range of surveillance equipment was mentioned in general terms in Chapter 6 on intelligence, and in the discussion of perimeter security in the previous section. In this section, particular attention will be paid to the possible effects of these techniques on civil liberties.

Few of the techniques so far described for perimeter control (other than those round West Berlin in Cold War days) pose civil liberties hazards unless they might involve excessive force. Within protected perimeters, both staff and visitors expect to be monitored by security lights, outdoor and indoor surveillance, beams, volume detectors, heat detectors, automated locks, cameras, identity checks, and so on. It is, however, in areas open to the public, such as shopping centres or football grounds, where civil liberties dilemmas arise; also in the use of mail or telephone interception, long-range eavesdropping or bugging.

Interception of mail and telephones can be authorized in every country, including Britain, subject to the police convincing the appropriate authority (a minister or a judge, depending on the country) that there is reasonable ground to suspect that the persons to be placed under surveillance are contemplating or have committed an act of terrorism or serious crime. This power is clearly capable of being misused and, in Britain at least, it is possible to take legal action against those responsible if there is evidence that it was done without good cause.

Bugging is subject to stricter control. Only in exceptional circumstances is this authorized, and then only with the personal authority of the Home Secretary. An example of this occurred in 1986, after a series of bombing and incendiary attacks had been made on individual scientists, laboratories, food and pharmaceutical companies which were alleged to be using live animals to develop or test products

before use by the public. Suspicion was aroused that further attacks were being planned by an Animal Liberation Front (ALF) cell operating in the Midlands. Police surveillance was targeted on known or suspected ALF activists, who were seen to be using a certain house for their meetings. This was bugged and their discussions were recorded on audio tape, confirming the suspicion. Arrests were made in a raid in which other evidence was found and those planning the attacks were charged with conspiracy and sentenced to prison terms of up to ten years.

Long-range cameras and sensitive eavesdropping devices beamed on windows are tools more commonly used by investigative journalists or private detectives than by police and intelligence services. Unless specifically authorized and tightly controlled, they can amount to a gross abuse of civil liberties.

The morality of such techniques must be judged in the same way as other intelligence techniques (discussed in Chapters 6, 7 and 8). If they succeed in preventing terrorist or criminal acts which seriously endanger life and property, and in securing the conviction of those who committed or were conspiring to commit them, then safeguarding the civil liberties of the actual or potential victims of those crimes may justify them.

CLOSED CIRCUIT TELEVISION (CCTV)

CCTV and telephoto high resolution cameras are the commonest systems used in deterring or preventing crime in public or sensitive premises and in securing the evidence to convict the criminals.[5]

Both still and CCTV cameras have been used for more than ten years in countering football hooliganism. It is now normal, in matches in which hooliganism may be likely, for cameras to be mounted by the police covering the stands on the opposite side of the field. If known football hooligans are spotted, their movements are watched and video taped for use in evidence in the event of incidents occurring. Also, where an incident does occur, participants using violence (recognizable or otherwise) can be photographed, either for evidence for prosecution or future recognition as likely offenders. This capability was further added to in 1996 by the introduction of 'photophone' equipment, whereby the police on different grounds where matches are in progress can call to other grounds or to police headquarters for photographs to be transmitted to them which can help them identify people in the vision of their cameras who have aroused suspicion.

These measures proved to be such an effective deterrent that, in the 1990s, football hooliganism became rare within the grounds themselves, but it still occurred in fights between rival fans on the approaches to the ground before and after the match, or in the streets and pubs in the town. Placing CCTV coverage at selected points on these streets or premises have used the same tactics and techniques as are used in deterring and detecting theft in shops, shopping precincts and high streets, and in detecting drug trafficking (see Chapters 4, 6, 7 and 8).

A substantial number of arrests and convictions have been made on the evidence obtained by these means. CCTV covering a shopping precinct in Bootle, Liverpool, for example, gave leads to the arrest and conviction of two 10-year-old boys who abducted and murdered a 2-year-old toddler, James Bulger, in 1993. Blurred pictures showed one of the boys leading the child by the hand, and his size, appearance and clothing matched the descriptions by eye witnesses who had seen the three children on the roads approaching the scene of the murder.

A problem may arise over how long the video tapes from CCTV security cameras should be kept before they are washed off and re-used, because detection and arrest of offenders may take several weeks or months. Tapes from police cameras in public places will be kept for some time as a matter of course, and even cameras positioned at traffic bottlenecks may help weeks or months later in tracing the movements of, say, a vehicle carrying a bomb. Commercial firms such as banks and department stores using CCTV within their premises will be reluctant to incur the expense of keeping too high a proportion of their tapes out of use. The Home Office has requested that tapes should be kept for possible evidential use for 31 days.[6]

Civil liberties issues may arise over the use of CCTV cameras to record demonstrations and aggressive picketing, which can help to identify and convict people who use or incite violence or who cause criminal damage. This may also raise the issue of the right of demonstrators to conceal their identity by using masks or balaclavas (as bank robbers often do). Following a series of violent demonstrations, the German government tried to introduce legislation in 1987 to make this a criminal offence but it was vetoed by the minority party in the coalition (the Free Democrats). It can be argued that, in a democracy, the purpose of freedom of assembly is to enable people to demonstrate a point of view, and that demonstrators who intentionally conceal their identity are abusing this freedom; or they may be contemplating breaking the law by use of violence or intimidation and the police may fairly ask why they want to conceal their identity.

On the other hand, any restriction on freedom to demonstrate, and the arrest and prosecution of demonstrators for concealing their faces, by whatever means, might arouse resentment against the police and lead to more violence. Such restrictions are probably best avoided unless violence by disguised demonstrators or strikers becomes a serious problem.

Perhaps the best answer would be to make it an offence to conceal identity in the commission of a crime, or while engaging in activities 'such as would cause a person of reasonable firmness present at the scene to fear for his personal safety', that is amounting to riot, violent disorder or affray, as defined in POA 1986 (see pp. 120–1). As is customary in Britain, the police would be allowed to use their discretion in deciding whether to take action in each particular case.

17 Search Techniques

BODY SEARCHES

People may be picked up at any checkpoint carrying guns, explosives, jewellery (including watches) and drugs, on or inside their bodies and clothing, but the bulk of body searches are done at frontier exits and entries, especially at airports.

The simplest check is the magnetometer arch at the entrance to the departure lounge at airports. This detects only certain metals and its sensitivity can be adjusted. It should be sensitive enough to pick out the smallest gun but if it is set to be too sensitive it will give too many false alarms, picking up every ballpoint pen or belt buckle. It is usual to hand metal objects such as keys or spectacle cases to the staff, to bypass the arch. Passengers can also be frisked using portable metal detectors or by hand.

If security staff have serious doubts or suspicions, strip searches can be conducted by searchers of the same sex in search booths but this is done only rarely, as it is time consuming, humiliating, causes resentment and arouses accusations of harassment, victimization and abuse of civil liberties. Airport managers have to walk a tightrope to preserve a reputation for good security without driving passengers or airlines away by harassment or humiliation. In any case, hand searches will not find drugs sealed in condoms and swallowed, to be excreted later (see p. 40).

For people carrying drugs or explosives, vapour detection may be the most effective. At its simplest, an instant hand sniffer is run over the body, but these will not detect low vapour explosives, such as Semtex, some of which exude only one part of vapour in a million million (10^{12}) parts of air;[1] most hand-held sniffers are unlikely to detect anything less than one part in 100 million (10^8).

More efficient is a small vapour sampling booth with sealed doors in which the passenger stands for about half a minute while a sample of vapour is sucked out through an adsorber (filter) which is then tested in a more sensitive and more expensive machine, but testing the sample is likely to take at least half a minute per person, probably more.[2] This may be too much at peak time in a busy airport.

Dogs have extremely sensitive noses (a million times more sensitive than human noses) and they can be trained to detect drugs and explosives, including Semtex. For drugs, they can sniff people's clothing (but again will not pick up swallowed condoms); for Semtex explosives, the dog sniffing an adsorber from a vapour chamber may be more effective, because the sniffing can be done in conditions in which the dog is less likely to be distracted.

LETTER AND PARCEL BOMBS

Drugs are seldom sent by mail but terrorists often post letter and parcel bombs to their victims. A simple and cheap X-ray machine may pick up wires and metal detonators but some forms of ignition are free of metal. As well as hand-held vapour sniffers, there are hand-held 'gamma ray backscatter' detectors, costing much the same (about £10,000) which, held close up against the letter or parcel, emit nuclear particles which bounce back and are read by the same detector head that emits them. These, however, require careful handling as their radiation can be dangerous to human beings.

On a larger scale, the vapour can be sucked from a closed mail van or from mail bags in a sealed container, through an adsorber, and analysed by sensitive detectors or dogs (as described in the previous section). If there is a positive result from the van or container as a whole, then the letters or parcels can be tested individually.

An experienced mail sorter may be able to spot a letter or parcel bomb without using equipment. The sorter can handle them fairly freely, as they will have been designed to survive rough handling in the post. They may seem heavy for their size, or feel unusual (unless, as is often done, the device is concealed in a hard covered book). A wrongly written address or the lack of a sender's address may arouse suspicion.[3] As in many forms of detection, fingers, eyes, noses and common sense may be best of all, with equipment as a useful supplement.

BAGGAGE

Hand baggage, especially in airports, and sometimes at the entrances of offices or stores under special threat, is usually checked only by metal X-ray, but would be better checked by enhanced X-ray machines which indicate both metal (showing blue) and explosives (showing red). Hand-held sniffers and gamma ray backscatter detectors can also be used, and so can dogs. Again, if there is doubt, the bag should be hand searched in the presence of the owner.

Terrorists in recent years increasingly put their bombs in radios or cassette players, because the firing circuits are almost impossible to detect among the existing electrical circuits. It was a bomb like this, with only 10 oz (300 g) of Semtex which blew up an aircraft over Lockerbie in Scotland in 1988, killing 270 people. Carrying electrical equipment of this type in hold baggage is now normally banned. It is best picked up by detecting the explosive. Any electrical equipment revealed by X-ray of hand baggage can be removed and subjected to explosive detection by enhanced X-ray, vapour sniffers or dogs, supplemented by hand search.

Air baggage checked for the hold, except for high risk flights, is often subjected only to random search, which is quite inadequate. In the most modern air terminals, however, it is subjected to a double test while moving along the automated conveyor system in the baggage loading hall. It first passes through an enhanced X-ray detector, such as VIVID, in which the operators detain it for a few seconds, during which they can apply various detection modes which are highly sensitive, and most unlikely to allow false acceptance of a bag containing drugs or explosives. The price of this, however, is a high false alarm rate (see pp. 190–1).[4] If there is a negative or doubtful scan, the operator presses a button and the case is diverted through a side chute to a search area in which it is checked by a highly sensitive vapour or particle detector, such as EGIS, which involves taking and analysing a sample. Allowing for handling, this will take at least a minute per bag. If it passes this second test it is returned to the main conveyor for delivery to the loading point for its aircraft. If, however, there is still any doubt, it is diverted to a quite separate hand search area to which its owner is summoned, to unlock it and witness the search.

Most machines with this high sensitivity for enhanced X-ray or vapour detection cost a lot (half a million or a million dollars) so they, and the complex conveyor systems, are economically possible only at large airports handling a large number of flights every day. On smaller airports, a much higher proportion of personnel is needed for hand search. An effective alternative is to line up the baggage beside the boarding gangway and load it only after the owner has identified it and boarded the aircraft. There are no known cases of such owners blowing themselves up, but of course this system would not be possible at large international airports.

A system of reconciliation of passengers with their baggage is increasingly used by the big airlines at major airports and will, it is hoped, become internationally standardized within the next few years. This should ensure that no aircraft can take off, after initial loading or after loading more passengers and baggage at a transit stop, if there is a bag in the hold without its owner being aboard. Failure to do this in Canada in 1985 killed 329 people when an Air India flight blew up over the Atlantic.

At the major British airports now, the passenger's boarding card and the hold baggage label are marked with identical barcodes. This is done at the check-in desk, and recorded on the database in the baggage control office. Hold baggage is normally loaded before passengers board but they will, of course, have received their boarding cards before their baggage goes onto the conveyor. When the bag reaches the point for loading into the trolley for its specified flight, it is checked by a reader and will not be loaded unless a matching barcode on a boarding card has been issued. Then, as the passengers board the aircraft, their boarding cards are passed through a reader. If, when boarding is complete, there is a bag in the hold whose owner has not boarded, the computer will flash and go on flashing its number on the screen. If the owner is not found, then the bag, whose trolley number is also recorded, will be located and removed from the hold. In a well-designed system, this should take only about 20 minutes, even when the bag is in the hold of a fully loaded jumbo jet. The computer will not stop flashing until the bag is removed, and the aircraft can then take off.

CARS

Large numbers of cars, loaded to the roof with families, baggage and duty-free liquor, cross frontiers, enter the Channel Tunnel or drive off ferries every day. If there is a high alert, there will usually be some indication as to the car or cars subject to suspicion. Otherwise, there will be no attempt to check every car. At the customs barrier (which is before entering the Channel Tunnel or after leaving a ferry) security will depend largely on the experience, diligence and hunches of the customs officers. They aim to speak to all drivers, even if only for a few seconds and, by instant profiling in their minds, they can eliminate most cars from suspicion. Other cars are diverted to a search bay, and can be searched with similar equipment to that already described. Selected cars can, when necessary, be passed through a hermetically sealed search chamber (without driver or passengers) to be scanned by enhanced X-ray equipment and/or vapour sampling tests as described earlier. Handling each car will take a few minutes, so the number which can be checked is limited. At the EU frontiers with former Communist countries, the delay is longer because of the need to check the documentation of the car and its driver to counter the massive theft of cars from the West by organized criminal gangs.

In some cases, customs may judge it necessary to unload and hand search the car, using hand sniffers, dogs or gamma ray backscatter detectors. There is, however, no practicable way to search every car without unacceptable disruption of traffic, any more than it would be practicable to search every car entering London in the morning rush hour.

To check a car, van or coach suspected of carrying drugs, explosives or human beings hidden in the baggage compartment, the best way is probably to suck out all the air through an adsorber which is then checked by a dog or a sensitive vapour detector.

HEAVY GOODS VEHICLES, CARGO AND CONTAINERS

It is equally impracticable to search every heavy goods vehicle (HGV) and container crossing frontiers or leaving or entering seaports. Governments appoint a number of cargo handling agents who are responsible for supervising the packing of cargo consignments, HGVs and containers. Rotterdam handles 2.5 million containers every year, of which only about 10 per cent contain cargoes destined for the Netherlands. Of 6000 containers arriving on an average day, only 7 or 8 are searched, all from among those destined for the Netherlands.[5] They are searched for illegal immigrants as much as for drugs and other contraband, and the best method, once again, is to suck out the air through one of the ventilation holes. Human smells are among the easiest to detect, and some containers (especially from Asia) have been found to be fitted out as living rooms, with chemical toilets and feeding arrangements.

At the Channel Tunnel terminals, a proportion of HGVs are passed (as was described for cars) through a sealed search building using enhanced X-ray and vapour sampling.[6] Again, the ferry terminal staff have to select the vehicles for search by profiling, after examining the documentation and talking to the drivers. Many of the offending vehicles and containers successfully detected at the ports and tunnel terminals, however, follow intelligence leads, particularly those smuggling drugs or illegal immigrants. As in every sphere of fighting crime, intelligence is the best weapon.

CIVIL LIBERTIES IMPLICATIONS

The casualties from bombs in aircraft and the disruption caused by hijacks have been sufficiently shocking for most passengers to cooperate without complaint with search procedures and to accept the inconvenience and delays with a good grace (for example, when it is explained that there is a bag aboard without its owner). The incidence of both aircraft bombings and hijacks, however, have declined since 1990, chiefly as a result of the Middle East Peace Process. There is still a serious threat from Islamic fanatics, especially

Algerians, but if such incidents cease to be perceived as a threat, some passengers might become less patient.

Another factor, especially in aviation, is the cut-throat competition between operators. Airlines fear loss of passengers and airports fear loss of traffic, every time there is delay or disruption. For every security measure, finance directors need to be convinced that it is essential and worth the cost. The same applies to the operators of ferries and the Channel Tunnel. Threats to these have been rare so far, and less spectacular than attacks on aviation, but this could change.

Drug searches cause the most resentment and harassment. As described in Chapter 4, a large number of small-scale couriers smuggle drugs from the Caribbean and Nigeria, many of whom are cynically exploited; most are naive and vulnerable and are often accompanied (as a tactic) by young children. It is normal routine to do vapour checks with dogs and sniffers of passengers arriving from these areas. These may lead to body searches. If the police or customs officials questioning passengers become suspicious, due to their demeanour, that they may be smuggling drugs within their bodies (say, by swallowing condoms) they may detain suspects in the hope that the crime will be revealed when they defecate. The couriers will probably have taken powerful constipating agents for this reason, and the police may encourage them to take food or drink with laxative effects, though it would be illegal to force them to do so. Suspects can be detained for only a limited period unless charged with an offence. If the police had other grounds for charging them, suspects could conceivably be held until they defecated. Otherwise, the police know that, if they are released with the condoms still inside them, they will be able to get rid of the drugs even if they do not risk delivering them. There is a great deal of scope here for tension, resentment and hysteria and, since couriers from Nigeria or the Caribbean will almost certainly be black, for accusations of racial discrimination. This will be especially so if they are in fact innocent, so the police have a very difficult job.

Part VI
Conclusions

18 Striking the Balance

YOUNG CRIMINALS: WHY? WHAT CAN BE DONE?

Among the problems of crime in Great Britain, by far the most serious is the prevalence of juvenile crime. The long-term implications of this are daunting. The fact that nearly half the serious (indictable) crimes are committed by young people under 21 is worrying enough; but more serious is that, each year, a substantial new intake of young children is starting on the inexorable progress through truancy to petty crime and experience with drugs at primary school, producing teenagers already so far behind in education that they may have no hope and no intention of earning a living by working for it. They are programmed for either the frustration of unemployment or living by crime.

Of males reaching the age of 30–35 in 1994, over 13 per cent (one in seven) had appeared in court before the age of 21, and 8 per cent before 17. Of these, 75 per cent had been convicted for a second offence within two years.[1] A large proportion of these will have come from deprived families.

Some of the blame must fall on the policies of the Conservative government in the 1980s. It managed the economy so that the 90 per cent of people in work became steadily richer each year (and re-elected the government at the next general election) but the other 10 per cent got poorer and poorer, many becoming long-term if not permanently unemployed. Since a reasonably competent burglar or drug seller can earn £1000 a week, the route they looked for thereafter is not surprising. Some of these may prosper, but they will not bring up responsible children; the others, who continue to have miserable lives on unemployment benefit, are also unlikely to make good parents.

The seeds of trouble are sown earlier than at school. There is a close relationship between parents who left school with no qualifications and the odds on their children being illiterate or semi-literate and themselves failing at school. This underlines the importance of play schools and nursery schools; also of including good parenting in the curriculum of teenagers at secondary school.

Society must be tougher on truancy, since truants not only fall a lap behind in their education, but also spend their days away from school among gangs of older children learning the arts of petty crime. The police should be authorized and encouraged to question children seen on the streets in school hours; persistent truants should be moved to special schools where they can be taught to become self-disciplined and catch up on their education.

It is not in children's interest to let them rot – or start a life of crime – on the streets. If this is allowed to happen, they may be beyond hope of recovery by the time they get to secondary school. Nevertheless, the battle to get them away from crime must be carried forward into their late teenage. It is encouraging that all three major political parties agree on expanding the availability of nursery schools and crèches. If Britain is to check this slide it will be necessary to spend more on education at all levels, especially on paying teachers enough to attract first-rate people and making provision for retraining or dismissal of those who are inadequate.

DRUGS AND CRIME

Drug abuse is inextricably linked to crime, since 90 per cent of the money spent on drugs is acquired by crime and 50 per cent of thefts and burglaries are committed to get money to buy drugs. By the age of 16, 22 per cent of boys and girls have experimented with drugs and 6 million people (11 per cent of the population) take some illegal drugs each year. Half a million young people attend raves each week, many taking Ecstasy, which can be as dangerous as heroin or crack cocaine. Even more damaging are the criminal drug trafficking gangs – again mainly young. Those who become importers and distributors can make over £250,000 a year.

One solution would be to import drugs direct, to be sold by qualified dispensers under licence. This would cut out most of the criminal drugs gangs because the price, even if heavily taxed like alcohol, would be cut to about one-sixth of the current street price, but this might send the wrong signal and encourage more addiction. It would not in any case solve the teenage problem; no government would license the sale of drugs to people under 18, but the teenagers would still want them, so some of the criminal gangs would continue to operate to provide that market; and the teenagers would continue to steal to find the money to pay. Nevertheless, present methods are failing so we must be ready to experiment with radical alternatives.

Organized criminal gangs thrive on international crime, smuggling not only drugs but also other valuables, illegal immigrants and child prostitutes from East Europe and Asia. There is also a huge trade in counterfeit money and goods, and a growing amount of fraud and other white-collar crime by highly sophisticated criminals.

It is estimated that 10 per cent of the money passing through the City of London is laundered money from the proceeds of international crime. Money laundering depends largely on rapid electronic transfers between international banks which guarantee client confidentiality. Many of these are in fiscal havens (often independent offshore islands) whose governments, to attract lucrative trade, make it illegal for a bank to give information about customers' accounts. Many Western countries have laws which oblige banks to give police or Inland Revenue access to accounts on a court order, if the police can present good grounds for suspicion that they may contain criminal money (though some of the banks manage to get round the law). These laws also allow such accounts to be frozen and the assets confiscated in the event of a conviction. In a reversal of the normal rule of 'innocent until proved guilty', the onus lies on the accused to prove a legitimate source for the money. This is not, however, an erosion of civil liberties, because people are already liable to be called upon to prove the source of their assets to the Inland Revenue.

INTELLIGENCE

The prevalence and sophistication of crime now calls for proactive intelligence-led policing, which depends on first finding out where to look. This generally involves three overlapping processes: background intelligence to get leads to criminals; specific intelligence acquired by targeting these criminals for surveillance; and the recruitment and handling of informants within or with access to the criminal gangs.

Background intelligence comes mainly from routine police patrolling and encouraging the public to give information. This can be enhanced by employing 'intelligence developers' to provide additional eyes and ears for the police; these are often retired police officers and other responsible members of the public. The first leads often come from spotting who talks to whom and who lives or goes where. The subsequent surveillance is done by targeted observation by police officers, and equipment such as CCTV. The possible civil liberties hazards of some of the surveillance technology is discussed later (p. 228).

Informants are seldom 'infiltrated' but are recruited from within or on the fringes of criminal organizations. Most often they are people who have already committed crimes, have been detected and are anxious to mitigate the consequences; they may also be rewarded for information leading to the arrest and conviction of other criminals. If their lives are put at risk, they may be relocated, with their families, in a safe place under a new name. However little they seem to deserve these things, their information may save lives and reduce the threat of further crimes. The cost of the rewarding, relocating and ongoing protection of informants can be high, but it may achieve more than much higher expenditure on other police and intelligence work.

Informants can seldom be called as witnesses in court, nor must their identity be revealed. Unless they can be sure of this there will be no informants. They often lead the police to find circumstantial evidence or other witnesses who can safely be called to give evidence.

If informants have been used in preparing a case, the CPS should mention this in advance to the trial judge, saying that it is not intended to call them or to use any information obtained from them as evidence. A defence counsel who suspects that an informant has been used may request that the informant appears as a witness, knowing that if the judge accepts this request the police will have to abandon the case.

Informants must be very tightly controlled; their names must be known only to their handler and to two at most of the handler's superior officers. Informants may give false or exaggerated information to gain advantage for themselves or to settle old scores. They are by nature often duplicitous, so great care must be taken that they do not prejudice a fair trial or other people's civil liberties.

PREVENTION OF TERRORISM

Following a study by Lord Diplock in 1972, it was decided that terrorist offences in Northern Ireland should be tried without jury by a single judge (the 'Diplock Court').[2] This was because intimidation, and sometimes murder, of witnesses or jurors made normal trials impossible. Confessions by the accused were acceptable unless they were obtained by torture or inhuman or degrading treatment. Written evidence could be accepted from witnesses who could not be produced in court for 'specific reasons'. The police and the army were given special powers to stop and search people and vehicles; also for entry, search and seizure in premises if it was suspected that arms, explosives or hostages were being held there. The onus was on the people found in possession of these things to prove that they were unaware that they were there.

Early in 1974, this prompted a leaflet from NICRA (which in the past was alleged to have had links with the IRA) listing ways in which they thought that the Act was being used to curtail civil liberties (see pp. 102–3), but claimed that evidence to prove this was almost impossible to obtain. This is an inevitable hazard when emergency powers have to be introduced, and preventing abuse depends on police training and supervision and a fair complaints procedure.

The Diplock Courts convicted many prisoners on their own confessions or on the evidence of defectors from the IRA and Protestant terrorist movements (notably the 'supergrass trials' of 1981–83). The Court of Appeal, with three judges, usually quashed the convictions unless the defectors' evidence was corroborated.

By contrast, several hundred left- and right-wing terrorists were convicted in Italy on the evidence of defectors (the *pentiti*). Most of these convictions were upheld because the much larger number of defectors (389) enabled enough corroborative witnesses to be called. The same applied in the later mass trials using Mafia *pentiti*.

In France, all terrorist offences are tried without juries by a senior judge sitting with six junior judges (examining magistrates). This kind of court is also employed in the Netherlands, where juries are not used in any case.

In Britain, all judges are selected from barristers or solicitors with many years of experience, so there are no equivalents to examining magistrates or junior judges. It would make sense if the single-judge Diplock Courts were replaced by a judge sitting with two barristers or solicitors as assessors; an alternative idea would be for juries to be anonymous and protected from view, sitting in a separate building with video cameras. (This idea is discussed on pp. 165–7.)

On a wider field, it must be questioned whether the hallowed British adversarial system is any longer fairer and more effective than the continental inquisitorial system. The work of British criminal lawyers, until they become judges in middle age, consists entirely of seeking and making the most of evidence for one side only of a case. Young French or Dutch lawyers in their 20s or 30s may be investigating cases as examining magistrates, gathering and weighing the evidence on both sides and seeking the truth. They will also serve under senior judges as junior members of the court – again seeking the truth. Logically, this seems a much better career background for a senior judge. It also seems to result in fewer of the guilty going free.

In 1974, following the explosion of two large IRA bombs killing 21 people in Birmingham, measures were introduced (PTA 1974) to allow more time for detention and investigation of terrorist suspects entering the country, two days or up to a total of seven with the Home Secretary's approval. This extra time was needed because the IRA based itself outside the UK, in the Republic of Ireland, with cells in the USA and West Europe. This led to complaints on civil liberties grounds, but the numbers detained for long periods have always been small, and the PTA has been renewed every year by Parliament whichever party was in power. There were only 20 votes against it in March 1996 in the wake of the IRA's sudden breach of its 'total and permanent cease-fire'.

PUBLIC ORDER

Britain's unrivalled record of over 300 years (since 1688) of government without any unconstitutional change owes much to the tradition of free assembly and protest.

The 1970s and 1980s saw a marked increase in violent clashes between rival left- and right-wing demonstrators and a rise in violent industrial mass picketing. These led to three Employment Acts (1980, 1982 and 1984), which curbed violent picketing, and the Public Order Act 1986 which increased the powers of police and local authorities to impose conditions and control the routes of processions. It also introduced powers to control 'trespassory assemblies'. This Act was used in the 1990s to control animal rights protesters, hunt saboteurs, travellers, vagrants and demonstrators aiming to obstruct the building of new roads. The aim was to stop the violence from getting out of hand. Further provision was made in CJPOA 1994 to enable police to exercise control over raves, at which drugs such as Ecstasy were consumed, sometimes resulting in deaths. The effect of all these measures has been, not to prevent the assemblies, but to minimize the risk of damage and casualties. In this respect, the legislation seems to have succeeded.

ARREST, TRIAL AND CONVICTION

Two Acts – PACE 1984 and CJPOA 1994 – revised the laws concerning arrest, bail, detention and interrogation. One of the more controversial changes affected the historic right to silence, both under interrogation and in court. The right to silence remains, but the prosecution is now permitted to draw attention to the fact that the accused declined to answer questions and for courts and juries to draw 'such inferences . . . as appear proper'. This has resulted in changes to the wording of the standard police caution, particularly drawing attention to inferences to be drawn from failure by accused persons to mention any fact relied on in their defence which they could reasonably have been expected to mention.

It is suggested (pp. 141–2) that the problems arising from this change would be largely removed if interrogations on serious offences were all to be video taped, a copy of the tape being given to both prosecution and defence, either of whom could use any part of the tape as evidence. The defence could use it as evidence of improper interrogation (by threats, bullying or improper inducements) and the prosecution to draw attention to the demeanour of the accused in declining to answer questions, just as they can draw conclusions from his or her demeanour in court.

Another problem was tackled in the Report of the RCCJ in 1993. This was the obligation on both the prosecution and the defence to disclose before a trial any evidence they plan to use at the trial. This was being abused by some defence lawyers to demand to see, and request inordinate time to peruse, *all* existing documentary evidence. At the same time, a number of convictions of alleged IRA bombers in the 1970s had been overturned by retrospective appeals in the 1980s and 1990s on the grounds that there was evidence which the prosecution did not use but which could have been of use to the defence in undermining the case for the prosecution, for example in throwing doubt on the reliability of scientific forensic evidence. The prosecution is now obliged to make all such evidence available to the defence before the trial. However, except where this factor applies, the prosecution is not obliged to disclose evidence which it does not propose to use at the trial.

The problem of intelligence from informants whose identity must not be disclosed was mentioned earlier (pp. 220–1). If the defence lawyers are aware of the existence of such intelligence, they may demand to see it, knowing that this would lead to abandonment of the case against their clients. Provided that this information is not going to be used as evidence, the trial judge may rule that neither the existence of the information nor the identity of the informant need be revealed.

Another controversial area is evidence of previous convictions. The defence may use almost any evidence to discredit a prosecution witness but the prosecution cannot draw attention to the previous record of the accused until the jury has announced its verdict. In certain trials, notably for rape and violence, this has resulted in perverse acquittals of people whose records are such that the jurors have been appalled to find that they have released an extremely dangerous person to commit further offences against future victims. It is suggested (pp. 151–2) that judges should be given more discretion in such cases, where they believe that this evidence should be fairly taken into account in reaching a verdict.

Chapter 12 discusses the problem of criminal lawyers who knowingly distort or fabricate evidence to secure acquittals where the weight of evidence would overwhelmingly justify conviction. This should be regarded as seriously as the crime of police officers planting or fabricating false evidence to secure a conviction. Both of these types of crimes need to be tackled.

The perversion of justice by intimidation or corruption of witnesses and juries, which necessitated the changes in the judicial processes in Northern Ireland, has now become a serious problem in England. While trial by jury and examination of witnesses in public has been the fairest process of law, it cannot be carried out if criminal or terrorist gangs, and sometimes their lawyers, set out to make the process unworkable.

The protection of informants was discussed earlier (pp. 220–1). Protection may also have to be extended to witnesses who would otherwise not dare to give evidence. This may be achieved by concealing their identity and by giving them protection and even relocating them after the trial. The cost – inevitably falling on the taxpayer – may be necessary in order to avoid the greater loss of civil liberties by enabling dangerous criminals to go free.

One means of continuing jury trials in the face of organized intimidation and corruption would be for jurors to be anonymous, sitting in a separate building watching by video, with five CCTV screens in the jury room, showing the faces of the accused, witness, judge and both prosecution and defence counsel. This would present a number of civil liberties problems: counsel would lose their right to object to the selection of jurors on grounds of prejudice and this duty would have to fall on the trial judge or on an ombudsman; the opportunity for jurors to participate by asking the trial judge questions would be lost; and the process might seem to erode the principle of 'justice being seen to be done'.

As has already been essential in Northern Ireland, it might be necessary for the identity of witnesses also to be concealed. Screens alone will not give confidence if the threat is serious. One possible compromise would be for threatened witnesses to give evidence by video, with CCTV screens provided only for the judge and jury. Unfortunately the abuses of ethics by a minority of criminal lawyers (described in Chapter 12) might preclude them from being allowed to see the witness, and some witnesses might be fearful of giving evidence if they were. None of these restrictions is desirable, but they are better than justice being denied by intimidation and corruption.

PRISON AND ITS ALTERNATIVES

Of the four purposes of imprisonment (rehabilitation, custody, retribution and deterrence), rehabilitation should be the primary aim for all first offenders and generally remain so for second offenders but, for those who commit a third offence, custody to protect the public must take overriding priority.

The application in parts of the USA of the 'three strikes and you're out' rule has led to some bizarre results and, if applied to the UK, might vastly increase the prison population, which is already too high. The proposal for statutory sentences for second and third offences has been vigorously opposed as curtailing the discretion of judges. A possible answer would be for Parliament to enact guidelines for minimum and maximum sentences for serious crimes committed a second or third time, with a right of appeal by the Attorney-General if the sentence seemed to be unduly below the guideline. The final decision would then be in the hands of the judiciary – the Appeal Court, not a politician.

Nevertheless, sentences should escalate more steeply than

they do, especially for third and subsequent offences. A serious crime is a gross violation of the civil rights of the victim for the gain or gratification of the criminal, and criminals who repeat them a third time have no *moral* right ever to be free to persecute the community again. In some cases, life imprisonment should really mean life. But the chief sufferers from this would be the prison officers, so special arrangements would be needed in top security prisons to make their task possible (see pp. 176–8).

For first and second offenders, community service has given better results than prison and costs far less. Every effort should be made to avoid putting young people into custody with other offenders, which is more likely to advance their career in crime than to stem it. But after a third offence, offenders have made their attitude clear, and public safety must take priority; they deserve no further sympathy. But punishment is less important than arrest and trial. The expectation of conviction is the real deterrent.

TECHNOLOGY AND CIVIL RIGHTS

Concealment of identity for honourable purposes is rare, and it is doubtful whether it should be classed as a civil right. But impersonating someone else is certainly *not* a civil right; doing so by theft or forgery is a crime.

Britain will one day almost certainly need to join the other countries of the EU in a harmonized ID card system, for its own security. This will probably best be done by combining it with the new driving licences, with openly recorded personal data, as on the new passports, in machine readable (OCR) lettering. It should initially be voluntary but should offer so many advantages that almost everyone would want to get one, as has happened in the voluntary systems in France and Italy. These cards should, in addition, carry biometric data unique to the holder in digital form. Trials so far suggest that hand geometry is probably the most reliable, cheapest and simplest to use.

Biometric data should also be incorporated in passports and visas. These, with the ID cards, should enormously help the police in detecting criminals, drug traffickers and illegal immigrants in spot checks to compensate for the relaxation of national frontier controls.

ID cards should not, however, contain any confidential data at all – such as police and medical records or benefit entitlement – which would cause anxiety to some people. They are in any case quite unnecessary. The machine readable personal particulars (name, place and date of birth, card number, date of expiry) are sufficiently unique for the police, NHS or benefit agency to call up their own databases for the information they need, to which they alone would have access. The biometric data on the card will have only one purpose – to prove that the person presenting it is the authorized holder – though effective measures will be needed to prevent forgery of biometric data, like any other data.

With these precautions, the only possible abuse of civil liberties will be malicious harassment by officials repeatedly and unnecessarily demanding identification, for example from young people or minority groups, but modern computer systems should make it easy to prevent or detect such abuse.

Surveillance is another area in which technology could cause abuse of civil liberties. Techniques for espionage (such as bugging and the intrusive use of long-range cameras) must be strictly controlled so that they can be used only for targeting people whom there is strong reason to suspect of criminal activities.

CCTV cameras have, however, brought far more benefits than hazards. Several IRA bombers and the two children who murdered James Bulger were caught with the aid of CCTV cameras placed in shopping centres to deter and prevent petty crime. CCTV cameras covering traffic bottlenecks also record other things.

Long-range CCTV or still cameras beamed into private property – abused by the media and private snoopers rather than by police – can severely infringe civil liberties. But the monitoring of who goes where in shopping centres and other public places should cause no anxiety except to people who are contemplating or carrying out criminal, dishonest or disreputable activities, and it will enhance the civil liberties of the community if criminals are deterred or detected.

Detection of drugs and explosives, especially by sensitive vapour detectors and dogs, is increasingly effective against terrorists, drug traffickers and other criminals. The only likely abuse of these, as with other police surveillance, may arise from malicious harassment.

THE ULTIMATE CIVIL RIGHT

The ultimate civil right is the right to life; close behind it comes the right to live in peace and tranquillity. The greatest threat to civil liberties in Britain comes from crime. In some countries an even greater threat comes from the use of violence or intimidation to bring about political change. All over Africa, in parts of Asia and Latin America and south-east Europe, untold suffering has been caused by civil wars and revolutions, to refugees and to people who have seen their loved ones killed or do not know where they are; or who have been deprived of all their possessions and left homeless and destitute. Mercifully, British people have been spared that for the last 300 years.

Britain, however, has suffered much from terrorism since the mid-1970s, though this has not inflicted damage comparable to that from crime, except in Northern Ireland. Crime more than doubled during 1981–93, but has shown a slight decrease during 1994–96. If the tide does prove to have turned, this will be the result of a change in police philosophy, to intelligence-led policing.

Britain should give priority to two main targets: first to stem the flow of a minority of young people into drug abuse and crime, by starting their education earlier, before school, and improving its quality all the way through. It is in the interest of the community to spend more on education and to pay the necessary taxes to do so. In particular this must focus on the deprived 10 per cent who grow up believing that they have few options other than to turn to crime.

The second priority is to tackle persistent criminals. Prison should be avoided if possible for first offenders, but penalties for second offences should escalate sharply, with a warning that, if there is a third, they will forfeit any moral right to walk free until they have proved beyond doubt that they are no longer a threat to the community.

The civil rights of victims must have priority over those of criminals. Only 1 in every 50 crimes leading to conviction is not enough. Freedom for a minority to kill, maim and destroy must never be allowed at the expense of the right of the majority to live in peace.

POSTSCRIPT

In October 1996 the British Government introduced radical changes in gun laws following the report by Lord Cullen on the cold-blooded massacre fo 16 primary schoolchildren and their teacher with a handgun in Dunblane School gymnasium. Their killer, who allegedly did it for the sadistic pleasure of seeing lightly clad children writhing in agony, had a gun licence and kept several guns at home. In response to highly emotional public outrage, a total ban was placed on keeping handguns at home. Only low-calibre 0.22 pistols of the type used in Olympic competitions could be privately owned at all (about 40,000 of them), and were to be kept and used only in heavily secured gun clubs. Apart from guns for police and armed forces, only single-shot sporting rifles and shotguns could be kept at home, under much stricter licence and registration than before. Automatic weapons (already banned since 1988) and higher-calibre handguns were banned from private ownership altogether. These restrictions were strongly opposed by shooting enthusiasts, by the 2500 gun dealers who stood to lose 10,000 jobs, and by the 2000 gun clubs. They felt that their civil liberties were being infringed by depriving them of an honourable recreation. As in the USA, they argued that this would not stop criminals getting guns and other weapons, including knives. These arguments were countered by the stark contrast between the USA and the UK – 70 times more per million killed by guns each year (see pp. 19–20). In the USA, one household in four contains guns, which are also regularly carried in cars. Guns breed more guns. Lawyers say that public emotions make bad law but the new laws checked the spread of US gun culture in Britain; and handguns are designed to kill – the ultimate denial of civil liberties.

Notes and References

After the first reference, a short title is normally used (see Bibliography).

1 QUESTIONS AND DILEMMAS

1. The facts and figures quoted in this introduction are discussed more fully in later chapters, with other related material. Their sources are given in those chapters rather than here. This one is in Note 11 to Chapter 2.

2 PATTERNS OF CRIME

1. G. C. Barclay (ed.), *Information on the Criminal Justice System in England and Wales*, London, Home Office, 1993, cited in NACRO (National Association for the Care and Resettlement of Offenders), *Crime and Social Policy*, London, NACRO, 1995, p. 9.
2. NAPO (National Association of Probation Officers), quoted in *The Times*, 13 October 1995.
3. Jon Silverman, *Crack of Doom*, London, Headline, 1994, pp. 189–98, gives a description of 4 rival gangs in Manchester, between 30 and 60 strong, mainly trafficking in drugs with links to Jamaica.
4. Anthony Daniels, *Sunday Telegraph*, 12 November 1995, in a review of Tony Thompson, *Gangland Britain*, London, Hodder & Stoughton, 1995.
5. BBC 1, *Here and Now*, 12 February 1996.
6. Richard Clutterbuck, *Drugs, Crime and Corruption*, London, Macmillan, 1995, p. 159, gives accounts of two attempts to establish Mafia cells in the UK, by Francisco di Carlo in 1985 and David Medin in 1987. Neither lasted long.
7. Alison Jamieson, *The Modern Mafia: Its Role and Record*, Conflict Studies no. 224, London, RISCT (Research Institute for the Study of Conflict and Terrorism), September 1989; also 'Mafia and Political Power', *International Relations* 10 (1) May 1990, and 'Mafia and Institutional Power in Italy', *International Relations* 12 (1) April 1994, comprehensively analyse the Italian Mafia. For a briefer account, drawing on these, see Clutterbuck, *Drugs*, pp. 131–7.
8. Christopher Ulrich, *The Price of Freedom*, Conflict Studies no. 275, London, RISCT, October 1994.
9. These are quoted from CSO (Central Statistical Office), *Social Trends, 1996*, London, 1996 (mainly 1994 figures) and from Metropolitan Police, *Report 1994–95*, London, 1995.
10. The 'clear-up rate' is the proportion of reported notifiable offences

resulting in a charge or caution, or the equivalent in the juvenile courts.

11. Jack Straw, Shadow Home Secretary, quoted in *The Times*, 13 October 1995.
12. CSO, *Social Trends*, pp. 162–3.
13. Ibid.
14. Ibid, p. 166.
15. Ibid, p. 164.
16. Clutterbuck, *Drugs*, pp. 129–30 and 175. There was an encouraging fall in the number of murders in New York in 1994 (20 per cent) and 1995 (25 per cent): *The Economist*, 6 January 1996.
17. Met Police, *Report*, pp. 69 and 72.
18. Clutterbuck, *Drugs*, pp. 124–30.
19. Met Police, *Report*, p. 83.
20. Ibid, pp. 73–80.

3 WHY YOUNG PEOPLE TURN TO CRIME

1. Desmond Morris, *The Naked Ape*, London, Cape, 1967.
2. CSO, *Social Trends*, pp. 66–7.
3. DSS (Department of Social Security), *Households Below Average Incomes*, London, DSS, 1994, in NACRO, p. 39.
4. J. Douglas, *Young Children with Behaviour Problems*, 1990, in NACRO, p. 48.
5. NACRO, p. 48.
6. L. J. Schweinhart and D. Weikart, *A Summary of Significant Benefits: The High Scope Perry Pre-School Study through Age 27*, 1993, in NACRO, p. 48.
7. M. Thomas, E. Goddard, M. Hickman and P. Hunter, *General Household Survey 1992*, London, HMSO, 1994, in NACRO, p. 49.
8. Harriet Wilson and G. W. Herbert, *Parents and Children in the Inner City*, London, Routledge & Kegan Paul, 1978, in NACRO.
9. NACRO, p. 49.
10. Ibid.
11. Centrepoint, *Youth Affairs Briefing*, 1994, in NACRO, p. 50.
12. R. Walmsley, L. Howard and S. White, *National Prison Survey 1991: Main Findings*, Home Office Research Study no. 128, London, HMSO, 1992, in NACRO, p. 42.
13. DSS in NACRO, p. 29.
14. R. G. Wilkinson, *Unfair Shares: The Effects of Widening Income Differentials on the Welfare of the Young*, London, Barnados, 1994, in NACRO, p. 29.
15. Joseph Rowntree Foundation, *Inquiry into Income and Wealth*, York, 1995, in NACRO, p. 29.
16. Ibid.
17. NACRO, p. 30.
18. Rowntree in NACRO, p. 44. Right-wing activists ask, 'Then why did they come, and why don't they go home?' Most of them were born in the UK and now have few links with their homelands; and, from

what they hear, their standard of living back there would be lower even than on unemployment benefit in the UK.
19. Runnymede Trust, *Multi-Ethnic Britain: Facts and Trends*, 1994, in NACRO, p. 44.
20. NACRO, p. 44.
21. Ibid, p. 44.
22. D of E (Department of Employment) figures quoted in NACRO, p. 30.
23. NACRO, p. 31.
24. Ibid, p. 31.
25 Ibid, p. 32.
26. Ibid, p. 32.
27. Eurostat, *Unemployment in the European Union*, no. 12, Brussels, EC Commission, 1994, in NACRO, p. 26.
28. NACRO, p. 26.

4 DRUG TRAFFICKING IN THE UK

1. Alison Jamieson, *Drug Trafficking after 1992*, Conflict Studies no. 250, London, RISCT, April 1992.
2. Metropolitan Police, interviews with author 1994–95.
3. CDCU (Central Drugs Coordination Unit), *Tackling Drugs Together* (Green Paper) (Cm 2678), London, HMSO, 1994.
4. John Grieve, Paper presented to the London Drug Policy Forum, 18 March 1994.
5. *The Economist*, 13 November 1993.
6. Release, quoted in the *Sunday Telegraph*, 5 June 1994, estimated that 85 per cent of drug users in Britain were taking only cannabis.
7. Silverman, p. 129.
8. Frances Crook, Director, Howard League for Penal Reform, in an interview with the author, 1 September 1993.
9. Jon Silverman, op. cit., gives a fuller description of drug smuggling, especially on pp. 155–63.
10. ACJDTU (Andean Commission of Jurists, *Drug Trafficking Update*) no. 43, Lima, November 1993.
11. Silverman, pp. 189–204.
12. The ideas in this chapter are more fully explored in Clutterbuck, *Drugs*.

5 MONEY LAUNDERING

1. Nicholas Dorn, Karin Mur̆ji and Nigel South, *Traffickers: Drug Markets and Law Enforcement*, London and New York, Routledge, 1992, pp. 28–9.
2. Alison Jamieson, *Global Drug Trafficking*, Conflict Studies no. 234, London, RISCT, September 1990, p. 25.
3. Jamieson, CS 250, p. 32.

4. Albert Pacey, Director, NCIS, quoted in *Computers*, 14 March 1996.
5. Silverman, p. 171.
6. Jamieson, CS 234, p. 37.
7. Jamieson, CS 250, p. 19.
8. Ibid, pp. 19–20.
9. Interpol is the International Police Organization, of which 176 countries are members. It provides an excellent facility for exchange of information on organized crime and individual criminals, but the wide membership inevitably restricts its involvement in sensitive political and intelligence matters.
10. DTOA (Drug Trafficking Offences Act) 1986 and CJA (Criminal Justice Act) 1988.

6 INTELLIGENCE ORGANIZATION AND BACKGROUND INTELLIGENCE

1. HAC (Home Affairs Committee of the House of Commons), *Third Report: Organized Crime*, London, HMSO, 17 July 1995, paras 93–6.
2. Ibid, paras 96–105.
3. JIC (Joint Intelligence Committee), *Central Intelligence Machinery*, London, HMSO, 1993.
4. Since 1992, TREVI has been incorporated into the 'Third Pillar' of the EU under the Maastricht Treaty.
5. Richard Clutterbuck, *Terrorism, Drugs and Crime in Europe after 1992*, London and New York, Routledge, 1990, pp. 61–7.
6. Author's visit to Europol, The Hague, April 1995.
7. *The Economist*, 14 November 1992.
8. Richard Clutterbuck, *Terrorism in an Unstable World*, London and New York, Routledge, 1994 (pp. 74–6) examines the prospects and limitations of computers in the police intelligence field more fully.
9. HAC, para 158.

7 INFORMANTS AND PRECISE INTELLIGENCE

1. Bruce Page, David Leitch and Philip Knightley, *Philby: The Spy Who Betrayed a Generation*, Harmondsworth, Penguin, 1969, p. 317.
2. Richard Clutterbuck, *Riot and Revolution in Singapore and Malaya*, London, Faber & Faber, 1973, Chapters 1 and 2 discuss Lai Tek's role.
3. Ibid, p. 358.
4. ACPO (Association of Chief Police Officers), *Report on Operational Intelligence*, 1986, quoted in Dorn, pp. 157–8.

8 CASE STUDIES – INTELLIGENCE

1. Silverman, pp. 190–3.
2. Dorn, p. 107.

3. Ibid, pp. 108–10.
4. Silverman, pp. 64–76.
5. Ibid, pp. 193–7.
6. Ibid, pp. 1–35.
7. Ibid, p. 1.
8. Clutterbuck, *Riot*, pp. 188 and 211–19. This book also gives a detailed account of the operations, built around informants, to bring about the collapse of a major guerrilla district organization, pp. 211–49.
9. Ibid, pp. 252–5, gives a fuller account of the operations involving Hor Lung and of the handling of some of the hardline terrorists.
10. In retrospect, there was a press report in Peru in June 1994 that there had been a tip-off in August 1992 from another SL member, who was rewarded under the 'Repentance Law', that Maritza and her husband were accommodating 'an important SL leader'. If true, this would have given confirmation of the suspicions and illustrated the value of the incentives offered for giving information.
11. Clutterbuck, *Drugs*, p. 21. This book also gives more details, with sources, of the operation to capture Guzman (pp. 30–4).

9 PREVENTION OF TERRORISM

1. Lord Diplock, *Report of the Commission to consider legal procedures to deal with terrorist activities in Northern Ireland*, London, HMSO, December 1972.
2. Richard Clutterbuck, *Protest and the Urban Guerrilla*, London, Faber & Faber, 1973, pp. 97–8 describes this case more fully. The bus driver, Sidney Agnew, had made a deposition, of which a copy was given to the defence, and the judge ruled that this deposition was admissible as evidence. The terrorists were convicted, but this incident made witnesses extremely reluctant to give evidence in other trials, and highlighted the hazards of the prosecution having to make evidence available to the defence in advance of a terrorist trial.
3. The French have a similar list of offences, in their case including those affecting national security as well as those connected with terrorism, which are tried without jury. For these offences, a judge sits with up to six assessors, some of whom are professional judges. Under the French system, there is an ample supply of young judges available for this duty, their normal work being as examining magistrates, or *juges d'instruction*. Various other possibilities for dealing with the intimidation of witnesses and juries are discussed in Chapter 13. See also Clutterbuck, *Europe*, pp. 64–7.
4. The 'balance of probabilities' is the standard of proof required in reaching a decision between litigants in a civil case, as distinct from 'beyond reasonable doubt' normally required for conviction for a criminal offence.
5. NI(EP)A (Northern Ireland (Emergency Provisions) Act) 1973 Clauses 1, 6, 5 and respectively.

6. Ibid, Clause 4.
7. Ibid, Clauses 12, 13 and 14.
8. Ibid, Clauses 15, 16 and 17.
9. Ibid, Clauses 18, 22 and 19.
10. NICRA (Northern Ireland Civil Rights Association), *The Emergency Provisions Act and why it should be repealed*, Belfast, NICRA, 1974.
11. Ibid.
12. Lord Gardiner, *Report of a Committee to consider in the context of civil liberties and human rights measures to deal with terrorism in Northern Ireland* (Cmnd 5847), London, HMSO, 1975.
13. Article 6 is printed in full in Diplock, *Report*, 1972, p. 8.
14. Diplock, *Report*, p. 9.
15. Ibid, para 12.
16. Gardiner, *Report*, paras 16 and 17.
17. Ibid, para 21.
18. Ibid, paras 30–33.
19. PT(AP)B (Prevention of Terrorism (Additional Powers) Bill) 1996.
20. PTA (Prevention of Terrorism (Temporary Provisions) Act) 1989, Secs 2 and 3.
21. Ibid, Secs 5–8.
22. Ibid, Secs 9–11.
23. Ibid, Sec 12.
24. Ibid, Sec 13.
25. Ibid, Sec 14.
26. Earl Jellicoe, *Review of the Operation of the Prevention of Terrorism (Temporary Provisions) Act, 1976* (Cmnd 8803), London, HMSO, 1983, pp. 21–2.
27. Ibid, p. 129.
28. PTA 1989, Schedule 5.
29. Ibid, Sec 17.
30. Ibid, Sec 18.
31. Lord Shackleton, *Review of the Operation of the Prevention of Terrorism (Temporary Provisions) Acts, 1974 and 1976* (Cmnd 7324), London, HMSO, 1978.
32. Ibid, Secs 65–8.
33. Jellicoe, *Review*, pp. 84–9.
34. House of Commons Debate on Renewal of the PTA, 14 March 1996.

10 PUBLIC ORDER

1. Richard Clutterbuck, *Britain in Agony*, Harmondsworth, Penguin, 1980, gives an analysis of violence in the 1970s.
2. Home Office, *Review of the Public Order Act 1936 and related legislation* (Green Paper) (Cmnd 7891), London HMSO, 1980, p. 2.
3. Ibid.
4. Ibid.
5. Ibid.

6. Home Office, *Review of Public Order Law* (White Paper) (Cmnd 9510), London, HMSO, 1985.
7. POA (Public Order Act) 1986.
8. CJPOA (Criminal Justice and Public Order Act) 1994.
9. Home Office, *Review POL,* pp. 5–6 and POA 1986, Secs 1–10.
10. Home Office, *Review POL,* p. 7.
11. POA 1986, Sec 14A .
12. *The Economist,* 13 November 1993.

11 ARREST AND INTERROGATION

1. PACE (Police and Criminal Evidence Act) 1984, Sec 1.
2. CJPOA 1994, Sec 60.
3. Ibid, Secs 34–5.
4. CE(NI)A (Criminal Evidence (Northern Ireland) Act) 1988
5. CJPOA 1994, Secs 34–5.
6. Robert Mark, *In the Office of Constable,* London, Collins, 1978, p. 274
7. Jeremy Bentham, *An Introduction to the Principles of Morals and Legislation,* cited by Mark, p. 274.

12 TRIAL

1. Bernard Levin in *The Times,* 22 March 1996 and letter to *The Times* from DPP, on 26 March 1996, reinforcing author's impressions on a visit to China in 1975.
2. PACE 1984, Secs 76–8.
3. Ibid, Sec 76 (8).
4. Ibid, Sec 27, 'police powers' being defined as in the Police Act 1964, Sec 64.
5. PACE 1984, Secs 76 (4) and 78.
6. CJPOA 1994, Sec 35.
7. Alison Jamieson, *Collaboration: New Legal and Judicial Procedures for Countering Terrorism,* Conflict Studies no 257, London, RISCT, 1993, p. 17.
8. CJPOA 1994, Sec 48.
9. RCCJ (Royal Commission on Criminal Justice), *Report* (Cm 2263), London, HMSO, July 1993.
10. HAC.
11. City Forum Conference on *Security and Integrity in the Financial Services Industry,* London, 12 June 1995.
12. RCCJ 1993.
13. Ibid, Chapter 6, paras 34–42.
14. Ibid, Chapter 6, paras 59ff.
15. Home Secretary's Statement in Parliament, 16 May 1995 Column 162, reported in HAC, para 150.
16. Under the adversarial system, the defence lawyers may already be thinking ahead to the possibility of an appeal. If they are convinced

that their client is likely to be found guilty, they may look for some piece of evidence which was not disclosed but which they can later use as the basis for an appeal. It is very rare for a retrial to be ordered for a person whose conviction is quashed on appeal, so this may be their best hope.
17. HAC, para 151.
18. PACE 1984, Sec 74 (3).
19. Mark, p. 155.
20. Ibid, p. 151.
21. Ibid, p. 156.
22. Ibid, pp. 157–8.
23. Ibid, p. 148.
24. Ibid, p. 159.
25 Ibid, pp. 148–9.

13 WITNESSES AND JURIES

1. HAC, paras 161–9.
2. Ibid, para 161.
3. Ibid, para 162.
4. CJPOA 1994, Sec 51.
5. HAC, para 168.
6. NI(EP)A 1973, Clause 4.
7. PACE 1984, Sec 68.
8. Diplock, *Report*, paras 93–100.
9. CJA 1988, Sec 23.
10. HAC, para 167; the HAC is an all-party committee.
11. Ibid, para 151.
12. Home Secretary's Statement in Parliament, 16 May 1995, reported in HAC, para 150.
13. RCCJ 1993, Chapter 6, paras 45–8.
14. Diplock, *Report*, paras 39–40.
15. Clutterbuck, *Europe*, pp. 63–6.

14 PRISON AND ALTERNATIVES

1. *The Economist*, 23 December 1995.
2. Sir Ivan Lawrence, QC, MP, Chairman of the House of Commons Home Affairs Committee, quoted on BBC Radio 4, *The World Tonight*, 5 March 1996.
3. Home Office, *Protecting the Public: The Government's Strategy on Crime in England and Wales* (White Paper) (Cm 3190), London, HMSO, April 1996.
4. *The Times*, 4 April 1996.
5. *The Times*, 21 March 1996.
6. *The Economist*, 23 September 1995.
7. *The Economist*, 9 December 1995.

8. *Sunday Telegraph*, 7 January 1996.
9. Ibid.

15 IDENTIFICATION AND IMPERSONATION

1. Home Office, *Identity Cards* (Green Paper) (Cm 2879), London, HMSO, 1995, p. 3.
2. Ibid, p. 8.
3. Ibid, p. 37.
4. *Intersec* 5 (6) June 1995, describes Iriscan, coding and digitalizing the eye on a database requiring 256 bytes, checking it against a 4000 record database in three seconds.
5. Ibid, describes Technology Recognition Systems facial thermal system.
6. WTTC (World Travel and Tourism Council), FAST (Future Automated Screening of Travellers) *Report*, 2 March 1994.
7. INS (Immigration and Naturalization Service, USA), INSPASS (INS Travel Pass) *Report*, August 1995, in WTTC, FAST *Report*, 11 January 1996. The rejection rates for JFK and Newark Airports were not available at the time of writing.
8. WTTC, FAST *Report*, London, 11 January 1996.
9. APC (Advance Passenger Clearance) Project leaflet, Department of Immigration and Ethnic Affairs, Canberra, 1996
10. WTTC, FAST *Report*, 11 January 1996.
11. Ibid.
12. Home Office, *ID Cards*, 1995, pp. 7–9.
13. Ibid, p. 10.
14. Ibid, pp. 10–14.
15. Ibid, p. 15.
16. Data Protection Act 1984, summarized in Home Office, *ID Cards*, 1995.

16 SURVEILLANCE AND ACCESS CONTROL

1. Brian Walters, 'Airport Boundary Security', *Intersec* 5 (6) June 1995, pp. 208–10.
2. This description is based on author's visit to East and West Berlin, 1971.
3. Christine Meyer, Jennifer Duncan and Bruce Hoffman, *Force on Force Attacks: Their Implication for the Defence of US Nuclear Facilities*, RAND Note N-3638-DOE, Santa Monica, RAND Corporation, 1993, assesses the problem of defending especially sensitive targets.
4. Brian M. Jenkins, *The Lessons of Beirut*, RAND Note N-2114-RC, Santa Monica, RAND Corporation, 1994, gives an account of this incident and lessons to be drawn from it.
5. Stephen Ulph, 'CCTV Surveillance', and John Morton, 'CCTV Cameras', *Security Industry*, February 1996, pp. 23–8 and 35–8, give an up-to-date account of CCTV technology.

6. Home Office, *Bombs: Protecting People and Property*, London, HMSO, 1994, p. 19.

17 SEARCH TECHNIQUES

1. This is roughly equivalent to a glass of whisky in Loch Ness.
2. Clutterbuck, *World*, pp. 55–63 and 194–200, gives a fuller description of search equipment and its use.
3. Home Office, *Bombs*, pp. 10–11 and 36.
4. John D. Baldeschweiler, 'Explosive Detection for Commercial Airport Security' in Paul Wilkinson (ed.), *Technology and Terrorism*, London, Frank Cass, 1993, pp. 81–102, gives a comprehensive analysis of current techniques.
5. EAASP (European Association of Airport and Seaport Police), *Report*, Annual Conference, Rotterdam, April 1995.
6. Richard Clutterbuck, *The Channel Tunnel: Security Threats and Safety Measures*, Conflict Studies no. 269, London, RISCT, April 1994, gives a fuller analysis.

18 STRIKING THE BALANCE

1. CSO, *Social Trends*, 1996, p. 163.
2. NI(EP)A 1973.

Bibliography

BOOKS, ARTICLES AND DOCUMENTS	(*Short title*)
ACPO (Association of Chief Police Officers), *Report on Operational Intelligence*, 1986	(ACPO, *Report*)
ANDEAN COMMISSION OF JURISTS, *Drug Trafficking Update*	(ACJDTU)
BALDESCHWEILER, JOHN D., 'Explosive Detection for Commercial Airport Security', in WILKINSON, PAUL (ed.), *Technology and Terrorism*, London, Frank Cass, 1993	(Baldeschweiler)
BARCLAY, G. C. (ed.), *Information on the Criminal Justice System in England and Wales*, London, Home Office, 1993, in NACRO	(Barclay in NACRO)
CDCU (Central Drugs Coordination Unit), *Tackling Drugs Together* (Green Paper) (Cm 2678), London, HMSO, 1994	(CDCU)
CE(NI)A (Criminal Evidence (Northern Ireland) Act) 1988	(CE(NI)A 1988)
CENTREPOINT, *Youth Affairs Briefing*, 1994, in NACRO	(Centrepoint in NACRO)
CJA (Criminal Justice Act) 1988	(CJA 1988)
CJPOA (Criminal Justice and Public Order Act) 1994	(CJPOA 1994)
CLUTTERBUCK, RICHARD, *Protest and the Urban Guerrilla*, London, Faber & Faber, 1973	(Clutterbuck, *Protest*)
CLUTTERBUCK, RICHARD, *Riot and Revolution in Singapore and Malaya*, London, Faber & Faber, 1973	(Clutterbuck, *Riot*)
CLUTTERBUCK, RICHARD, *Britain in Agony*, Harmondsworth, Penguin, 1980	(Clutterbuck, *Britain*)
CLUTTERBUCK, RICHARD, *Terrorism, Drugs and Crime in Europe after 1992*, London and New York, Routledge, 1990	(Clutterbuck, *Europe*)
CLUTTERBUCK, RICHARD, *Terrorism in an Unstable World*, London and New York, Routledge, 1994	(Clutterbuck, *World*)
CLUTTERBUCK, RICHARD, *The Channel Tunnel: Security Threats and Safety Measures*, Conflict Studies no. 269, London, RISCT, April 1994	(Clutterbuck, CS 269)
CLUTTERBUCK, RICHARD, *Drugs, Crime and Corruption*, London, Macmillan, 1995	(Clutterbuck, *Drugs*)
CSO (Central Statistical Office), *Social Trends 1996*, London, HMSO, 1996	(CSO, *Social Trends*)
DIPLOCK, LORD, *Report of the Commission to consider legal procedures to deal with terrorist activities in Northern Ireland*, London, HMSO, December 1972	(Diplock, *Report*)

DORN, NICHOLAS, MURJI, KARIM and SOUTH, NIGEL, *Trafficking: Drug Markets and Law Enforcement*, London and New York, Routledge, 1992 (Dorn)

DOUGLAS, J. *Young Children with Behaviour Problems*, 1990, in NACRO (Douglas in NACRO)

DSS (Department of Social Security), *Households Below Average Income*, London, DSS, 1994, in NACRO (DSS in NACRO)

DTOA 1986 (Drug Trafficking Offences Act 1986) (DTOA 1986)

EAASP (European Association of Airport and Seaport Police), *Report of the Annual Conference*, Rotterdam, April 1995 (EAASP, 1995)

EUROSTAT, *Unemployment in the European Union*, no. 12, Brussels, EC Commission, 1994, in NACRO (Eurostat in NACRO)

GARDINER, LORD, *Report of a Committee to consider in the context of civil liberties and human rights measures to deal with terrorism in Northern Ireland* (Cmnd 5847), London, HMSO, 1975 (Gardiner, *Report*)

GRIEVE, JOHN, Paper presented to the London Drug Policy Forum, 18 March 1994 (Grieve)

HAC (Home Affairs Committee of the House of Commons), *Third Report: Organized Crime*, London, HMSO, 1995 (HAC)

HOME OFFICE, *Bombs: Protecting People and Property*, London, Home Office, 1995 (Home Office, *Bombs*)

HOME OFFICE, *Identity Cards* (Green Paper) (Cm 2879), London, HMSO, 1995 (Home Office, *ID Cards*)

HOME OFFICE, *Protecting the Public: The Government's Strategy on Crime in England and Wales* (White Paper) (Cm 3190), London, HMSO, April 1996 (Home Office, *Protecting the Public*)

HOME OFFICE, *Review of the Public Order Act 1936 and related legislation* (Green Paper) (Cmnd 7891), London, HMSO, 1980 (Home Office, *Review 1936*)

HOME OFFICE, *Review of Public Order Law* (White Paper) (Cmnd 9510), London, HMSO, May 1985 (Home Office, *Review POL*)

HUTTON, W., *The Shape We're In: Why Britain is in Crisis and How to Overcome It*, London, Cape, 1995 (Hutton)

INS (Immigration and Naturalization Service, USA), *INSPASS Report*, August 1995, in WTTC 1996 (INS in WTTC 1996)

JAMIESON, ALISON, *The Modern Mafia: Its Role and Record*, Conflict Studies no. 224, London, RISCT, September 1989 (Jamieson CS 224)

JAMIESON, ALISON, 'Mafia and Political Power, 1943–89', *International Relations* 10 (1) May 1990 (Jamieson, Mafia 1990)

JAMIESON, ALISON, *Global Drug Trafficking*, Conflict Studies no. 234, London, RISCT, September 1990 (Jamieson, CS 234)

JAMIESON, ALISON, *Drug Trafficking after 1992*, Conflict Studies no. 250, London, RISCT, April 1992 (Jamieson, CS 250)

JAMIESON, ALISON, *Collaboration: New Legal and Judicial Procedures for Countering Terrorism*, Conflict Studies no. 257, London, RISCT, January 1993	(Jamieson, CS 257)
JAMIESON, ALISON, 'Mafia and Institutional Power in Italy', *International Relations* 12 (1) April 1994	(Jamieson, Mafia 1994)
JELLICOE, EARL, *Review of the Operation of the Prevention of Terrorism (Temporary Provisions) Act, 1976* (Cmnd 8803), London, HMSO, 1983	(Jellicoe, *Review*)
JENKINS, BRIAN M., *The Lessons of Beirut*, RAND Note N-2114-RC, Santa Monica, RAND Corporation, 1994	(Jenkins)
JIC (Joint Intelligence Committee), *Central Intelligence Machinery*, London, HMSO, 1993	(JIC)
MARK, ROBERT, *In the Office of Constable*, London, Collins, 1978	(Mark)
METROPOLITAN POLICE, *Report, 1994–95*, London, Metropolitan Police, 1995	(Met Police, *Report*)
MEYER, CHRISTINE, DUNCAN, JENNIFER, and HOFFMAN, BRUCE, *Force on Force Attacks: Their Implications for the Defence of US Nuclear Facilities*, RAND Note N-3638-DOE, Santa Monica, RAND Corporation, 1993	(Meyer)
MORRIS, DESMOND, *The Naked Ape*, London, Jonathan Cape, 1967	(Morris)
MORTON, JOHN, 'CCTV Cameras', *Security Industry*, February 1996	(Morton)
NACRO (National Association for the Care and Resettlement of Offenders), *Crime and Social Policy*, London, NACRO, 1995	(NACRO)
NICRA (Northern Ireland Civil Rights Association), *The Emergency Provisions Act and why it should be repealed*, Belfast, NICRA, 1974	(NICRA)
NI(EP)A (Northern Ireland (Emergency Provisions) Act) 1973	(NI(EP)A 1973)
PACE (Police and Criminal Evidence Act) 1984	(PACE 1984)
PAGE, BRUCE, LEITCH, DAVID, and KNIGHTLEY, PHILIP, *Philby: The Spy Who Betrayed a Generation*, Harmondsworth, Penguin, 1969	(Page)
POA (Public Order Act) 1986	(POA 1986)
PT(AP)B (Prevention of Terrorism (Additional Powers) Bill) 1996	(PT(AP)B 1996)
PT(TP)A (Prevention of Terrorism (Temporary Provisions) Act) 1989	(PTA)
RCCJ (Royal Commission on Criminal Justice) *Report* (Cm 2263), London, HMSO, July 1993	(RCCJ 1993)
ROWNTREE FOUNDATION, JOSEPH *Inquiry into Income and Wealth*, York, 1995 in NACRO	(Rowntree in NACRO)
RUNNYMEDE TRUST, *Multi-Ethnic Britain: Facts and Trends*, 1994 in NACRO	(Runnymede in NACRO)

SCARMAN, LORD, *The Red Lion Square Disorders of 15 June 1974* (Cmnd 5919), London, HMSO, 1975 (Scarman)

SCHWEINHART, L. J. and WEIKART, D., *A Summary of Significant Benefits: The High Scope Perry Pre-School Study through Age 27*, 1993 in NACRO (Schweinhart in NACRO)

SHACKLETON, LORD, *Review of the Operation of the Prevention of Terrorism (Temporary Provisions) Acts, 1974 and 1976* (Cmnd 7324), London, HMSO, 1978 (Shackleton)

SILVERMAN, JON, *Crack of Doom*, London, Headline, 1994 (Silverman)

THOMAS, M., GODDARD, E., HICKMAN, M. and HUNTER, P., *General Household Survey 1992*, London, HMSO, 1994 in NACRO (Thomas in NACRO)

THOMPSON, TONY, *Gangland Britain*, London, Hodder & Stoughton, 1995, reviewed in *Sunday Telegraph*, 12 November 1995 (Thompson)

ULPH, STEPHEN, 'CCTV Surveillance', *Security Industry*, February 1996 (Ulph)

ULRICH, CHRISTOPHER, *The Price of Freedom*, Conflict Studies no. 275, London, RISCT, October 1994 (Ulrich, CS 275)

WALMSLEY, R., HOWARD, L. and WHITE, S., *National Prison Survey 1991: Main Findings*, 1992, in NACRO (Walmsley in NACRO)

WALTERS, BRIAN, 'Airport Boundary Security', *Intersec* 5 (6) June 1995 (Walters)

WILKINSON, PAUL (ed.), *Technology and Terrorism*, London, Frank Cass, 1993 (Wilkinson, Paul)

WILKINSON, R. G., *Unfair Shares: The Effects of Widening Income Differentials on the Welfare of the Young*, London, Barnados, 1994, in NACRO (Wilkinson, R. G. in NACRO)

WILSON, HARRIET, and HERBERT, G. W., *Parents and Children in the Inner City*, London, Routledge & Kegan Paul, 1978, in NACRO (Wilson in NACRO)

WTTC (World Travel and Tourism Council), *FAST Report*, Brussels, 2 March 1994 (WTTC 1994)

WTTC (World Travel and Tourism Council), *FAST Report*, Brussels, 1 January 1996 (WTTC 1996)

JOURNALS AND NEWSPAPERS

Computers
Conflict Studies
The Economist
International Relations
Intersec
Security Industry
Sunday Telegraph
The Times

Index

Where acronyms are shown in the list of abbreviations (pp. xv–xviii) the acronym rather than the full title is normally used in this index.